"With his honest, empathic, and pragmatic approach, Dr. Rubin demystifies what makes some children well-liked and accepted by peers while others are not and, more important, teaches parents to support their children in becoming socially adept but without blaming them for their children's struggles. Required reading for the parent of every child."

—Roni Cohen-Sandler, co-author of *"I'm Not Mad, I Just Hate You!"* and author of *"Trust Me Mom—Everyone Else Is Going!"*

"A balanced, reflective discussion of a subject that many parents wonder about. Rubin's clear prose clarifies this complex theme."

—Jerome Kagan, Ph.D., professor of psychology, Harvard University

"This highly readable book fills a significant void in the parenting literature. Dr. Rubin draws on his extensive knowledge of child development research to offer useful recommendations about ways to facilitate children's peer relationships. Parenting is too important to do without friendly guidance and we all will benefit from this fine book."

—Steven Asher, professor of psychology, Duke University

"*The Friendship Factor* is packed with engaging real-life scenarios as well as specific strategies and techniques, from early childhood through adolescence, that parents can actually use to help their children become socially successful. Unlike other books about parenting, this one is unique in that it is solidly based on many years of basic research as well as parenting techniques that are effective in helping children to become socially competent."

—Cathryn L. Booth, professor, department of family and child nursing, School of Nursing, University of Washington

PENGUIN BOOKS

THE FRIENDSHIP FACTOR

Kenneth H. Rubin, Ph.D., an internationally renowned researcher in child development, is Professor of Human Development and Director of the Center for Children, Relationships and Culture at the University of Maryland. He is a past president of the International Society for the Study of Behavioral Development and has served as an associate editor of *Child Development*, the major journal in his field. His research on the topics of peer and parent-child relationships has been featured in such publications as *USA Today*, *The New York Times Magazine*, *Parents* magazine, and *Better Homes and Gardens*. He has appeared on *20/20*, NPR, and many other popular television and radio programs. The father of two young adult children, he lives with wife Margo in North Potomac, Maryland.

Andrea Thompson is a freelance writer based in New York City. Her articles have appeared in *Good Housekeeping*, *Redbook*, *McCall's*, *Parents*, and other magazines. She has collaborated on many books, including *You and Your Only Child*, *Tired of Nagging?*, and *Familyhood*, with the late Dr. Lee Salk.

The Friendship Factor

Helping Our Children Navigate Their Social World—
and Why It Matters for Their Success and Happiness

KENNETH H. RUBIN, PH.D.

with Andrea Thompson

PENGUIN BOOKS

PENGUIN BOOKS

Published by the Penguin Group

Penguin Putnam Inc., 375 Hudson Street, New York, New York 10014, U.S.A.

Penguin Books Ltd, 80 Strand, London WC2R 0RL, England

Penguin Books Australia Ltd, 250 Camberwell Road, Camberwell, Victoria 3124, Australia

Penguin Books Canada Ltd, 10 Alcorn Avenue, Toronto, Ontario, Canada M4V 3B2

Penguin Books India (P) Ltd, 11 Community Centre,
Panchsheel Park, New Delhi – 110 017, India

Penguin Books (N.Z.) Ltd, Cnr Rosedale and Airborne Roads,
Albany, Auckland, New Zealand

Penguin Books (South Africa) (Pty) Ltd, 24 Sturdee Avenue,
Rosebank, Johannesburg 2196, South Africa

Penguin Books Ltd, Registered Offices:
Harmondsworth, Middlesex, England

First published in the United States of America by Viking Penguin,
a member of Penguin Putnam Inc. 2002
Published in Penguin Books 2003

3 5 7 9 10 8 6 4 2

THE LIBRARY OF CONGRESS HAS CATALOGED THE HARDCOVER EDITION AS FOLLOWS:
Rubin, Kenneth H.
The friendship factor : helping our children navigate their social world—and why it matters
for their success and happiness / Kenneth H. Rubin, Ph.D., with Andrea Thompson.
p. cm.
Includes index.
ISBN 0-670-03018-X (hc.)
ISBN 0 14 20.0189 9 (pbk.)
1. Friendship in children.   2. Interpersonal relations in children.
3. Parenting.   4. Social skills in children.   I. Thompson, Andrea.   II. Title.
HQ784.F7 R8 2002
303.3'2—dc21   2001046561

Printed in the United States of America
Set in Adobe Garamond
Designed by Nancy Resnick

To my parents
Sunny & Jerry Rubin

Acknowledgments

There are many people to whom I am indebted for making this book possible. To begin with, during my thirty-year career as a developmental scientist, I've had the distinct pleasure of working with a group of stimulating, bright, and highly productive scholars. These friends have shared with me their valuable insights about what makes kids "tick," about the importance of peer acceptance and good friendship, and about the very meaning of social competence. At the same time, they have helped me discover what it is that gets kids into trouble with their peers and parents—valuable information that serves as a guide in prevention and intervention. These colleagues include Linda Rose-Krasnor, Shelley Hymel, Xinyin Chen, Rob Coplan, and Kim Burgess. From Cathryn Booth, Rosemary Mills, and Paul Hastings, I've learned about the significance of early parent-child attachment relationships, and of parenting beliefs and practices insofar as normal and abnormal social and emotional development are concerned. Thanks to Nathan Fox, I have come to appreciate the power of biology and infant/toddler temperament—the absolutely alterable foundations for all that follows. My mind would be a muddle if all these conversational partners and research collaborators spoke in independent tongues. My partners and I, after all, have studied a great many diverse topics. But diversity does not mean scattershot independence. The guiding spirit who has, through his elegant writings, allowed me to put all the diverse pieces into a single developmental framework is Robert Hinde.

The backbone for the studies and stories you will find described herein derives, in no small part, from the institutions that have provided my colleagues and me with the financial support to gather our data. These institutions include the National Institute of Mental Health, the National Institute of Child Health and Human Development, the Social Sciences and Humanities Research Council of Canada, and the Ontario Mental Health Foundation. And of course, there would be no data, and no stories to tell, were it not for the dedication and commitment of the children, parents, and teachers who have worked with us over the years.

I am indebted also to Meg Schneider and Lynn Sonberg of Skylight Press for enduring my frequent forays into "journal-speak" despite our collective goal of creating a readable book for parents. Meg, in particular, made me toe the line throughout the writing process. At Viking Penguin, Janet Goldstein and her capable staff offered highly engaging, helpful, and reinforcing comments. They made me feel that the book in the making was truly meaningful—something that scientists don't often hear from their professional colleagues. Of course, this book would not exist without the collaborative spirit of Andrea Thompson. Andrea and I spent countless hours in my office at the University of Maryland. She would ask endless questions and I would do my best to answer them into a tiny, ancient tape recorder. From the questions and answers and from Andrea's clear understanding of my professional, jargon-riddled writings came the text of this book. Thank you, thank you, Andrea!

Last, I turn to the Rubin family. I am grateful to Margo for showing me firsthand how and why parenting matters. Anyone who writes otherwise should have lived in our house when our now-adult children were still at home. And I am eternally indebted to Amy Joy and Joshua. They have demonstrated ably that if parents stick with their children through the perturbations of snow, sleet, and thunder that invariably occur, on and off, from childhood through adolescence, the glow of the sun will eventually find its way to warm the parents' hearts and spirits. My children are my role models.

Contents

The
Friendship Factor

Part I

The Friend/Parent Mosaic

Chapter 1

You, Your Child, and Your Child's Friends

What Parents Should Know About Children's Social Lives

Once upon a time, a child's world of peers tended to be misunderstood, undervalued, or even largely ignored. A generation or two ago, mothers and fathers didn't worry all that much about their children's social lives. While parents genuinely hoped for the best, as long as a child wasn't getting into fistfights and his school grades stayed decent, the friendships he formed or didn't form were not a matter of great interest. Teachers and other adults who worked with children likewise remained largely silent on the subject of peer relationships.

That picture has changed. Today it's not unusual, for example, for a child to be referred for professional help not only because of failing grades or an inability to pay attention in class, but because of bullying and other aggressive behaviors. The gloves are off. Most parents are attuned to subtler indications of social and emotional difficulty as well—recognizing when a child has few friends or the friendships don't last, or she seems to *feel* disliked by other kids.

This changing picture is all to the good. From my own experiences in the world of child-development research, I can state unequivocally: Your child's friendships are tremendously significant. At times in the passage from toddler to teenager, his friends may take center stage. More, perhaps, than any other individuals, they will have the power to cause your child to feel truly happy or absolutely miserable; more even than Mom and Dad, your child's friends may be the people he turns to for feedback on how to get through the day.

But friends are critical not only because having them makes life more pleasant. Our research has demonstrated powerful connections between how well a child fares socially and how successful she is in other areas of life. We know, for instance, that

- Children, especially good friends, help one another think things through more clearly and competently.

- From one another, they learn lessons about what's right and wrong, about loyalty, and about what happens if you hurt someone's feelings or betray someone's trust.

- The better able children are to form good, sustaining friendships and to be accepted and valued within their peer groups, the more apt they are to do well in school—and, in the long run, in life.

So yes, friends *do* matter; it *is* appropriate to pay attention to that aspect of your child's growth and development, and to think about what you can do to promote it. From my talks with parents, however, I know that this worthwhile focus can often lead to troublesome thoughts:

"When the children in her first-grade class are playing, my daughter seems to be kind of an outsider. I wonder if she does something that turns off other kids."

"My daughter is miserable because she's not in the popular clique in her school. I wish I could help her feel better about the whole thing."

"My sweet, funny, bright thirteen-year-old hangs out with a group of boys whom I find cocky and obnoxious. He acts that way, too, when he's with them. And I don't like it!"

These are typical of comments I've heard from parents countless times. Perhaps one of them strikes a responsive chord in you, or maybe you have a different worry. I would guess, in any case, that *something* about your child's life among other children is causing you grief or at least raising some level of concern:

- Why isn't she being invited on more playdates?
- Why is he always being teased by other kids?

- Why is she so quiet and sullen when she gets home from school?
- What does he do when he's out with his friends? Where do they go?

When it comes to our children's friendships and peer associations, there seems to be a kind of cloud cover of unease hanging over our collective parental mind. I believe there are a number of identifiable, modern-day explanations for this. Here's why mothers and fathers may feel uncomfortable when they consider their children's social lives:

Almost from the cradle on, today's children are called upon to make social connections.

Whereas children of an earlier generation rarely got together with peers other than siblings, cousins, or neighborhood kids before formally entering school in kindergarten, many of today's infants are with groups of other infants for eight or more hours a day. Two- and three-year-olds are now meeting their agemates in settings that essentially compel them to get along well with others and even to make difficult decisions about whom they want to be friends with and whom they don't. Furthermore, they will remain in age-segregated groups *longer* than children have done at any previous point in history, in their schoolrooms and in all the extracurricular venues they go to as soon as school is out.

Learning to live comfortably in the company of peers is a necessary requirement for your child, a critical challenge that begins at a very early age and will continue for many years.

Parents and children don't spend a great deal of time together anymore.

Said one parent, "My mother was always there when my brothers and I came home from school. My dad arrived at six o'clock on the dot every evening. Dinner was at six-thirty on the dot. I wouldn't say that we were a cheery, happy little family all the time. But my folks were always around, we were always around, and that was true right until the time I went off to college." Her own son and daughter, in contrast, each entered day care at the age of eighteen months. Now, as fourth and fifth graders, both chil-

dren have, according to their mom, "a laundry list of things they do after
school and on the weekends. Their father and I feel like chauffeurs. Sometimes I think we're all ships that pass in the night."

It's a familiar story. In a culture in which more women than ever are
working, more are remaining in the workforce after having children, and
more are single parents—and in which both mothers and fathers are
working longer hours than ever—we simply don't see as much of our children. Family members can indeed feel like ships that pass in the night.
Mothers and fathers *can* feel more like chauffeurs than like parents, or at
least have an uncomfortable sense that they are on the periphery of their
children's day-to-day lives.

**In a competitive world, parents want their children to keep pace with
their peers.**

A father whose two young sons were involved in soccer in the fall and Little League in the spring said, "I sometimes wish they had a more laid-back
kind of life, more like I had as a kid. But being on teams is good for them.
Not only because it's fun and it's exercise, but because it helps them set
goals and learn to compete. And they're growing up into a tough, expensive, aggressive world." Besides, he added, "all the kids they know are involved in these activities, so they sort of have to be, too."

Like this dad, many parents perceive that their children are entering a
winner-take-all society. They want them to keep up with the children
down the block, the children in their school, the unknown children on the
other side of the country who are doing things in fourth grade that they
(or their parents) hope will get them into a particular college years down
the road or prepare them for a particular career. *Parents* feel the pressure;
children feel the pressure.

**Parents perceive the social world their children live in as being fraught
with difficulties, even dangers, they themselves never had to face when
they were in school.**

Parents' sense of being out of touch with their kids is not simply a result of
spending limited time with them. Said the mother of two preteens: "My

kids live in a hugely more complicated world than my friends and I did when we were their age. It's like a foreign territory!" She explained, "I know about raves, club drugs, Internet chat rooms. Some of my daughter's twelve-year-old friends look like eighteen-year-olds. I think it's so easy for these kids to get lured into things they're not ready for, or they can't handle."

Even more alarming are the tragic incidents we have begun to hear about with dismaying regularity on the news. "How do I really know what's going on with my son and his friends?" wondered one parent. "If these seemingly average, middle-class, normally brought up kids can come out of nowhere and even think about trashing a school or shooting someone, it feels like it could happen anywhere."

Children once got into trouble in the course of a school day for running in the hall, talking out of turn, or throwing food in the lunchroom. Today the stakes are higher: Many of our older children must pass through metal detectors before they can even enter their classrooms.

Parents believe that if something is going wrong with their child, they must correct it.

Many of the things that used to cause children problems are now fixable. Orthodontists, dermatologists, math and reading tutors, and myriad other specialists are ready to help us turn out the perfect child. A few thousand parenting-advice books have persuaded us that a child's "inner," psychological life can also be fixed.

Of course, it's a positive, loving parental impulse to want to make everything right for a child. But that good wish can weigh heavily when we think it's up to us to solve all of our children's problems. Contributing to that burden is the fact that in recent decades, "the experts" have insisted that when things *aren't* going right with a child, it's the parents who must carry the blame. Lately—just to add to the confusion and the pressure—some have advanced a contrasting argument: "Parents matter less than you think," a popular book advises us, "and peers matter more!"

No wonder today's mothers and fathers are feeling less than sanguine!

We have taken upon ourselves the admirable task of attending to our children's emotional and psychological well-being, at the very moment that they seem most vulnerable to powerful forces beyond our control.

The good news, I believe, is that social scientists have also been paying attention to all this. In recent years there has been an explosion of research into childhood friendships and relationships. How does a child make friends? What is the nature of a child's life within her peer group? What kind of parental attention seems to hinder or to facilitate her ability to get along well with other children? These are among the issues that have occupied my own career in developmental science for over twenty-five years.

From the start—as a graduate student in psychology at Penn State University, as well as in the early stages of my academic career at the University of Waterloo in Canada—I found myself involved in trying to understand how it is that children become social beings. At what point do they begin to take into account the perspectives or points of view of others, and what prompts them to do so? My initial studies, and those of other researchers, bore out one of the leading theories of the time, the thesis that being with other children, and engaging in play and pretend games with them, seemed to promote a young child's ability to think and act socially. For me, then, the next question was, What happens to children who, for whatever reason, do not fit comfortably into the world of their agemates?

So began what we called the Waterloo Longitudinal Project, a study in which my colleagues and I followed the same group of children from the beginning of kindergarten to the beginning of high school. It was this project that taught us how enormously significant peers are in a child's development.

In particular, our work supported the generally accepted notion that aggressive kids—that is, the children who, whether they were four, seven, or eleven, simply could not get a handle on other people's thoughts and feelings and who lacked empathy and helpfulness—didn't fare very well. More unexpectedly, we were able to show that shy, withdrawn kids were also having a great deal of trouble. Why is it, we wondered next, that some children grow up to feel confident and to act competently in their increasingly broad social worlds, while others don't? This new question led me to investigate two new areas, parenting and biology.

Between the mid-1980s and the mid-1990s, my colleagues and I organized several studies to gauge the impact of parenting on how children behave among their peers. As we followed these youngsters up into middle school, we began to discover the connections between the two. From our observations, the next question suggested itself: Why do parents differ so markedly in the ways they think about and develop relationships with their children? Is there something about the individual child that causes a mother or father to react in a certain way? So began my work (now in its twelfth year) with colleagues at the University of Maryland on the biological bases for infant and child social and emotional behaviors—work that has provided further confirmation of the fact that parenting *matters*.

More recently still, in the ongoing Friendship Study, I've been interested in finding answers about children's friendships and peer groups. Are some friendships good for a child and others less good? What happens to the child who is friendless? Why do some children feel lonely in their school settings, and others perfectly happy? When a child experiences stress, can he or she turn to friends for support? At what age does that begin? Do the kinds of relationships children form with their closest friends mirror the kinds of relationships they have with their parents?

I must add that I have learned a great deal about the importance and influences of peers and parents from my fifteen-year "career" as a hockey coach and my even longer one as a father. Observing kids on a hockey team form friendships and reputations over the course of a season, as they learn how to cooperate and how to compete all at once, has taught me a lot about child development—though nowhere near as much as has being a parent myself, watching my two children grow and engaging them in all manner of activities and experiences.

I've had the absolute pleasure of seeing my daughter and son survive each of the "stages" of childhood and adolescence. I've been privy to their experiences with their close friends. I've lived through *Grease* and *Star Wars*, U2 and Nirvana, blue hair (daughter) and black nail polish (son). As is so often the case, my children—both now young adults—are ever so different in many ways. But both are decent, kind, sensitive, highly active, and talented individuals. I'm proud of them—and knowing what I do about developmental science, I'm confident that their parents played a significant role in their development!

All of this is to say that at no previous point in my work (and life) could I have presented a more accurate picture of what goes on with a child as he or she moves through various peer worlds from preschool to high school. Certainly, as director of the Laboratory for the Study of Child and

Family Relationships at the University of Maryland, and through professional collaborations on several continents, I have become increasingly aware that children's developmental trajectories are both complex and largely predictable. We now know a great deal more than we ever did before about children's social and emotional lives.

Are peers instrumental in the process of children's growth? Absolutely. Are parents? Again, absolutely. My studies focus, like much of the most exciting other research in the field, on the connections between those two worlds or those two relationship systems, child/parent and child/peer. We are learning that the two feed off each other in subtle, powerful, and intriguing ways.

And so the time seems right for *The Friendship Factor.*

What I hope to accomplish in this book is, first, to ease parents' minds. I intend to assure you that you can and should be involved in helping your child form good, rewarding friendships with "good" kids, from toddlerhood right through adolescence. Parents wield tremendous influence over their children's social lives, even if much of what the kids themselves do appears to take place in a "foreign territory," and even during the early-teen years when they seem swept away by their friends.

In this book, I'll share with you the findings of the many recent and ongoing studies regarding children's psychological and emotional development as it relates to friendships and peer groups. Based on this research (a good deal of it carried out in my own labs in the United States and Canada), we can paint a portrait of what we call the socially competent child. I'm sure you already have a pretty good idea of what that means.

A socially competent child, after all, is what you want your son or daughter to be—that is, a child who makes good friends; who is generally accepted and well liked by other children; and who can meet the challenges of modern-day childhood head on, without being bowled over or crushed under by them. You want your child to be able to maneuver his or her way successfully, safely, and (at least most of the time) happily through complicated social worlds—worlds that encompass classrooms, lunchrooms, locker rooms, playgrounds, summer camps, friends' homes, and all the other places in which your growing youngster spends so much time before reaching young adulthood.

We have discovered through our work that most children can become socially competent. But each child will get there in his or her own manner. For some, from the earliest ages on, that competence seems to come naturally. These are the youngsters who head cheerfully and confidently off to meet their peers and who apparently have what it takes (or learn what they must learn) to draw others to them in pleasant and positive ways. For many other children, however, social competence does not come effortlessly at all. And when things aren't going well, *every* child will benefit enormously from parental help, which starts with parental understanding.

That means, first of all, accepting where your child is coming from. Even though I haven't ever met your son or daughter, I can say with some measure of assurance that he or she tends to behave socially in one of several ways—what we'll describe later as essentially *moving toward, moving away from,* or *moving against* others. No doubt you are keenly aware of these tendencies; parents know their children well. And yet my work with hundreds of families over the years has taught me that mothers and fathers, even with all the love and good intentions in the world, often resist or fight against what they know: They wish their child were someone different, and are frustrated and upset that he or she is not. They struggle with feelings of disappointment, and then perhaps with feelings of guilt and blame—"What's wrong with me that I get so annoyed and impatient with my kid?" But only by first embracing what is special about your child—what is fundamental or biologically based—can you truly be in a position to offer the appropriate response when he or she runs into difficulties with friends or in peer groups.

The Friendship Factor is all about those appropriate responses. I hope you will come away from reading this book with some concrete ideas—skills, strategies, or techniques—that will work for *your* child, that will encourage him or her to begin or continue to develop social competence. The fact is that while you cannot solve your child's problems for him or her, there *is* much you can do to be supportive and helpful. There is much you can learn about when, where, and how to step in if social life is going badly for your son or daughter, or even if things just aren't what they should be.

The themes described below form the core of this book. They are my wish list of what I'd like all parents to know about their children's social lives.

Biology matters.

Your child came into the world with a set of genes—which determined, for example, that she'd have brown eyes and curly hair—as well as a group of biologically based characteristics that can affect how she will act around other people. Doubtless you already have a pretty good idea about those aspects of your child that define her personality or temperament; in fact, qualities related to temperament can be measured even in infants. Before a child is walking and talking, and certainly long before she is having play-dates and going to birthday parties, we can begin to understand, for instance, whether she is likely to be outgoing and confident around other children or, in contrast, cautious, worried, and wary.

In other words, some of your child's core inclinations in terms of approaching other children have no connection whatsoever to anything you did or didn't do. That's a relief, isn't it? But parents nevertheless can—and should—mediate or moderate, soften or channel, shape or reinforce a child's inclinations in ways that will further his social competence.

In a later chapter, I'll take you through studies that my colleagues and I have conducted that track these biological beginnings through the early years of childhood and, more important, reveal how parents' responses to them can be either helpful or not so helpful. Yes, biology matters. If yours is a biologically inhibited child, you cannot "remake" her into a highly gregarious one. However, with the right guidance, your inhibited child can be happy, have friends, and be liked by her peers.

Socially competent children almost always have competent parents.

Competent moms and dads are those who are responsive to their children's nature and needs and to the lay of the land at any particular time.

But competent parenting is no simple matter; it's as much about what a parent *thinks* and *feels* as it is about what he or she does. Indeed, being the kind of mother or father who—or providing the kind of parenting that—helps a child make friends and get along well with other kids derives from a rather complicated dance, a dance in which both child and parent take turns leading and following.

Think back to when you first welcomed your youngster into the world or adopted him or her into your family and began to discover what this little person was all about. You recognized that a certain cry meant hunger or tiredness, that a crooked grin invited you for a cuddle. You may also have soon enough realized that the same kind of tossing into the air that had your first child shrieking with delight caused this one to wail unhappily—and so you learned that baby tossing can have different consequences with different children, even children born and raised in the same house by the same two parents. And you toned down the horseplay with this son or daughter, while at the same time you kept up the robustness of play that the older brother or sister enjoyed.

Right from the start, in other words, you began to clue in to your youngster's desires and needs, and adjusted your actions to meet them. You recognized that at this stage of the game, your infant or toddler was leading the dance.

Deciding whether a bottle, a nap, or a hug was called for was just the beginning. The dance continues throughout the years of childhood and into adolescence; it gets trickier and the stakes get higher when friends and peer groups come onto the scene. Keeping the dance going requires knowing when to take the lead by setting clear limits, defining expectations, and nudging your child forward along the paths to both independence and appropriate dependence on others.

Some of the research that I will share with you in chapters 3 and 4 concerns precisely this match between how a parent thinks and behaves and what his or her child is like characterologically. Making the right match can be exhausting and emotionally draining for parents, especially at those times when they wish they could just erase their youngster's unhappiness or struggles. But it is essential. We know from many studies that, for example, the parent who is unfailingly warm and affectionate but offers little guidance may end up with a child who finds herself on the outs with her peers. Similarly, the parent who demonstrates warmth and control in all the wrong places and at all the wrong times can actually make matters worse for the child who has trouble making friends or joining kids at play.

Normal behavior is knowable (and not always so nice).

First appreciate what is singular about your son or daughter, and then know what is typical when it comes to children's friendships and groups. In the middle part of this book, you'll see what the latter look like across the age span from toddler to teen.

Normal development can, in fact, encompass a wide range of difficult, troublesome, and shifting behaviors. What's viewed as normal at one age may not be seen that way a short time later. Likewise, some behaviors are considered socially and emotionally normal for boys but not for girls. (And for that matter, some behavior that is deemed normal in our North American culture isn't accepted as normal in other areas of the world.)

You will see what it takes for a child at each age, and of either gender, to make and keep friends and to be liked. If your preschooler can make himself understood through clear words and gestures, for example, he will probably have little trouble attracting playmates. For your middle-school child, not fighting, lying, or otherwise coming across in outstandingly negative ways is a key to social success. Somewhere during those years, having a best friend may become a crucial element in how your child feels about herself. For the adolescent girl, for example, being willing and able to talk over her emotional ups and downs is what matters most in her friendships.

Even when the passage *seems* relatively smooth, even when your child is basically getting things right, the peer world can be harsh and cruel. Almost all children are teased at times. Hierarchies dominate the life of the classroom and the locker room; cliques and crowds often rule the roost. Recognizing that some of these unpleasant experiences are part of the territory at any given age will give you, as a parent, a leg up. When you know *what* to expect *when,* you're ahead of the game! And you will gain a clearer sense of when to step in and when it's best to stay out of it and allow your child to learn—perhaps the hard way—his or her own social lessons.

Over the broad arc of your child's life from preschool to high school, you will almost certainly take on and then cast off a variety of roles—as social secretary or monitor, comforter or adviser, devil's advocate or ally. Later we'll look at the various parenting skills that come into play at different points in a child's development. Even small adjustments in your actions, or reactions, can make the world outside the family a more pleasant place for your youngster, whether he or she is a toddler or a teen.

Not every child can be popular.

And sometimes being popular is not all that wonderful.

Speaking about her daughter's misery at being snubbed by the popular girls in her seventh-grade class, one mother said, "This crowd is a group of pretty girls who have lots of clothes and lots of freedom. They are also mean and bitchy to other kids, as I've seen firsthand. And Molly wants to be part of this group, and isn't."

This mother went on to say that *she* felt almost as bad about the whole business as her child did, because it was quite awful for her to observe Molly's efforts to be accepted by a group of classmates who had formed a little exclusionary world unto themselves. Maybe you, too, are very much aware of such feelings. A child's seeming lack of popularity—the party invitations are few and far between, the phone doesn't ring very often—can take as much of an emotional toll on the parent as on the kid, if not *more* of a toll. But the fact is, there may be any number of reasons for a child's high status among peers, not all of them terribly admirable or terribly lasting.

You may recall the movie *Heathers* (if you haven't seen it, I recommend that you rent it at your local video shop), about three high school girls with the same name: Heather One, Two, and Three. Every kid in school knows that the Heathers are the leaders of the popularity pack. These girls have the best stuff; they act confidently; they wield a lot of influence. They are also cruel, or what psychologists call *relationally aggressive,* spreading rumors and playing rotten tricks on the unattractive and out-of-it kids. Others long for acknowledgment and acceptance by the Heathers, because this clique can ruin reputations and make life miserable for those they target. But virtually no one trusts them, and no one really *likes* them.

Many schools and classes have their own Heathers. Typically they're the most visible kids in the group—everyone is aware of them, and the confidence they appear to possess is much envied. That's a kind of popularity, however, that actually says very little about how successful or happy a child will be for the rest of her life. It says very little, too, about a child's ability to make good friends—in fact, the popular child may or may not have such a talent. And most children, even while temporarily longing to be accepted, can distinguish between the peer they respect as a person and the peer they admire, or fear, as the embodiment of social power.

This is not to say that during childhood and adolescence some children—such as twelve-year-old Molly, evidently—won't suffer from being ignored or even tormented by the classroom hotshots. And it's also not to say that it isn't painful being the parent of a seemingly "unpopular" child. What I hope you will take away from chapter 8 is a set of key notions that will help put this whole troublesome matter into proper perspective—so it'll be easier for you to extend appropriate sympathy and support to your child without getting caught up in all the emotional turmoil yourself.

Not every child can be popular, and not every child *has* to be. Some kids who aren't listed in anyone's popularity polls in fact don't suffer unduly because of their apparently invisible status within their groups—and these kids are capable of forming fine friendships. Other children have a greatly harder time of it, for any of a variety of reasons. These are among the children we call *rejected*. If not everyone can be popular, rejection is just not where any child should be.

Peer rejection is not a permanent "trait."

The parent who wondered if her child was doing "something that turns off other kids" told the following story. She served as a parent monitor on the first grade's all-day field trip, which gave her a chance to observe her daughter over several hours. "Megan was OK when there were structured and teacher-supervised things going on, like the three-legged sack race," said her mom. "But when the kids were on their own, running around and making up games, she wasn't included. I watched her circle this big field they were in, and sometimes approach little groups of kids, and they just ignored her."

It broke her heart, said Megan's mother, who called her daughter a shy kid. She had been painfully shy herself as a child, she said, and she thought Megan would just have to muddle through it for a while, as she had done, until she gained more confidence over time. And it's true that some kids like Megan may very well figure things out for themselves eventually—but that doesn't mean their parents can't offer them the guiding hand they need in the meantime.

For some other mothers and fathers, it's not a child's extreme timidity or fearfulness that's upsetting, but exactly the opposite kind of behavior. "Plain and simple, I think my son is a bully," said the mother of six-year-old Cody. "Playtime with another kid always degenerates into pushing, hitting, and bad roughhousing, with the other boy walking away." She described her son as a gregarious boy who had no trouble joining groups at play, though she noted that those initially positive connections usually and quickly turned sour. Cody had been born "a little battler," she said, "always bulldozing into things." Like Megan's mother, this parent believed that her child would in time learn more acceptable behaviors.

Cody's mother was quite right to be concerned about her son, and she may have been correct in assuming that he acted the way he did in part due to his biologically based temperament. She may even have been right that in time he'd learn from his playmates that intentionally rough stuff wasn't appreciated, and he'd cut it out. Much research, however, tells us that children like Cody may have trouble getting the peer message on their own and are likely to be ostracized by "normal" kids. Here, too, parents can take an active role in helping their children find the better path.

If yours is a shy child or "a little battler," he or she needs your help. If you are the parent of a son or daughter who perpetually struggles at the edges of acceptance by peers, who acts in ways that other children seem to find peculiar or disagreeable, you absolutely can guide your child toward a greater degree of social comfort and competence. And there are specific, well-substantiated ways to extend such encouragement and support, as you'll see in chapters 9 and 10.

Much of my own work in child development has focused on understanding the emotional lives of children like Megan, who shy away from their social milieus, and like Cody, who do battle with their interpersonal worlds. Other significant research has examined the strategies that seem to be most effective in helping a child become better accepted—and thus happier, more content, and more socially successful. There's good news to report: Life really can change for the better for many of these youngsters, at any age. Indeed, my colleagues and I would be out of a collective job if the kinds of problems children face in their peer groups could not be mended.

All of the suggestions in chapters 9 and 10 grow out of one essential developmental truth: Every child (and every adult, for that matter) must learn how to *regulate* his or her own feelings, thoughts, and behaviors. Children who are experiencing rejection aren't doing that kind of regulating very well. Suppose your shy, retiring son really wants to join the group of boys playing tag on the playground, but the idea of approaching them makes him terribly nervous. His inclination is to stay safe by hanging back, even though it means missing out on the fun. If he can learn to calm himself down, think through what he might do, and then take an appropriate action in spite of not feeling relaxed or confident, he may have some success. And social success does breed success, besides diminishing feelings of anxiety.

There is a learning process that all children must go through, one in which parents play a central role. It starts in infancy and toddlerhood, when you offer the soothing and calming-down that your youngster can't manage on her own. It is enhanced when you provide the kinds of opportunities that let your child test the social waters, explore her environment, and begin to figure out what works and what doesn't. Eventually, if all goes well, sometime during the early school years, *self-regulation* kicks in as your child gets better at controlling her *own* feelings, thoughts, and behaviors.

But even if the process hasn't gone so well—if your five- or six- or eleven-year-old often gets the brush-off in social interactions—there are ways you can help that child change the picture, as we'll see.

Not all "bad" behaviors are all that bad.

At the beginning of this chapter, I quoted the mother who disliked the "obnoxious" kids with whom her "sweet, funny, bright" son spent his time—kids who she believed were pressuring him to act in ways that weren't like him. Confronting thirteen-year-old Ethan with her impressions of his friends, including her disapproval of the way they talked, she told him she'd prefer it if he didn't hang out with them so much. Her son's response was the one that many self-respecting adolescents would have offered: "I have the right to pick my own friends." Insofar as his rights were concerned, Ethan was entirely correct. But where did that leave his parents?

When your child reaches the age at which cliques and crowds and friends seem to dominate his life, in school and out, you may find reason to dislike the kids he "hangs with"—especially if being with them seems suddenly to have produced a transformation from sweet and funny to brash and obnoxious. Such preteen or early-adolescent transformations may not run deep or last long (though a few months or close to a year can feel like an eternity), but they tend to send the mercury in a parent's anxiety-meter skyward, bringing concerns about "bad influences" and a child's "falling in with the wrong crowd" to the fore. And from there it becomes all too easy for the parent to assume that what may in fact be essentially innocuous behaviors on the part of a child and his friends will lead inevitably to disaster. Partly, I believe, this is a result of fear-inducing media reports that warn us of the dangers that lie in wait for such youngsters.

But what about the fear expressed by the parent I mentioned earlier, the one who fretted that when seemingly normal kids start coming out of nowhere and blowing up schools, "it feels like it could happen anywhere"? Again, I think in recent years we have been coerced into believing that young people are carrying on secret, volatile lives that are beyond the ken of the average parent and immune to parental control.

In chapter 11 I address some of these issues in a way that I hope will help you differentiate between normal (albeit disturbing or irritating or exasperating) activities and genuinely worrisome ones. While some deviations from adult-expected or -accepted behaviors cannot and should not be dismissed, others are simply not worth the fight. Parents just need to know which battles should be pursued in a reasoned fashion, and which are best conceded. There *are* lines that children should not be allowed to cross; there *are* signs that a child may be "in" with a group of friends who are headed for real trouble; and there *are* actions that parents can take. But it's also the case that "good" kids sometimes do "bad" things and in the long run will be none the worse for them.

Even when there's nothing terrible going on, however, *you* have your *own* rights (and responsibilities) as a parent, and it's perfectly appropriate for you to make clear to your child which behaviors you consider unacceptable, unadvisable, or disagreeable. I hope chapter 11 will give you some workable ideas on how to do that without alienating your teen or causing him to tune out.

When families are under stress, a child's life among peers may suffer.

Friends, biology, and parenting all contribute to a youngster's social competence, with each playing its own role in the development of healthy or unhealthy outcomes. But other factors figure in as well, including the neighborhood, the child's school, and, especially, the extent to which his or her family is either conflicted or peaceful.

In a day and age in which many adults are under stress and divorce is common, it's critical that parents understand the ramification that marital tension and changes in family structure can have for a child. Many research studies have shown that adult problems and upheavals can have a negative impact on a child's peer relationships. Witnessing persistent arguments and fighting between parents, or going home to a mother and father who are so distracted by their own difficulties that they're simply not able to parent very effectively, can cause even a formerly well adjusted, competent child to become either angry, suspicious, and resentful among his peers or silent, sad, and withdrawn.

A number of studies, as we'll see in chapter 12, have dramatically demonstrated how children react to and feel about displays of anger between their parents. In suggesting what children need most during times of family stress, the results of this research should be required reading for any parent who is in an unhappy marriage or struggling with the possibility or the reality of divorce.

Underlying these various points are a few key themes concerning the two relationship systems, child/parent and child/peer, and the connections between them. Take heart: The messages are hopeful and encouraging!

In the most important ways, children's peer relationships will
be a lot like their relationships with their parents.

Especially through the years of late childhood and adolescence, it's a good idea to bear in mind that your child's struggle toward self-definition and independence does not mean that she is repudiating the life lessons learned at home. This is a central truth for parents to understand and remember during the trying or puzzling times. And it's a truth that flies in the face of many popular notions that have had a place in our collective consciousness for some time.

For example, with the publication of his classic 1961 work *The Adolescent Society*, James Coleman attracted much attention by suggesting that what peers valued was antithetical to what parents valued, and that when these two rivals for a young person's soul went head to head, the peer group inevitably won out. It was perhaps the first widely read and influential assertion that a child's friends, or the crowd he hung out with, were the major force in determining the choices he made. Parents, Coleman's book implied, were in for the battle of their lives.

In the years since, many researchers have painted a radically different picture. We now know that in many ways, *peer values tend to be much like family values* (albeit in a different context), and *peer relationships tend to be much like the relationships children have with their parents*. If the members of your family treat one another with respect, support, kindness, empathy, and honesty, these are the relationship qualities your child will carry into her other interpersonal worlds as well. And likely she will expect the same in return from her friends.

Children can learn social skills, and parents can teach them.

Parents—and educators, too—often tend not to think of social competence as a skill that's *learned*. And yet, children acquire social competence much as they do an understanding of mathematics or science—through exploring by trial and error, through working out problems and practicing, and through building knowledge step by step, all with the help of friends and wise and responsive adults. As you begin to perceive your child's friendships and peer connections in terms of the necessary skills to be learned, your role in the process will become infinitely clearer.

In his book *Presentation of Self in Everyday Life,* the sociologist Irving Goffman introduced the wonderfully descriptive term *face work,* signifying the ability to present oneself successfully to others by putting on somewhat different faces for different audiences. The children who do the best socially are those with a talent for face work and the ability to maintain social repertoires that are wide and deep. They understand when to put on which face, without ever appearing shallow or false to others and without feeling like fakes or frauds. In short, these are children who are sensitive and responsive to social cues.

If your son is good at face work, for example, he may know that while it's OK to act in a goofy manner when he's with close friends, eating lunch or clowning around after school, that same silliness would be misguided and distracting to others in the classroom; he's aware that there he must present a more serious face, as a student. He accepts that in a group it's sometimes best to hang back and be quiet, to listen and observe; at other times, though, he can be the leader, out front. He learns to "read" his various audiences, to know what they're thinking about him (or whether they're thinking about him at all), and to shape his actions in ways that invite others to value him and seek him out. Face work is thus a central feature of social competence, which may be defined as the ability to achieve personal goals in social interactions while simultaneously maintaining positive relationships with others, over time and in a variety of situations.

Personal goals, it's easy to see, make up a vast inventory from toddlerhood through adolescence. Your youngster's goal at any point might be having the chance to play with a particularly neat toy or joining a group of kids in the sandbox; patching up a fight with her best friend or starting a conversation with someone she thinks she'd like to get to know; figuring out what to say when he's being teased or picked on or asking a classmate for help with homework; confiding her worries to someone she knows will be supportive or coming to the aid of someone who she sees is having problems; finding like-minded kids to befriend in a new school or refusing to go along with the crowd, while still preserving self-respect and strong friendships. Face work is real work. For your child, it means being flexible, resilient, and sympathetic to the needs of those closest to her—the surest way to make and keep good friends—and at the same time being all those things, in a somewhat different way, within the larger peer group as well. It takes heart, confidence, and—especially—skill.

That brings us back to the point: Social skills are central to making a child a good friend and well liked. And social skills are *learned*.

In childhood, friendship is where the action is!

The bottom line is, we are social beings; we need to establish satisfactory and satisfying human connections. Figuring out how to get along with people, how to initiate friendships, how to walk away from relationships that are no longer pleasant and maintain the ones that are enjoyable and valuable—these are the challenges at the core of our emotional lives, and childhood is when we must begin to meet them.

Witnessing your child confront these challenges successfully, and playing a role in the process, can be wonderful. It can provide the deepest satisfaction you'll ever have as a parent.

Chapter 2

The Power of Peers

How a Child's Friendships Form, What They Mean, and Why They're Critical

Peers are a powerful force in our children's lives, influencing their development in all sorts of ways. They encourage a child to think about what's right and what's wrong; they are central to his feelings of self-esteem; and they help him figure out which social behaviors are acceptable and which are not. In the simplest terms, having friends and decent peer connections benefits a youngster immensely; being friendless or not so well liked spells trouble.

How and why all this is true have been the focus of what I earlier described as the explosion of research over the past fifteen or twenty years into children's relationships. In our work, including the ongoing Friendship Study, we've gone a long way toward demystifying the social world of childhood by coming at it from some fresh angles. As a parent, you can do much the same thing in your own relationship with your child.

In a sense, parenting calls for being a bit of a psychologist, reading a child's signals with a dispassionate eye in order to provide support that is not only loving but also wise and genuinely helpful. In this chapter, I'll detail some of the ways we have been looking at children's behaviors, explain what our research has led us to believe about the power of peers in a child's life, and suggest how the perspectives we use can be of great value to parents in understanding their sons and daughters.

When friends clash: What's really going on?

Two parents—the mother of six-year-old Bobby and the mother of eleven-year-old Lily—talked about recent experiences involving their children and their children's friends. Both were puzzled.

Bobby had had two playdates in his home one week, each with a different kindergarten classmate. One date went swimmingly, while the other, said his mom, "was a disaster." The disastrous get-together included a lot of fighting between the boys, which was bad enough that the babysitter who was looking after them took them out for ice cream to settle things down and then dropped the playmate off at his home earlier than planned. That evening, when Bobby's mother asked him what had happened, he told her that the other boy, Alex, had taken all the toys and "acted mean." He added, "I hate him!"

This surprised her, because Bobby and Alex had always seemed to get along well at school, and it bothered her, because she and Alex's mother were friendly. "So I launched into a little talk about how I thought he and Alex could be friends and how we really shouldn't *hate* anybody," she said. The little talk was probably a mistake, she later reflected, "because Bobby just scowled and got silent." She thought she'd call Alex's mom and get his version of the afternoon. Then she wondered if maybe the two boys "just don't have good chemistry together."

Lily wasn't doing much talking, either, and her mother was sure something was up. She had always heard a lot about Marty, one of her daughter's closest friends, but then abruptly she stopped hearing her name. Over the course of several days, this parent noticed that the two girls were no longer on the phone together every night, as usual. So she casually brought up the subject with her daughter—"How's Marty these days?"—and got a noncommittal answer: "She's fine, I guess."

A few days after that, Lily's mom tried again. "I asked her if something had happened between her and Marty, if they'd had a fight or whatever," she said. Lily replied that they hadn't had a fight, but explained, "I just talked to some other kids, and Marty got all upset. She takes everything personally, like it's all about her." Forging ahead, Lily's mother asked her daughter if she'd said something that had hurt her friend's feelings. Lily responded, "Just forget it, OK, Mom? It's no big deal."

Mom let it drop, but she, too, was bothered, "because Marty's a sweet girl, and I wondered if Lily was giving her the brush-off. Besides, I knew this was really upsetting Lily. I thought she probably wanted to patch things up but just didn't know how." She added, "It's hard to sort of step back and take in the big picture."

I can't think of a more succinct way to describe what is probably a parent's best stance in situations like the ones these mothers described. But standing back and looking at the big picture is often the hardest thing to do when your child is having peer problems or just doesn't seem very happy, and you want to learn more. A lot gets in the way, including your own emotions. When your child is upset, you're upset. And if she takes that unhappiness out on you when you're only trying to be helpful, that can hurt, too, or make you angry. And anyway, how do you know what the real story is when your child can't or won't tell you in so many words?

Then, too, the shape of your child's world is always changing. Friends come and go. The broad scenes he is part of, whether involuntarily or by choice, shift. Things may be proceeding pleasantly, smoothly, and uneventfully at one moment, and then turn difficult, troublesome, or unsatisfying the next.

But here's a good starting point: It's much easier to see the big picture when you appreciate what a number of researchers describe as the three levels of social connection. In brief, children bring to any social exchange certain individual, biologically based characteristics—their nature or temperament—as well as social skills. These factors lead them to interact with others in particular ways. A child's *interactions* in turn predict the kinds of *relationships* he or she will form. And relationships, finally, occur within larger *groups* or networks. In a sense, the levels of connecting thus move from the simplest or most basic to the most complex and populated.

Sorting out and making sense of the levels will help you piece together a reasonably accurate picture of your youngster's social-emotional universe at any point in time, and enable you to figure out your own role in it. To put it another way, when things are going wrong you can't "treat" your child without recognizing his individual characteristics and interactional style; you can't influence that interactional style for the better without understanding his relationships and friendships; and you can't understand those relationships without knowing about group behaviors and norms.

Interactions

An *interaction* is a social exchange between two children, in which what *Child A* does is both a response to and a stimulus for what *Child B* does. Interactions occur with pals the child knows well and likes, with other children he or she hasn't met before, and with kids he or she knows and either doesn't much like or is indifferent to. It's easy to see that the definition "a social exchange between two children" covers a vast range of possibilities, from saying hello to arguing, from playing a game to telling a joke or gossiping about a classmate, and on and on.

It's also easy to appreciate that no interaction takes place in a social vacuum. Consider Bobby's playdate, for example. Maybe it started on its disastrous course when Alex grabbed a toy and Bobby retaliated with a shove. How this interaction continued—that is, what Alex did next—was based on a number of factors. Did Alex like Bobby and consider him a friend? Was either Alex or Bobby generally quick to anger? Were the two boys alone in Bobby's living room, or was the baby-sitter watching them? And what in fact *was* the "chemistry" between the two? Bobby's other playdate may have gone smoothly because he acted one way with that child and somewhat differently with Alex, perhaps because those two children had different characteristics.

In general, however, we can identify three broad childhood behavioral tendencies or interactional styles. If you were to watch your youngster among her peers, you could quite readily identify her as one of the following interactional types:

- The child who *moves toward other children.* This child is, by and large, appropriately involved with others and with what is going on at the moment.

- The child who *moves against other children.* This child is uninhibited and has trouble controlling anger, among other negative emotions.

- The child who *moves away from other children.* This child is inhibited and has trouble controlling fear and other negative emotions.

We can call such children *normal* (or *average*), *aggressive*, and *withdrawn*, respectively. Although clearly they hardly describe the whole child—normal kids, for instance, are often not as predictable or placid as the label might suggest; aggressive kids aren't necessarily always starting fights; and withdrawn kids are not "abnormal" simply because of their reticence—these three widely accepted terms are a useful guide for understanding how children make their way among their peers.

Relationships

Two kids who have a number of interactions over time and thereby get to know each other enter the next level of complexity in peer experiences: They have a *relationship*. Within a relationship, every interaction—a game played, an argument—is influenced in some part by what's happened between the participants in the past and by what each anticipates or hopes for in the future. In a close relationship, the friends are committed to and accept their connection to each other.

Of course, children also have close relationships with siblings, cousins, and others who are not classified primarily as peer friends. In our work, however, my colleagues and I focus on friendships, which we define according to specific criteria. To determine whether a friendship exists between two kids, we ask, Do the two spend time together? Do they clearly like each other? Are they acknowledged as friends by other kids? Do both feel that their relationship is intense, special, even unique? Do they recognize that if one calls off the friendship and walks away, the relationship is over?

Groups

Of course, a friendship doesn't exist in a vacuum, either. Separately and together, the two children belong to a *group* or several groups—the little knot of kids around the sand table, the third-grade class, the seventh-grade clique, the basketball team, the cheerleading squad, or one of the myriad "crowds" of high school. Some groups are decreed by the environment—for example, a third grader is a member of the third grade whether he or she wishes to be or not. Others form on their own, according to shared interests or perceptions or some other uniting factor. Each group has its own properties—it's understood, for instance, that everyone in one group cracks jokes about teachers—and members will tend to stick together and may exclude others. And within most groups, there's a pecking order.

From the day a child first joins a roomful of other little kids in day care, preschool, or kindergarten, looking excited or teary or something in between, every parent appreciates the place and the power of the group in the child's young life. Indeed, social-dominance research confirms what I'm sure you already suspect: Hierarchies can and do exist in gatherings of even the youngest children. Clear-cut win/lose episodes occur between children as young as two, with some youngsters emerging at the top of the social heap and others at the bottom. It is within that heady mix that children from toddlerhood on deem themselves to be liked and to have what it takes to be popular or, at least, to fit in.

The group has the power to affect relationships. To get the big picture of what was really going on between Lily and her once-good friend Marty, for example, Lily's mother might need to know that her daughter was trying to join forces with several girls who didn't especially like Marty, or that Marty had been on the receiving end of some basically good-natured teasing by a group of classmates one day and that Lily had said the wrong thing at the wrong time—or any number of other, similar scenarios.

Picking up on the clues

Understanding the nature of these various levels of connecting—disentangling the threads—has been a challenge for social scientists, and it's the core challenge *you* will have to confront as a parent hoping to be a force for good in your youngster's social development. But disentangling the threads is more than a means of identifying appropriate actions to take; it's also a liberating effort. That's because a lot of what transpires in your child's peer life is not entirely knowable, not within your control, and not your "fault."

Until fairly recently, much of what social scientists believed or assumed about child development was derived from adults' accounts of their childhood experiences, both good and bad—but mostly bad. Extrapolating from the revelations of adult patients in treatment, in other words, psychologists made inferences about what set children on a happy or unhappy path, and what kind of child-raising practices contributed to each outcome. Thus were born notions of the all-powerful parent—and, by extension, the all-to-blame parent.

Today we use a very different approach, one that has clarified the lines of influence among children, their peers, and their parents. To understand children's social lives, we now observe *children* in *social* settings, not adults in therapeutic ones. We also talk to children about their experiences with their friends and ask their parents and teachers for *their* impressions. We position ourselves close to the age of the child and close to the action, so to speak, and use a rich array of assessment "tools" to fine-tune the picture. These are tools that every parent should have at hand as well.

In telling you now a little about our research methods, my aim is to encourage you to adapt and embrace them yourself. If there are aspects of your child's social life that are beyond your control, you have everything to gain by obtaining as much information about them as you possibly can. Many of the suggestions provided on "parent skills" in the later chapters of this book have evolved from just such tactics. Basically it's a matter of picking up on clues by considering several questions:

How does my child act?

Watching children in their natural habitat, as it were—whether in school or in play groups or in structured laboratory settings—lets us code behaviors: Is this a youngster who gets pushed around? One who easily shares toys? Does this boy assume a leadership role with his peers, or is he more of a follower?

Observing your child—simply watching and thinking about what he is like when playing with a friend or in a group of kids—is the key to acquiring a real understanding of the strengths and weaknesses he brings to social interactions. That's the level at which you can make a powerful difference in whether your child moves toward, against, or away from other children. Observing behaviors and what they say about a child is the subject of the following chapter, in which I will invite you to "sit in on" my laboratory-based study of a number of youngsters we've come to know from infancy on up into their early school years. You'll see there some revealing demonstrations of the link between the two relationship systems, child/parent and child/peer, and learn how even small adjustments in a parent's actions or reactions can make things go greatly better for a child.

How do other adults perceive my child?

Teachers can tell us a lot about the social worlds of the children in their charge. Privy on a daily basis to the goings-on in their classrooms, these adults can offer objective impressions of which kids take a long time to settle down to work, which are frequently sought out by others for play, and so on. In some instances, it's true, teachers may not be so reliably clued in to the real story concerning the youngsters they teach—the pleasure of having a quiet, respectful child in the classroom, for example, may result in an "adultomorphic" perspective, one that effectively prevents the teacher from seeing that student the way his peers do (Since I like this child, the teacher may think, the kids must like him, too). But more often, teachers' impressions are accurate and can help researchers "map" classrooms according to broad behavioral profiles.

The other adults in your child's life, besides you and your spouse, almost surely have impressions of or information about her that it would be good for you to hear. A tuned-in parent, I have suggested, has to be something of a psychologist. The job description also includes being a competent news gatherer, because many, if not most, of a school-age child's behaviors happen *out there,* during all the hours of the day when she isn't with you. But as their children grow older, especially when they get to middle-school age and beyond, moms and dads, we have found, tend to drift away from actions that could tell them what's up with their kids— from talking to teachers, coaches, or counselors, to comparing notes with other parents, to simply being on the scene when possible and appropriate as interested observers. In fact, staying in touch in these ways is critical to getting the big picture.

What do other kids think about my child?

Through the use of questionnaires and rating scales, we're able to obtain an insider's view of the peer group. So, for example, we might ask children to name the classmates who are leaders, the kids who get things going, or those who are very shy. We want to know who's a show-off, who has a good sense of humor, who's the best person to seek out for help with homework. Clearly, children are often better judges of such aspects of the social landscape than their teachers.

In recent years, the development of new information-gathering techniques has enabled us to come up with more detailed assessments of what children think of one another. More than simply identifying who's the fighter in the group, for instance, or who likes to be alone, we can learn about forms of relational aggression (whether a child tries to hurt other kids by saying mean things about them or by keeping them out of activities) and determine whether the "loner" is that way because the group has deemed him a misfit or because he's happiest doing his own thing.

Our research has mostly focused on school-related relationships and reputations; we haven't gotten terribly far, unfortunately, in understanding those children whose primary connections are outside of school, either in the neighborhood or with others involved in extracurricular interests and activities. Even for children whose friendships are elsewhere, however, what goes on in the second-grade or sixth-grade setting certainly affects how they feel about heading out from home in the morning. Without a friend or two in school, the day can be long and miserable.

In particular, free times—right before classes begin, when kids are chatting and joking; at lunch, when having someone to sit with is so important; and right after classes end, moving through the halls or out the door and into the rest of the afternoon—are painful and terribly lonely for some children. School becomes an aversive place, where finding a friend can indeed mean the difference between night and day. So our mostly school-based friendship and popularity data, we believe, provide the most meaningful clues to how a child is doing socially.

In all likelihood, your child's school friends see her in action in ways that you can't. Of course, it would be unwise for you to pepper these young people with a lot of questions designed to reveal what they really think about your child. But welcoming them into your home, listening to what they have to say, and in other ways being an unintrusive but attentive presence will surely add to your store of information about the nature of your child's relationships and the groups of which she is a part.

What does your child say about his friendships and peer groups?

We can also learn a great deal about a child's social life by simply asking him to tell us about it. Certainly by middle school and the teenage years, when they're able to conceptualize the meaning of friendship in a fairly mature manner, children have thoughts and feelings about it, which they're often marvelously, touchingly willing to share with us.

One question we ask the preteens taking part in our current study is "What does friendship mean to you, or what do you think having a good friend is really all about?" Some youngsters tell us, "Well, it's having someone to have fun with, someone who likes the same stuff you do." And indeed, that's a big part of the story. From Jonathan, a thoughtful twelve-year-old, we heard a more sophisticated definition of the nature of friendship, the kind of definition we'd like to expect from someone his age. After pondering our question for a while, Jonathan said, "It's like, you're at the free-throw line in the basketball playoff game, and if you sink the basket, you win the game and your team wins the championship. And you're getting ready to take your shot, but you see that your best friend, over on the sidelines, is getting pushed around by some other kids. So you drop the ball and go over and help him out. That's the meaning of friendship."

As you consider Jonathan's statement, you may be wondering, Would this kid truly elect to pass up a chance at personal glory on the basketball court in order to aid his friend? If push came to shove in real life, is that, in fact, how he would act?

Maybe yes, maybe no. And maybe the answer doesn't especially matter. The response we get in a one-on-one interview with a twelve-year-old in a lab setting may indeed be very different from what happens when that same child is confronted with a difficult bit of business in everyday life— when he may feel the need to save face, or is with a group he's particularly eager to impress.

But here's what we consider a critical aim of our interviews with middle-school and older kids: We are looking for a child's ability to form ideas about and to articulate the subtler aspects of being and having a friend— from giving and receiving affection and support to having to put the needs of the relationship above personal needs on occasion. A young person who thinks that's what friends do, above and beyond just plain having fun together, will gravitate toward other young people whose understanding of friendship is equally mature and caring. Research tells us, as well, that children who are able to *reason* in relatively sophisticated or age-appropriate ways about friendship are generally well liked by their peers. And so we believe that we can learn as much from what comes out of the mouths of babes as we can from observing them in action.

Jonathan's definition touched on central aspects of friendship, and something more: He was telling us, we think, that for him that was what *all* close relationships were about—between friend and friend, parent and parent, parent and child. Many researchers would say that Jonathan had a good *internal working model* of what should happen between people—a model that has much do with a child's relationship with his or her parents. How that model develops is something we'll return to in later chapters.

One suggestion I'd like to make here is, *Do* keep talking to your child, not only about what happened in her day, but about the *meaning* of friendship generally—because what your child thinks is sometimes as important as what she does.

I must add that should you ask your son or daughter the same question—"What does friendship mean to you?"—it's unlikely that you'll receive a considered, measured response. He or she may give you a "Where is *this* coming from?" look instead. Kids don't talk to parents the way they might to a researcher in the course of a lab study. But every time you put into words the values that underscore a close and caring relationship— maybe the two of you have just watched a movie or read a book together, and you take a moment to say, "I liked the way that character stood up for his friend, because even though it wasn't easy, he knew it was the right thing to do"—you give your child a way to think about what it means to be a social being, connected to others. And children do listen, and hear.

In an effort to understand children's relationships, much research essentially weaves together the various methods of information gathering I have just described. The work that my colleagues and I are currently engaged in at the Laboratory for the Study of Child and Family Relationships may serve as a snapshot example.

Studying children and their best friends

Several hundred children, all of whom are making the transition into middle school, are taking part in the Friendship Study. This point of change is a very difficult one for many, many children, as they move from familiar surroundings in which they are the oldest students into a new place, usually a completely different building, where they are members of the youngest group. A sixth-grade "freshman" may find herself to be just a little girl among what are essentially young women.

Before we even met the participants, my colleagues and I had a pretty good idea of the different pairs we'd be working with in our study, based on a wide battery of assessment materials. Because we were interested in which children would have the easiest or most difficult transition to middle school, we began data collection in the final year of elementary school (grade five). We selected our participants by asking each fifth grader to tell us who was his or her very best friend. We searched through the questionnaires of close to six hundred children to see if each child's nomination was reciprocated: Did the child Joel named likewise choose Joel? We gathered, as well, information from the teachers and from the mothers of our best-friend pairs. And then we had each child visit our lab on two occasions in the fifth grade, once with his or her mother and once with his or her best friend.

Here is how one of the sessions with a friendship pair was designed:

First, the two friends had fifteen minutes of free play in our lab playroom, which was filled with all kinds of goodies, including a basketball net and construction activities—a veritable Toys "R" Us. After this warmup, we asked them to tell us a little about how they'd met, what they liked to do together, and the best fun they'd ever had. (Cameras operating behind one-way mirrors videotaped the entire session.)

Then we presented them with an intriguing proposition: "Say you had unlimited funds—money is no object—and your parents' permission to do whatever you wanted for one whole weekend. What would you do?" We were interested here in how the discussion got under way: Did one youngster throw out all the suggestions? Were the two responsive to each other's ideas of what constituted a great time? When they disagreed, did they do so in such a way as not to hurt each other's feelings?

After planning their fabulous fantasy weekend, the two friends were given the assignment of constructing an origami figure, which could be an easy flower, a somewhat harder boat, or a very-difficult-to-make frog. Whichever figure they decided to try, we told them, they had to do it together. Again, we considered what choice they made, how they made it, and how they got going: Did they criticize each other? Did one do all the supervising while the other did all the paper folding? Did they laugh and have some fun with the project?

When they had completed the origami flower or boat or frog, we presented the two friends with a famous scenario developed years ago by the psychologist Lawrence Kohlberg, which attempts to gauge children's levels of moral reasoning or sophistication. The scenario goes like this: Ed's wife is dying of a deadly disease. There is a drug that can cure her, Ed knows, but he can't afford it; the medication costs five thousand dollars, and he has only one thousand. He asks the pharmacist to sell him the medication at an affordable price, but the pharmacist refuses. Ed pleads with him—"My wife will die"—but to no avail. Should Ed steal the drug? we ask the two friends. If he does, why is it right for him to do so? If he doesn't steal the drug, why is *that* the right choice to make?

Again, we videotaped the youngsters as they tried to come to a common resolution. Did the leadership within the twosome start changing? Was the child who was great at making the origami boat or at sinking Nerf baskets less able to think philosophically? Did his friend bring special strengths to bear in this area, and did the first boy seem to appreciate those strengths? One purpose of this scenario, then, was to see how, and if, the friends were able to "co-construct" a workable answer.

Next we split up the two to answer questionnaires and be interviewed separately. And we presented each with another story:

Jack and Matt have been best friends since kindergarten. One day a new kid who has just moved into the neighborhood spots the two friends playing on the park basketball court and asks if he can join them. Jack and Matt say, "Sure." Later, after the game ends and the new kid leaves, they talk about him. "What did you think about that guy?" Jack asks, and Matt answers, "He's kind of cool; I liked him." Jack responds, "Not me. He's pretty full of himself—he's a show-off." Jack and Matt then make plans for the following Saturday: they'll meet at Matt's house to build a new skateboard. That evening Matt gets a call from the new kid, who says he has tickets to a big basketball game and asks if Matt wants to go with him. "Sure," says Matt. "When is it?" It turns out the game is the following Saturday, skateboard-building time. (When our study participants were girls, the story characters were female, and the themes slightly different.)

We asked each child a number of questions: "What do you think Matt should do about this?" "If you were in this situation, and you could either hang out with your old buddy or go to the game with the new kid, which would you choose?" "Would you rather have one really close friend or a group of not-so-close friends?" And so on.

This mini-summary of the events of one afternoon in our Friendship Study lab should give you a good idea of the kinds of issues that interest us. They have to do with expressions of mutual concern; with the effects that two childhood friends have on each other as they think through a problem; with qualities of loyalty and feelings of betrayal; with evidence of affection and fun; and with how children display emotional bonds with their peers. In my ongoing studies, and in much current and recent research in the field of child development, these have been among the concerns occupying investigators, and we have learned and continue to learn a lot about them. We can now form an idea, for one thing, of the *characteristics* of a friendship.

Who is a friend?

A friendship is a reciprocal, voluntary affair. No external force such as a mom or dad, nor any fixed circumstance, decreed that these two should be pals. A brother and sister (or parent and child, or teacher and child) may do many of the same things that friends do together, such as playing or sharing ideas and feelings. But those family or adult-child pairings, according to developmental researchers, are significantly different from peer friendships.

In fact, psychologists who study individuals' "relationship inventories" (friend/child, parent/child, sibling/child, grandparent/child, and so on) define friendship as the one connection in a child's life in which both members have reasonably equal power. After all, while the sibling relationship is clearly more egalitarian than the parent/child one, an older sister can still pull rank on a younger sister.

And then, too, friends are friends because they like each other and want to spend time together. The underpinning of the connection is an emotional one, not born solely of similar interests or other factors independent of feelings. A child who's passionate about chess or soccer will find other kids with those enthusiasms, of course, and may well end up making friends among them. But mutual affection is at the heart of the matter.

These three elements are considered the basic criteria of friendship, which is thus defined as a reciprocal, voluntary relationship based on positive feelings. Much current research, however, is devoted to ascertaining the *quality* of children's friendships. For example, a youngster might be asked to describe what happens after she and her best friend have a fight. If the pair enjoy a high-quality friendship, each will put effort into weathering the conflict through discussion, compromise, and conciliation. Resolving the argument will in fact leave the friends feeling better about the relationship in general, and even strengthen their bond.

Kids are asked, too, about issues relating to caring, intimate exchange, companionship and recreation, help and guidance. "Are the following statements true (or not) about your best friend and you?" we want to know: "My friend makes me feel good about my ideas and sticks up for me if others talk behind my back." "My friend and I come up with neat ideas about how to do things." "We always sit together at lunch, pick each other as partners, and go to each other's house." "We talk about things that make us sad and tell each other our secrets."

Affection, trust, self-validation, the wish and willingness to get beyond arguments and conflicts—these, we believe, are some of the characteristics of high-quality friendships. In turn, having such relationships serves to promote and extend children's growth and adjustment in a variety of ways. We now know not only what constitutes a friendship, but what friends are good for.

What are friends for?

The father of a thirteen-year-old daughter said he could always tell on a Friday evening what the next couple of days would be like: "If she has something good planned with her friends, we're in for a sunny weekend. If there's nothing going on or, God forbid, if something's going on that she's not part of, we will live with storm clouds." Throughout the school years, every parent comes to realize that friends and social life have a lot to do with his or her child's prevailing mood at any moment. But in fact, that's only the most *visible* sign of the power of peers in your child's life. You should also know that:

Peers, and especially good friends, help your child think and reason.

In the 1930s, Jean Piaget, one of the most significant "fathers" of modern-day child psychology, proposed a theory of "constructivism," whereby a child builds an increasingly complex understanding of the world through experiences with his or her environment. You, of course, are part of your child's environment, as are his or her peers. And from those two sources, your child learns different things, in different ways.

According to Piaget's theory, children tend to accept what their parents (or other adults) tell them, not because they necessarily understand it but because their place in the scheme of things requires them to be obedient to grown-ups. Among peers, however, and especially with good friends, children feel freer to question, argue, negotiate over, and agree with or reject ideas, beliefs, and information—which in turn enhances their thinking and reasoning skills. Two children working together can thus solve problems that neither could solve on his own, or come up with the "best" answer— embodying a real-life, two-heads-are-better-than-one system.

Here's an example: The Kohlberg scenario I described earlier—in which a man can't afford the medication that will save his desperately ill wife—presents kids with a dilemma that requires thinking out black-and-white issues in a gray situation with no easy solution. A discussion between one of the pairs of friends in our study included this sequence of ideas: "Well, it's wrong to steal. It would be wrong for Ed to steal on an everyday basis, but this is a very unusual situation, because if his wife doesn't get the drugs, she'll die. Husbands and wives have to take care of each other, and she's more important to Ed than anything else right now. Ed could try again to work out a compromise with the pharmacist, one that would let him pay the money over time. But the pharmacist probably won't go along with that plan. So Ed should steal the drug and save his wife, but then he should confess what he did. If he has to go to jail, at least his wife will be OK. And maybe the judge will go easy on him."

That's a solution that takes into account everybody's interests, including what is "right" according to the world of rules and law, and what is "right" according to the needs of a personal relationship in which a human life is at stake; the good intentions that prompt Ed to do something recognizably "wrong," and the possibility of his reaching a rapprochement between the two.

When asked to come up with a joint solution, groups of children will thrash out a moral issue in much the same way, and here's what research has demonstrated: Not only does the group identify the largest range of issues to be considered; together, its members typically solve the problem at the highest level possible for children of a given age. Generally, kids will agree with the individual or individuals who propose the most mature response (which may still, of course, be a less sophisticated one than an adult would offer). Within the group, as within the pair, the leaders in complex thinking don't move down; the followers move up.

From peers, your child learns what's considered socially normal behavior.

For some decades, an accepted tenet of child development has been that children learn how to act from their parents. Only fairly recently have psychologists begun to explore the notion that a child also learns those lessons by observing the others in his social universe—significantly, other children. Modeling actions on other kids', he repeats them, abandons them, or adjusts them according to the reception they get. And it turns out that peers are powerful agents when it comes to reinforcing and encouraging or, conversely, discouraging a child's social behaviors.

Your child learns all manner of lessons about what works in his or her world in the company of peers, from when it's OK to act silly (and when it's immature and embarrassing to do so) to what's the accepted or cool way to say hello to someone—things about which you may be relatively clueless. One great value, then, of meaningful, high-quality friendships is that they give children—particularly during the years from middle childhood on—a safe place to test out behaviors, try things on for size, and maybe talk about successes or rebuffs in the social arena.

Children's friends help them feel good about themselves.

According to Harry Stack Sullivan, whose 1953 book *The Interpersonal Theory of Psychiatry* is a classic in the field, friends and peer relationships are essential to a child's sense of personal well-being. The child who is isolated from the group, who (especially at certain ages) is unable to find one or two really good friends, will consider himself or herself ineffectual, unwanted, and undesirable. Such a child, in Sullivan's view, will develop feelings of inferiority that will contribute to a sense of psychological unhappiness and loneliness—or, in Sullivan's elegant words, "the exceedingly unpleasant and driving experience connected with the inadequate discharge of the need for human intimacy."

Simply put, having friends makes your child happy.

"Making it" in the group

Consider two thirteen-year-olds, best friends. They enjoy a good, high-quality friendship: They support and rely on each other, they have fun together, they engage in neat, healthful, legal, age-appropriate kinds of activities. The obvious capacity that each child has to maintain a satisfying relationship, however, may reveal little about how he or she fares in the larger group. Either or both may be popular, and either or both may not be.

Popularity, often the bane or blessing of a child's existence, has been regarded as a trait that somehow "belongs" to the individual. But in fact, it's a phenomenon bestowed on each child by the group. Research on popularity status—that is, whether and how much a child is liked or disliked by his or her peers—has taken a leap forward in the past decade or so, thanks largely to new ways of measuring what children in any group perceive, think, and feel about one another.

Investigators have used the concepts of *social preference* and *social impact* to gauge children's popularity. A researcher might go into a school, for example, and ask kids to write down the names of the three classmates they most like and the three they most dislike. Of course, the children are always assured that their nominations will be kept in the strictest confidence and that no one other than the researcher and his or her colleagues will see their answers. From the data gathered, *preference* reveals a child's likability, as measured by the difference between the number of "I like" and the number of "I don't like" nominations he or she receives. *Impact* refers to how visible a child is to others, or how many nominations of both kinds, like and dislike, he or she receives. From this procedure have evolved five categories or classifications:

- Emily, let's say, gets many positive and few negative nominations, scoring high in both preference and impact; most of her schoolmates notice her, and most like her. Emily is *popular.*

- Mitch scores in the middle range, with neither unusually many nor unusually few plus or minus nominations; he is visible to some kids, and liked or disliked by some. Mitch is *average.*

- Celia receives few nominations of any sort; she is apparently not noticed much by others. Celia is *neglected.*

- Sam gets lots of positive and lots of negative votes; he has high impact and high but mixed likability. Sam we call *controversial.*

- Alice receives few positive and many negative votes; most kids are well aware of her, and most don't like her. Alice is *rejected.*

In a later chapter, we'll have a lot to say about these labels—what they really mean, and what you as a parent need to know in order to support your child in these often difficult worlds-within-worlds. For now, though, I'd simply like to repeat what I believe is the most important message to remember:

Not every child can be popular; not every child needs to be. And being popular, though it may bring with it social status, says little about a child's future prospects. Research findings do not suggest that popularity is the golden route to all manner of good things; there simply is not much evidence that it guarantees social or academic success in adolescence, young adulthood, or later life.

Conversely, all the evidence in the world does indicate—to parents, counselors, teachers, and others who influence the lives of children—that we must absolutely be concerned about one particular status category, that encompassing *rejection.* Rejected children typically have not been able to adapt to the norms of the peer milieu, and their classmates know it.

We do have a pretty clear picture of where, in most cases, rejection comes from; it has at least two central profiles. You'll remember those three broad behavioral tendencies, the kinds of interactions that are typical of the normal, aggressive, or withdrawn youngster. Rejected kids, we know, most often fall into the latter two categories.

Moving against/moving away from the world of peers

In the mid-1970s, in an effort to identify school problems, vast numbers of third graders in one state were rated on a variety of scales, including health, based on how often a child was absent or had to visit the school nurse; general intelligence, as determined by IQ scores; achievement, according to class grades and standardized test scores; and family structure, tied to parents' marital status. Teachers contributed observations as well, and the children were asked about themselves and one another.

Among the questions posed to the children was this one: "Imagine that we will be putting on a play, with a number of characters. Who in the class would you pick for each part?" The various roles described included some undesirable ones—"a bully," for example, another character "who can't get others to listen," and "someone who is shy."

Around the same time, by pure coincidence, a psychiatric registry was begun that recorded the names of individuals across the state who received public or private psychiatric care. This record laid the foundation for a quite remarkable payoff some time later, when those third graders reached the ages of nineteen, twenty, and twenty-one, and researchers were able to check the profiles that had been drawn up more than a decade earlier against the psychiatric registry. You may not be completely surprised to learn (as the investigators were not) that the children who had been considered "different" in third grade were much more likely than their "normal" peers to be experiencing some social and emotional difficulties as young adults (as measured by the incidence of psychiatric treatment).

What *did* startle the researchers was something else: Being perceived in third grade as socially different—as typified by nomination for the role of the bully in the pretend play, or someone who acts babyish, or someone who is very shy; in other words, being a kid whom most other kids didn't like very much—was the *one* measure that consistently correlated with later problems. Getting sick a lot and missing school, earning so-so grades, having a disrupted home environment—none of those other markers of a third grader's life and progress pointed as clearly to future rough water as did classmates' thoughts about a child.

It is not overstating the case to say that those findings sent social scientists rushing to search for possible connections between a child's relative popularity and how he or she fared in later life. Where the follow-up to the original class-play study linked "proxy" childhood peer acceptance with one specific outcome—whether or not a person underwent psychiatric treatment—many other studies have since broadened the picture. In particular, the evidence is strong that aggressive kids who get along poorly with their classmates are more likely than others to have academic problems and to commit juvenile offenses.

This is not to suggest that rejection is a cut-and-dried predictor of academic failure or juvenile delinquency; not every disliked child is a dropout- or delinquent-to-be. But that the rejected-aggressive child is at a greater than average *risk* for such outcomes is something we can't ignore. In addition, children who do battle with their worlds may become depressive, as they come to realize over time that they actually are not faring well at all in school, at home, or in life in general.

Aggressive, chip-on-the-shoulder kids are hard to miss. But timid, fearful children who are unable to join forces with others in ways that their peers recognize and value are also rejected—and up until very recently, we have not known much about this group. My own studies, and those of other psychologists, are filling in the picture. We're learning, for example, that fearful, withdrawn children who are unhappily left on the sidelines of peer activity often have a quite accurate sense of their position in the social scheme of things, and blame themselves for it. Recognizing their own shortcomings, they come to regard themselves poorly, and those negative thoughts and emotions are further reinforced by the inadequacy of the social "bag of tricks" they have at their disposal to relate in friendly and happy ways to other kids.

We know, too, that by the middle years of childhood, or from ages seven to ten and up, solitude becomes noticeable to other children. Whereas withdrawn two- or four-year-olds are left alone or ignored, withdrawn eight- or ten-year-olds—especially boys—are seen by other children as acting in a less-than-normal way, and are shunned by the group or considered "easy marks." And finally, we have discovered that early-childhood withdrawal, social failure, negative self-regard, and rejection by peers can very often predict loneliness, depression, and feelings of insecurity in adolescence.

Unlike most aggressive-rejected children, however, many shy and inhibited youngsters let us know that they're lonely and give us clues that they are open to receiving help. Some acknowledge, for example, that they would welcome a chance to talk over their social dilemmas with a counselor.

To return to where we started in this discussion of the "big picture":

Children's interactions—the way a child shares a toy, approaches a group of peers who are playing, or works on a joint project in the classroom—reveal a great deal about their social style, or how easy they find it to make friends and be liked by others. Those behaviors are the product both of a child's nature (what an individual starts with) and of his or her skills (what he or she learns). And parents are right in the middle of that mix.

In the next chapter, we will zero in on these origins and connections. What goes on among the children you're about to meet is not influenced by the fact that they are friends, or attend the same school, or have some other common frame of reference; in fact, they've never seen one another before. They've come to our labs for a few hours to engage in some games and activities, and to provide us with a "bare-bones" overview of the interplay between the two systems, child/parent and child/peer.

Chapter 3

Nature and Nurture

The Earliest Ties Among Temperament, Parenting, and a Child's Social Style

As we have seen, throughout the school years, the child who's most likely to be rejected is either the inhibited, shy, *moving-away-from* individual or the uninhibited, aggressive, *moving-against* type. This is the outcome that research has suggested to us again and again. But what causes children to come across in ways that lead to rejection? Is it just their nature, or do parents unwittingly encourage feelings and behaviors that keep such children out of sync with others their age? Among their peers, when and how do rejected children cross the line that distances them from other kids?

In this chapter we will look at some answers to these questions, derived from the result of a long-term project that my colleagues and I are conducting in our labs in Canada and the United States, as well as in other countries the world over. The pages that follow focus on the stories of Derek, Brett, and, somewhat in the background, several other youngsters who have also taken part in the study. Derek, as you'll see, acts in ways that are typical of the inhibited and fearful child; Brett, in ways that are typical of the uninhibited child. Their various play partners at different stages behave in ways we've come to expect from the *normal* or average child.

I've chosen to spotlight Derek and Brett for several reasons. First, they are rather "extreme" cases—in the sense that each consistently demonstrates behaviors that are pretty much at the far end of the continuum—and so they provide clear examples of these two recognizable pathways by which children can fall out of step with their peers. Second, as boys, they illustrate another point. While our study participants are equally distributed by gender, and while the girls we've observed act in very much the same manner as the boys (though they tend to be less physically aggressive), they seem to run into fewer difficulties overall. Specifically, evidence suggests that being inhibited, anxious, and withdrawn carries more severe "costs" for boys than for girls. The fearful boy is more often rejected by his peers and comes to have a poorer view of his own social skills and relationships.

Finally, and most important, Derek's and Brett's parents play a significant part in the small dramas that unfold around their children. Through their example, you'll see some of the parental attitudes and actions that are most helpful for a child who either tends to be on the shy and wary side or, conversely, is uninhibited and impulsive.

Derek and Brett, age seven

Seven-year-old Derek and seven-year-old Brett have just entered a playroom with two other boys, also second graders. Derek, Brett, David, and Jeff were in fact all born within days of one another, but they've never met before. As the other boys look around, Derek watches them, scoping out what they're doing. He seems to be waiting for a subtle signal—from anyone—that it's time to get down to the business of playing. Brett is meanwhile running around, scouting out the territory.

And it's an interesting territory! We have outfitted the room with the hottest toys on the market—some build-it, create-it sets, some materials that require the activity of more than one youngster, and others that are best used alone. In short order Brett, clearly a gregarious fellow, introduces himself to David and Jeff in the most casual of boyish ways, and then the three of them settle down at one of the games designed for a group. Somehow Derek seems to have missed the signal he was waiting for; finding himself a niche in a corner of the room, he begins to construct something from Lego blocks.

During the fifteen-minute free play session, Brett, David, and Jeff engage in play and some talk, pausing every once in a while to check out other materials in the room. For this threesome, Derek is either nonexistent or not worth approaching. It seems they have reached a silent but unanimous decision that this kid is a loner or in some other way not quite with it. Derek, for his part, looks increasingly uneasy as the minutes go by.

Now a researcher enters and asks the boys to pick up after themselves—by putting the toys and games on shelves or in baskets—and David and Jeff begin to comply. Brett continues to play; by his example, he seems to be discouraging the others from straightening up the room, though they do stick with it and eventually stow everything away. Derek stands to one side and watches.

Once the room has been made tidy, the researcher asks the boys to sit along a wall backed by a floor-to-ceiling mirror. Along the opposite wall is a matching mirror. The researcher now invites the boys to stand up one at a time and tell the others a bit about themselves—their names, where they go to school, their favorite activities, and so on. Each seven-year-old is thus confronted with the need to present himself to an audience, while at the same time he can hardly escape looking at himself in the mirror. It's a pointedly uncomfortable situation, one that we've designed specifically to test the limits of children's ability to control their shyness and social wariness.

Brett is the first to jump into action, speaking his piece with no obvious discomfort. He's a boys' boy, an athlete, a tough guy—these are the impressions he gives. David and Jeff follow in turn; though each tugs a little at his pants leg or talks to his shoes rather than directly to his audience, both make it through the exercise. With each passing minute, Derek is looking more and more upset. By the time his turn comes around, he's worked himself into a tizzy, bottom lip quivering, brow furrowed. When the researcher asks if he'd like to tell the others something about himself, he shakes his head.

Next the boys are asked to sit around a table on which is placed a neat, already constructed Lego model; at each boy's place are a bunch of Lego blocks. The youngsters are instructed to re-create the complicated model, a task that will require everybody's blocks. In short, in order to build the model, all four boys must participate.

David at once assesses the problem to be solved and begins by setting out two of his blocks as the base. After some discussion, he and Jeff place some more blocks in the appropriate spaces. The several pieces that must go next are in Brett's pile, but he isn't paying much attention. He's staring at the toys he was playing with earlier, apparently either uninterested in the task at hand or simply clued out.

So David and Jeff take turns putting Brett's blocks into the proper places. Meanwhile, Derek is obviously intrigued—he is *the* Lego expert in this group, as it happens—and yet he refrains from displaying his expertise, impeded by what psychologists refer to as an approach-avoidance conflict. He really could help here, and thus gain peer-reputation points, but instead he allows David and Jeff to continue arranging all the blocks until the model is finished. Brett, who's left his seat and meandered over to the other games, has contributed nothing but wise-guy remarks.

The researcher comes back in, congratulates the boys on their accomplishment, tells them they can play on their own for a while, and leaves again. Now David and Jeff are a twosome, engaging in conversation and constructive activity. Clearly wanting to join them, Brett attempts to get their attention by making clownish gestures and obscene sounds; after a minute or two he abandons that effort and tries to peek through the one-way mirror. Derek is back in a corner, his comfort zone.

After five minutes, the researcher returns again, this time holding a special toy—a computerized jet-wing fighter plane that can be used by only one boy at a time—which he places on a table before exiting the room. You can probably guess which boy is the first to reach the toy and refuses to share until he has had his fill of it—Brett to the fore. Eventually Jeff takes charge of the fighter plane, then hands it off to David. After a while, David holds the plane out to Derek, inviting him to have a turn. A look of joyful anticipation flashes across Derek's face, but just for an instant; almost immediately, clear-cut facial and bodily expressions betray his profound wariness. Soon after, the researcher comes in to end the session. Derek has not played with the toy at all; when the boys are told they can rejoin their mothers, he is the first to bolt.

You have just read an account of the sort of "stuff" that child-development researchers study with much interest. The "stuff" comprises such phenomena as *internalizing problems,* including anxiety and fearfulness; *externalizing problems,* such as oppositional behavior and attention difficulties; and *socially competent behaviors,* typified by cooperation and concern for others. It's a story with several different beginnings and endings, and I will provide you with a sense of those bits and pieces over the next pages.

My colleague Nathan Fox first met Derek and Brett when they were just a few months old; over the following years, we had several opportunities to observe them, both with their mothers and with other youngsters. Our observations enabled us to piece together the factors that we believe put these two children on their separate developmental paths and caused them to interact with their peers in the ways they did. Let's look at what those factors were, beginning with Derek.

Baby Derek

Derek and his family joined our research project when he was six months old. During this earliest meeting, and in others that followed some months later, our aim was to characterize the baby boy according to his temperament. Was he easily upset? Soothable or difficult to soothe? Sociable? Persistent? Highly active?

We noted at once that this was an unusually *reactive* infant, one who got quickly and easily stirred up. During his first visit, for example, we set in motion an electronically turning mobile that was suspended from the ceiling above him—a colorful, benign, common sort of baby toy. We also played an audiotape of two pleasant voices speaking at different volumes. Derek responded to both types of stimuli with highly agitated, jerky leg and arm movements, as well as fussing and fretting.

When Derek next came to visit, at nine months, he stood out from the majority of babies his age for a couple of reasons. The first of these was the data provided by his electroencephalogram (EEG), a simple test that traces variations in brainwaves. While at rest, relaxing comfortably in his baby seat, Derek exhibited greater relative activity in the right than in the left frontal part of his brain. To many researchers, such a measurement indicates that an individual will be more likely to respond with fear to stressful situations. That Derek was fearful was confirmed by several behaviors he demonstrated.

During the visit, again while resting, Derek was approached by one of Dr. Fox's assistants, a female graduate student. His immediate response was to cry, shrink away from her, and turn to his mother in a clear signal for help. Later, when we asked his mom to leave the room briefly, Derek "tightened up," cried some more, and remained immune to the assistant's efforts to comfort him with smiles and calming sounds. For the duration of the session, he never stopped looking extremely unhappy.

But, you're probably thinking, *most* babies will fuss and cry if their mothers leave them alone in an unfamiliar place with someone they don't know. And you're right: A typical nine-month-old may very well make it obvious that he's not at all pleased about his mom's leave-taking. Indeed, most babies in our study *did* become upset when their mothers left them, and many responded by withdrawing from the adult "stranger." Very few, however, had reacted with distress, as Derek had, to the mobile and the audiotape in the earlier session—and all of those who did either managed to self-regulate (or quiet themselves) or were easily calmed down by their mothers.

Emotional reactivity and regulation were two factors Nathan Fox examined when Derek next visited, at fourteen months. During this session, he ran what is known as the Strange Situation, an experimental scenario developed by the psychologist Mary Ainsworth to assess the quality of the parent-child relationship in early childhood.

Briefly, the Strange Situation begins with a period of free play involving mother and child. After that comes the following sequence of events: An unfamiliar adult (a member of the research team) enters the room, and the mother exits for a short period of time, leaving the child alone with the stranger; then the mother returns and the stranger leaves. Next the mother departs once again, so the child is on his own; then the stranger returns; and finally the mother comes back as the stranger leaves. Clearly, this is a very, very strange situation!

Ainsworth designed the scenario to test how a child will act when, first, he is approached by someone he doesn't know; second, his parent goes away; and third, he is reunited with his parent. From the range of infants' reactive behaviors, Ainsworth concluded, several *attachment classifications* could be postulated. Fourteen-month-old Derek, for example, fitted the classification of an insecure attachment relationship designated as *anxious-resistant*.

When he was first introduced to the playroom, Derek seemed to want no part of any of it. He clung to his mother, refraining from exploring the toy-filled space. A bit later, when the stranger entered the room, Derek not only stuck right next to his mom but even pulled at her clothing, seeking further reassurance or closeness. As you might guess, when his mother then left, Derek became inconsolable; efforts on the part of the stranger to engage him in play were to no avail. He looked thoroughly miserable.

And now you might assume that Derek would be overjoyed at the sight of his mother returning, but such was not the case. When his mom came back, Derek responded with both passivity and anger. Although he had been distraught at her departure, he didn't run to greet her but instead remained sitting unhappily. He let his mother pick him up, but when she did, he turned his back on her, looking very upset.

What we learned about baby Derek

Combining information gleaned from our research with the results of other studies conducted in recent years, we might begin to sketch a picture of Derek, and other children like him, as follows:

- Derek appeared to be "hard-wired" to behave in inhibited ways.

    Many researchers who study brain activity would say that Derek is biologically predisposed to react to unfamiliar situations, even only mildly stressful ones, with fear and anxiety. Excessive right frontal brain activity when an individual is at rest is, they believe, a marker of an underlying disposition, rather than an indication of a current emotional state. Simply put, the EEG taken while Derek was dozing in his infant carrier reflected something *basic about him,* not something about how he was feeling at the moment.

    Studies have also demonstrated that youngsters with excessive right 'frontal brain activity have what is known as low *vagal tone,* a measurement of heart rate and the overall efficiency of the nervous system in terms of both general reactivity and its ability to regulate their level of arousal. Toddlers who have low vagal tone or a consistently high heart rate—and Derek was one of these—tend to be more behaviorally inhibited.

- Derek appeared to have an insecure attachment to his mother.

    The Strange Situation that fourteen-month-old Derek experienced—unfamiliar place, unfamiliar person, Mom leaves, Mom returns—is designed to determine the quality of the emotional connection between parent and child. The explanation goes like this:

A one-year-old who has a *secure* attachment to his mother will tend to stay near her in the face of perceived danger, which to such a young child may be simply something or someone he's never seen before. During this test, on entering the unfamiliar playroom or, later, when the stranger comes in, the secure child may scurry toward his mom or at least look over at her for some signal that all is OK. He will use his parent, in other words, as a known and trusted base from which to push off to explore and play in an unknown yet tempting environment—in this case our lab room, where lots of playthings are ready and waiting for him. When his mother leaves, the secure child will try to tag along after her; he may become upset, but not so upset that he can't settle down after a minute or two and then let himself be pleasingly distracted by the toys. Upon his mother's return, this child will generally run up to her happily, glad to see her and eager for a hug.

Fourteen-month-old Derek fitted a different profile, that of the *anxious-resistant* youngster, who typically clings to his mother, does not check out the toys, weeps miserably when his mother is gone, and reacts both passively and angrily when she comes back.

The root cause of both sets of behaviors, according to attachment researchers, lies in the style of parenting a child experiences during the first year of his or her life. The secure youngster, it is thought, gets that way through responsive and sensitive attention; his mom or dad, or both, can from the start recognize his emotional signals and respond promptly and appropriately to his needs. The youngster develops the belief that his parent is someone who can be relied on for protection, nurturance, and comfort. From that belief system or secure *internal working model,* in turn, grows his sense of trust in relationships in general.

The anxious-resistant, insecurely attached child, in contrast, experiences a parenting style that is somewhat unpredictable—and usually also is characterized by intrusive control and overinvolvement in his activities. Biology and parenting work together here: Fearful babies such as Derek probably evoke in their parents the desire to shield them from "danger." In a well-intentioned effort to keep these children from feeling anxious and upset, then, the parents become overly protective and controlling. And those actions may in turn intensify the youngsters' biological tendencies.

We might surmise the following emotions churning in young Derek:

He wanted out of that room, right from the start. He had, in the course of his young life, become accustomed to having his mom come to the rescue at his first sign of distress and ease his natural anxieties. In this instance, however, not only did his mother not let him escape; she left him alone and compelled him to confront an unknown person all by himself. Later, he made his unhappiness with her over that "abandonment" very clear.

What parents should know

• "Hard-wiring" doesn't have to be measured.

Before you run to your pediatrician with a request for "baby-EEG" and vagal-tone tests, you should know that it doesn't require a professional to recognize a young child's temperament! Sensitive parents can make a quite adequate assessment all on their own, by watching how their children act and paying attention to the clues. The great majority of youngsters like Derek—the children who are made most unhappy by new things and people—can be calmed and settled down with some help from a responsive parent. Derek, as I said at the start, was a pretty unusual baby, in that he was both highly emotionally reactive *and* difficult to soothe.

• "Attachment" is not etched in stone.

Reading my description of attachment theory—explaining how the behavior of an unusually wary and inhibited youngster may have its roots in what his mother did or didn't do pretty much from day one—may have set off in your mind a disconcerting series of thoughts like the following: "Well, my daughter is clearly on the fearful and timid side, so I guess something went wrong back then, but what can I do about it *now?* If for some reason she failed to develop a secure attachment within the first year or two, is the case closed?"

In fact, nothing so immutable happens in those earliest months. Mother/child attachments can change over time, and other factors come into the picture as well. Significantly, John Bowlby, the "founding father" of contemporary attachment theory, used the term internal *working* model to indicate his belief that thoughts and feelings about relationships are subject to change—meaning that the child who doesn't feel terribly secure or confident can become more so over time. Any parent who worries that her shy youngster "got" that way because of missed and unduplicatable experiences in infancy would do well to consider what psychologists call *felt security,* a subject we'll return to in the next chapter.

Derek as a toddler

When Derek and his mother came to our lab again, shortly after he turned two, we took him through what is known as the Inhibition Paradigm, an experimental situation developed by the Harvard psychologist Jerome Kagan. Like the Strange Situation, the Inhibition Paradigm stresses a child to his or her limits. Here's how it went in this instance:

Upon entering the room, Derek's mother was asked to sit in a chair and complete a series of questionnaires. Derek, though free to play as he wished, never left his mother's side, and she did not encourage him to do so. After a few minutes, one of our researchers entered the room, sat down on the floor, and began to play with a truck and some blocks. We wanted to see if Derek might spontaneously approach this stranger who seemed to be having such a good time with the tempting toys. No go; Derek kept clinging to his mother's leg.

The stranger left, only to return a minute or two later with a really neat robot. After pushing a button or two, she had the toy circling wildly about the room, making a robotish noise. Now Derek nearly jumped out of his shoes; when the researcher asked if he'd like to push the buttons and move the robot himself, he began to wail. His mom responded to this display of misery by pushing her son behind her back, as if to protect him from impending doom.

At one point during the session, we asked Derek's mother to sit with him on the floor and play. Instead of playing with him, however, she gathered him into her lap, hugged him, and stroked his hair. After a little while, the research assistant returned and asked her to get Derek to straighten up the room by putting all the toys into a large basket. Derek's mother asked her son to pick up the toys, but he didn't move; she then quickly busied herself in getting the room cleaned up while Derek sat and watched.

One last challenge: We more or less repeated the Strange Situation of the earlier session, asking Derek's mother to leave the room for a short period. Again, Derek was one unhappy little boy, and all attempts by our researcher to comfort him were unsuccessful. Yet just as he had done before, Derek displayed a noticeably mixed reaction to his mother's return, first moving toward her and then turning away as she reached for him.

The toddler peer visit

We had been seeing Derek and his agemates for almost two years by the time of the toddler peer visit, so by then we had a pretty clear idea of the differences among our youngsters. Now we brought different pairs together, matching an inhibited toddler with an average one, a very uninhibited child with an average child, and so forth, to see how they got along. Accordingly, about two months after Derek's initial toddler visit, his mother brought him back to the lab for a play session with another two-year-old, "average" Matthew.

At the outset, the playroom was divided in half by a large, two-sided bookcase that extended across two thirds of the width of the room. Derek and his mother were shown to the far side of the bookcase, where we had already placed six toys and a chair for mom. Next Matthew and his mother were brought in to the near side of the bookcase, where there were six similar but not identical toys and another chair. Both mothers were asked to remain seated during the play period that would follow.

For the next ten minutes, the two little boys could play with the toys and wander around freely. Derek, as he had done in our earlier session, stayed beside his mother, playing with one of the toys set out for him, a school bus. Two-year-old Matthew, in contrast, quickly and confidently made his way around the barrier to case out what was on the other side. Within a minute or so, he attempted to start up a toddler game—showing Derek a yellow ball, bouncing it, then kicking it at the wall—but despite these overtures, Derek kept up his solitary scooting of the toy bus, next to his mom.

When the ten minutes were up, two researchers entered the room and began setting the stage for the next act, pushing the bookcase/barrier against the wall, opening up the space, and placing all the toys in the middle of the room in one-to-one correspondence, with each boy's toys opposite the other's. We were interested in seeing now whether the youngsters would play together or, alternatively, either exchange or try to take each other's toys. The typical toddler, we know, is beginning to define his or her "self," so he or she is likely to test limits by staking a claim on objects and settings, declaring them "mine."

Matthew behaved as expected, at once carrying Derek's bus over to his own territory, near his mother. While he played with this newfound treat, Derek sat quietly and watched; though he didn't complain, he did gaze at his mom, as if to ask, "What am I supposed to do now?"

Matthew went on to explore all of Derek's toys during the rest of the session. Each time he settled on a new one, he gave his mom a look and a grin; she returned her son's gaze and offered smiles and nods that encouraged him to keep exploring. Indeed, the small exchanges between child and mother were much like a coordinated symphony, with the child playing the role of conductor: Matthew rolled a ball in her direction, then stopped and looked at her as if to say, "Your turn"; his mom picked up on his cues by getting out of her chair to retrieve the ball, then rolling it back to him. Their little game went on for some time, punctuated by smiles, giggles, and affectionate banter.

When Derek's mother noticed the other mom playing with her child, she asked Derek to bring another ball over to her. She stayed seated while making this request, which got no response from her son; he was intently watching the other two at their game. Derek's mom then asked him whether he'd like to come sit near her and play, at which point he picked up a toy dinosaur, plunked himself down by her chair, and began galloping the dinosaur around on the floor. Derek's mother returned to reading her magazine.

Free play for Derek, Matthew, and their mothers was over; the session ended with a fifteen-minute snack time. A low table was brought into the room, and juice and cookies, along with coffee and tea for the moms, were set out.

At snack time, parents typically make certain, first, that their children are comfortably occupied, with juice and cookies in hand. They then usually chat between themselves; each will often focus a bit on the other's child, trying to start a "toddler-speak" conversation. That's just what Matthew's mother did. Derek's mother also began by seeing to it that her son was settled in with a cup of juice and a cookie or two. Soon, however, Derek was looking unhappy and climbed off his chair to go to his mother, apparently with the goal of distancing himself from his peer. He accomplished that when his mom pulled him up into her lap and fed him a cookie.

What we learned about Derek as a toddler

- Like many inhibited children, Derek tended to be anxious in any kind of novel situation.

  This young child's behavior during the peer visit demonstrated clearly that his wariness was not limited to any one setting, nor was it evoked only by unfamiliar adults; unfamiliar children also made him nervous. Another youngster's efforts to entice him into some joint fun seemed to make Derek feel more uncomfortable than tempted.

- Derek's mother acted in an overly solicitous manner with her child.

  During both sessions, Derek's mom offered him a level of affection and cosseting that was not really necessary in that context. In a word, she was smothering. Rather than involving her child in the clean-up or scooting him out to discover this, that, or the other thing—including another little boy just like him!—she mostly concerned herself with making sure he felt comfortable. Although warm and demonstrative, she was also overly intent on shielding her son from distress, even when it was neither appropriate nor sensitive to do so.

What parents should know

- Inhibited youngsters such as Derek are not very good self-starters, but they can get going with a little help.

  An inhibited child can often seem stalled, or emotionally paralyzed into inaction, when confronted with a new task or a new person—even when it's a peer with whom he really might have some fun. Such a child needs encouragement to move forward, some form of gentle reassurance that, on the one hand, his parent is not about to abandon him, and, on the other hand, it's necessary—and it may even be pleasurable—to take action.

- Too much parental demonstration of affection offered at the wrong time or in the wrong circumstances will not enhance a child's sense of confidence.

  Parents of fearful children need to resist their understandable urge to provide constant comfort and reassurance through hugs and kisses. Most such children in fact wish their parents *would* tone it down! Interestingly, Derek, in his way, showed at the end of the Inhibition Paradigm that he wasn't entirely thrilled about his mother's efforts to make him feel better—because even children as young as two *know* instinctively that the affectionate relationship endures and does not have to be demonstrated per se all the time. They *know* that there are times for closeness and comfort, and other times when what's needed is a push to get them out there in the world. And in our lab settings, the world is only an eight by ten room, full of toys.

Derek as a preschooler

Two years later, we invited Derek to our lab again. A quartet of four-year-old boys gathered in our playroom, getting to know one another through the initial fifteen minutes of free play.

We had selected those four carefully for this part of our study. After reviewing the previous toddler data, we had chosen two youngsters, Billy and Andy, whom we had identified back then as being average. The third child, Jake, had been extremely uninhibited and sociable at age two. And then there was Derek. The session was set up along much the same lines as the one described at the beginning of this chapter, with then-seven-year-old Derek.

Billy suggested right off that the group play a competitive game in which "hungry hippos" swallow marbles, and Jake and Andy immediately joined in. Derek stood with his back to a corner and watched the others for the first ten minutes or so; then he slowly slid along the wall toward the door, opened it, and called for his mother. His mom, looking embarrassed, came to the rescue with some cuddling and told him he needed to return to the playroom.

When the free time was up, the boys were asked to stand up one at a time (as the seven-year-olds would be), face the others (and a wall-length mirror), and tell everyone about their birthday parties.

Jake jumped up to start, and boldly announced to the group that his party had been held at Chuck E. Cheese and that his family and friends had brought him loads of gifts. Billy and Andy followed in sequence, both displaying some nervousness but nonetheless managing to describe their parties, presents, and guests. But when it was Derek's turn to tell the little audience about *his* party, he lowered his head and began to weep. The researcher comforted him.

Eventually the boys were told they could do as they wished, at which point Billy and Andy paired off to play with action figures. Occasionally Jake sat down beside them and took part in their game, though more often he ran around the room, either pretending to be Batman or bouncing a ball. Derek spent the rest of the session in his corner, at one point finding a puzzle to put together. None of the other boys approached him.

About two months later, Derek returned to the lab with his mother. Now we wanted to see how the two of them interacted in a variety of contexts.

The parent visit

We explained to Derek's mother how we wanted the session to unfold. After a period of free play, she was to ask her child to clean up the room; then she was to help him create a house out of Lego blocks, exactly matching a model we would set before them on the table. She was not to build the house for him; in fact, she was to refrain from even touching the Lego pieces herself (instructions that proved rather difficult to follow for many parents!).

This session with Derek and his mother, like all the sessions I've described, was videotaped. In our lab, cameras are installed in the ceiling, hidden behind darkened "bulbs" and controlled from an observation room separated from the playroom by a one-way mirror; it is in this observation room that my colleagues and I station ourselves during the visits. Thus, though mother and child both knew they were being taped and observed, the facts that the cameras were not visible and that the taping and watching were being done from behind the mirror allowed them to behave in a relatively unencumbered fashion.

Derek's mom at once picked out the toys they would play with, all the while acting warmly affectionate toward her son. At the same time, however, she also appeared hypervigilant, always on the alert (which is basically how one might describe Derek, as well). When clean-up time came around, Derek complained that he'd rather continue playing, a response that most little kids would offer. So his mother, as in an earlier session, did the tidying up for him. Mother and son then set about the Lego construction, a task in which the parent is essentially asked to assume a teaching and guiding role. When Derek seemed stymied by the assignment, his mother, to our surprise, abruptly expressed real impatience, sounding genuinely annoyed as she chastised him for not working on their project. Realizing that the task had to be completed in one way or another, she took it upon herself to make certain that her child didn't "fail," and stacked the blocks herself. It must be noted that Derek's mother completed the Lego model quite nicely.

What we learned about Derek as a preschooler

- While some preschoolers will choose to play by themselves, Derek seemed to remain uninvolved in the group's activities without wishing to be.

  For many years, psychologists believed that once children reached the age of four or so, they spent much if not most of their time in cooperative play. A child who played on his own, then, was deemed "immature." Our own work in the 1970s and 1980s challenged that long-held belief; one of our arguments was that not all playing-alone behaviors were the same, and not all were necessarily undesirable or immature.

  Some children who often played on their own even among other children, we found, were engaged in examining objects or creating things—building a block castle, painting a picture. We called such behavior *solitary-passive* activity, a label that we felt nicely described the quiet, gainfully employed nature of what the child was up to. It later occurred to us that children who were painting pictures or building castles were hardly being "passive"—a more accurate term would be *solitary-constructive*—but once the earlier label had been published in scientific journals, it "stuck."

  Refining the label, then, we can say that young children who play on their own when among peers seem to be cut from different kinds of cloth. Some exhibit an object-centered nature, in that they seem to prefer things to people. Yet these children don't shrink from exploring the unfamiliar, and when approached by others, they generally respond in a competent and positive fashion. Other children who engage in solitary-constructive play appear to be demonstrating an ability to cope with the stress of social anxiety—that is, when they're feeling wary or fearful in the midst of a group, these children find things to do.

Derek's solitary play, in contrast, was *not* constructive. As a toddler and as a preschooler (and later still, as one of our group of seven-year-olds), he engaged in mostly unoccupied and onlooking behaviors when among others his age. Indeed, he seemed always to be peering over his shoulder, distracted by peer activities that he couldn't figure out how to join. When others approached him, however, he shied away.

We would call Derek *socially reticent.* By the time he was in elementary school, his peers saw him as a loner; because they did not find his behavior particularly appealing, they chose to avoid him. In sum, what began as Derek's maintaining a "safe" distance between himself and others evolved into the sad situation of others' keeping their distance from him.

- Derek's mother perceived her two-year-old as being shy and vulnerable; Derek the four-year-old acted in withdrawn and inhibited ways with other children.

As a toddler sharing a playroom with another two-year-old, Derek would not interact with the other boy, even when he tried to interest him in a little game with a bouncing ball. When he was four, and with a larger group of peers, Derek was noticeably uncomfortable—sliding down the wall toward the door and escape, not talking to the others, getting weepy. The fact that his wariness as a toddler had escalated a couple of years later into an obvious inclination to move away from other children had a great deal to do, we believe, with his mother's actions.

In turn, her actions—not encouraging him to play, keeping him by her side, taking over for him when he had difficulty with a task—stemmed from the way she *perceived* her child: Derek is defenseless, sensitive, and easily upset and hurt, she seemed to believe, and I must shelter him, remove him from precarious positions, and make sure he does well. Perhaps she saw her function as helping her fearful son to feel less so by keeping him well within the range of her own psychological and physical protection, or providing a "quick fix" for his distress.

Derek was becoming accustomed to having a grown-up tell him

what to do and how to do it, and otherwise make things happen for him. Our studies show that when children such as Derek have difficulty joining peer activities, they inevitably turn to adults for help. In short, they become overly reliant on their moms or dads—and later, during the early school years, on their teachers—to get them through their social dilemmas.

- Derek's mom acted in an overly controlling manner with her child.

When we reviewed the mother-child session later on our videotape, we coded this parent's behaviors in particular ways. Among other things, we were interested in determining the following:

Was she *negatively controlling* of her child? Negative control is manifested in ill-timed, excessive, or inappropriate intrusions into whatever the child is doing. In this case that meant interrupting him, doing the job for him, taking away a toy, pulling him aside.

Was she *positively controlling?* If a youngster is unoccupied, for example, a positively controlling mom might suggest something for him to do, or explain about an activity and offer guidance. Positive control denotes well-timed, supportive assistance that facilitates a child's own behaviors.

Derek's mother behaved in a manner consistent with the behaviors of many parents of inhibited and socially reticent preschoolers. During free play, she tended to be both positively and negatively controlling, though control of any kind should not have been necessary in that context. Instead of encouraging Derek to explore the room on his own or simply letting him find his own way, she basically told him what to do and how to do it. Remember, we're talking here about *free* play! Faced with clean-up and the model building, she took over in order to meet the requirements we had spelled out. Although she was mostly warm and pleasant, she demonstrated intrusive and negative control as well as, on occasion, uncalled-for criticism.

What parents should know

- How parents *think about* a child's social style can influence whether or not they respond to it in helpful ways.

Sensitive parenting, as I noted earlier, is as much about what you think and feel as it is about what you do. This rather subtle point is one we see powerfully demonstrated in studies involving children like Derek. Here's what we have learned: Most parents of temperamentally inhibited children quite accurately perceive their two-year-olds as rather timid. But they see their youngsters not as shy, helpless, and vulnerable, but rather as tentative, "hanging-back" types who need extra encouragement to try things out. Accordingly, they try to set up opportunities that will gradually alleviate their children's fearfulness. They gently urge them to connect with their peers, and applaud and approve their efforts in this direction. And as a result, *these* kids, at age four, do *not* display excessively inhibited behaviors around other children. They've learned something about what it takes to be successful in their social worlds.

Some parents, however—and Derek's mother was one of them—perceive their inhibited toddlers as helpless souls. These parents may be concerned and embarrassed when their youngsters shrink away from other kids and desperately seek parental reassurance, as Derek did in the company of his fellow four-year-olds. When we dig a bit deeper in an attempt to find out *why* these parents think their inhibited children act this way, the answers typically relate to a fixed and *internal, dispositional* cause—"He was born that way," they'll say, or "She's always been shy." In other words, for these parents, the reason for the child's behavior is to be found within the child and is seen, in a sense, as a permanent fixture of his or her personality.

My point is this: Parents of inhibited children should try to stop seeing their youngsters as being "painfully shy," and their social shortcomings as immutable character traits. The better, more hopeful mind-set says, "This is a cautious and careful kid who needs to learn some social skills, and I can help him do that."

• A child's persistently solitary activity may be his way of avoiding people.

What we call solitary-constructive players, the children who like to do things by themselves, are often teachers' favorites! Many of these quiet, well-occupied girls and boys are not especially wary or anxious in social settings. When asked to give their little speeches in our lab, for example, or requested to help with our tasks, they do just fine.

For others, like Derek, it's a different story: Social interactions cause them great discomfort, and they deal with those feelings by *hiding* among objects and things. Objects, of course—whether games, building blocks, or computers—are far easier to explore, understand, and "relate to" than other children. Significantly, our studies show that *parents* (as well as teachers) often do not regard these children as having social or emotional difficulties. But the children themselves, from early elementary school on up, recognize their troubles all too well—and they report to us that their parents are unsupportive. They are asking for help, but no one is listening.

The signs and signals of the "hider," which we will take a closer look at later, are not that hard for the sensitive parent to spot. For now, what parents should remember is that inhibited children of any age can be encouraged to broaden their worlds. And the skills they need to do that can be learned and honed.

You'll remember Brett as the gregarious, impulsive seven-year-old who loved taking the floor to tell everyone about himself and was the first to glom onto the best toy in the room. Like Derek, Brett joined our study as an infant, and subsequently participated in the same sequence of sessions in our lab. Here now, in abbreviated form—and with some comparisons along the way to what we saw with Derek, his seeming counterpoint—is Brett's story:

Baby Brett

Strange places and unfamiliar people did not scare Brett. When our research assistant entered the room where the nine-month-old and his mother were waiting, Brett immediately looked the stranger in the eye and flashed a baby grin, as if in greeting. He gave no signal to his mother of impending danger, and evidenced no need for help or comfort.

What was most noticeable about this little boy was the fact that attempts to control his behavior seemed to make him angry. He was a baby with a short fuse!

At one point during their respective nine-month visits, we asked Derek's and Brett's moms to reach out to their children in identical fashion, grasping the boys' arms firmly at the wrists. Derek's response was to gaze at his mother as if this were just the sort of closeness he desired from her. Brett, in contrast, reacted to the wrist-hold by flailing away, kicking and crying. He appeared not to appreciate confinement of any sort. From their earliest visits, then, the two boys displayed very different behaviors, though both could be said to be easily unsettled and difficult to soothe (and indeed, both mothers had described their children in that way). Derek, it was clear, was upset because he was frightened; Brett, for his part, became upset due to felt frustration, a characteristic that would become increasingly obvious a year or two later.

In the interim, however, we observed Brett and his mother in the Strange Situation.

From the first minute, fourteen-month-old Brett was the picture of independence. Encountering our toy-filled lab room, he scurried away from his mom, sat down on the floor, and began to investigate all that neat stuff. He did not seem to mind when his mother left the room, and had no qualms about interacting with the stranger who came in to play with him. But when his mom finally returned after the several separations and reunions that comprise Ainsworth's experimental scenario, Brett's behavior was striking. Rather than approach her for a reassuring hug, he remained seated on the floor, occupied with his playthings, barely giving her a glance. When his mother attempted to pick him up, Brett turned his back on her and kept right on with what he was doing.

What we learned about baby Brett

- Brett appeared to be "hard-wired" to behave in uninhibited ways.

  Brett's resting EEG measurement showed relatively greater activity in the left than in the right frontal lobe of his brain. According to many psychologists, both "approach tendencies"—that is, the desire to get into the action—and anger are typical of children with this pattern.

- Brett appeared to have an insecure attachment to his parent.

  Like Derek, Brett could be said to have an insecure attachment to his mother; in his case, though, it was not an *anxious-resistant* attachment but an *avoidant* one. Here is how such a connection might develop:

When an infant signals a need for closeness or help in the face of distress or perceived danger, and a parent repeatedly fails to come through with comfort or support, the child will begin to feel frustrated, rejected, unhappy, and frequently angry. At the same time, uncertainty about the parent's responsiveness or availability is likely to make the child apprehensive and easily bothered by stressful events.

To protect against such uncomfortable emotions, the psychologist John Bowlby suggested, the child develops ego-defense strategies, excluding from conscious thinking any information that has in the past made him or her angry or anxious. In such a situation, then, the youngster blocks all awareness and processing of thoughts, feelings, and desires associated with the need unmet by the parent. In other words, when stressful situations do stir up that need, the child activates particular coping strategies based on what he or she has come to expect from Mom or Dad.

In the Strange Situation, Brett acted as if he weren't really counting on his mother to come back, and so just wasn't going to think about her at all. Attachment theorists, as I've mentioned, believe that such feelings and assumptions are internalized and carried forward into subsequent relationships. Later on, with peers, insecure-avoidant youngsters such as Brett are guided by previously reinforced expectations of frustration and rejection; viewing other kids as potentially hostile, they tend to strike out proactively and aggressively.

This was a pattern we would observe in Brett in a later visit.

Brett the toddler

When Brett was two, he and his mother took part in the Inhibition Paradigm. Here again, Brett's behavior was remarkably different from Derek's.

Upon entering the playroom, Brett at once charged off from his mother's side, plunked himself down on the floor with his back to her, and busied himself with the toys. When our research assistant came in and began to play with a truck, Brett stopped what he was doing, looked over, and then made his way to within arm's reach of the unfamiliar adult. Soon he was pointing with a crooked finger, as if to say, "Can I have that truck?"

When the stranger left the room to get the animated robot, Brett trailed her right to the door, as if to suggest that he'd follow her anywhere.

The robot that had so terrified Derek transfixed Brett. When it began to whir, he jumped up and down excitedly; then, without waiting to be invited, he approached the stranger and asked, in toddler-ese, if he could hold the mechanical toy. In short, all the comings-and-goings and noises that had made Derek shrink back in fear appeared to have exactly the opposite effect on this child.

Given his enthusiastic attempts to play with the toys and the research assistant, it was entirely predictable that when his mother asked him to clean up the room, all hell would break loose. Brett simply refused to cooperate; dropping onto his back, he kicked his feet in the air and gave a perfect demonstration of what the terrible twos are all about. Now Brett's mother, looking both embarrassed and very angry at her son's behavior, announced that they could not play any more unless he got the room tidied up. The standoff lasted for some time, until finally Brett caved in and began picking up the toys.

When his mother, in our repeat Strange Situation, left and came back, Brett again took little notice.

The toddler peer visit

Our foursome this time comprised Brett and his mother and "average" Adam and his mom, all of whom were shown into the playroom with the room-dividing bookcase and the two sets of toys.

Right after settling in, Brett gathered up all "his" things and carried them to the end of the bookcase, from which vantage point he was able to see that another child and mother were on the other side of the room, and that there were a lot more toys over there as well. Adam soon busied himself with a bus filled to the brim with Sesame Street characters. Brett's bus didn't have those figures; instead, it contained little animals.

Brett watched Adam for a while and then approached him. When Adam put his bus down on the floor for a millisecond, Brett made a grab for it. Adam responded in kind—no one was going to take "his" bus—and a little tug of war ensued, a typical toddler conflict over a desirable object. After Adam reclaimed his bus, Brett picked up a rubber ball and walked directly over to where Adam was seated. Everyone on our side of the one-way mirror agreed that this was a fairly mature gesture; it appeared that Brett was going to trade the ball for the use of the Sesame Street bus. Instead, however, Brett first made eye contact with Adam and then bounced the ball directly at him. It seemed to be a signal: "Give me that bus or else!"

Paying him no attention, Adam continued to play. Now Brett approached the other toddler, looked right at him, and, after turning his Yankees baseball cap around so the visor was in the back, proceeded to head-butt him. This was as clever an act of aggression as we had seen any of our two-year-olds attempt. Here was a child, after all, who had the presence of mind to let his putative victim know that he was asking for trouble—bouncing that ball as a "warning"—and who furthermore wanted to punish him: Had Brett not turned his cap around, he wouldn't have been able to hurt Adam!

At this point Adam's mother came to the rescue, consoling her child and then sitting on the floor and trying to get the boys to play together— a tall order for a pair of two-year-olds, especially when one of them had just been on the receiving end of a head butt.

What we learned about Brett the toddler

- Brett's mother believed that an *authoritarian* manner was most likely to get her son to follow her requests.

    Neither Derek's nor Brett's mother was successful in her initial attempt to persuade her youngster to tidy up the playroom. But whereas Derek's mother then did the job herself, Brett's mother demanded that her son do as he was told, requiring from him a level of compliance that could not reasonably be expected from a toddler.

    Compliance is an excellent marker of any child's developing abilities to regulate his or her emotions and actions. But recognizing a request and then inhibiting the impulse to do what one wants in order to do as others ask are fairly sophisticated behaviors. Most two-year-olds find it next to impossible to be compliant, unless Dad or Mom offers a helping hand in meeting the desired goal (for example, cleaning up that room).

- Brett reacted strongly and aversively when thwarted in a common kid conflict.

As any parent of a young child knows, there is no shortage of conflicts among toddlers. Such set-tos in a sense amount to ego testing, asking, What can I, the conflict initiator, get away with? And aren't possessions a key determinant of who "I" am?

The typical toddler conflict usually has to do with obtaining a desired thing, and toys are like magnets to two-year-olds, bringing them into contact with one another for better or worse. Quite often, it's for better, as a youngster recognizes that the moving thing in the room that's in possession of the coveted toy bus is a little person just like him, someone to play with. In our lab, we have frequently seen toddler scuffles over toys lead to bouts of play and giggles. In this case, however, Brett was clearly on the attack, and we guessed that his actions with Adam were representative of his behavior with other children as well.

We have already characterized Brett as uninhibited. We can say, too, that like Derek, he was *emotionally dysregulated,* though the feelings that tended to get the better of him were not, as with Derek, fearfulness and wariness, but rather frustration and anger. Another referent that is often applied to the Bretts of the world is *difficult temperament,* meaning they are disposed to express anger in many situations and are unable to stop themselves from charging ahead when upset—a definition that nicely describes how Brett acted when he couldn't get his hands on that Sesame Street bus.

Such displays of difficult temperament, it should be added, are more typical of a Brett than a Bonnie: The two-year-old boys in our studies are much more likely to initiate conflict than the two-year-old girls. This finding merely supports what researchers have reported time and time again, both in North America and in most of the rest of the world. (This does not mean that girls don't also act in combative or belligerent ways; their aggressive displays, however, are usually not physical. Later we'll look at the various types of aggression typically displayed by boys and girls.)

What parents should know

- Children who react quickly and angrily when thwarted need their parents to react in the opposite way—with patience, warmth, and support.
  Kids like Brett usually have a great deal of trouble settling down to

tasks, working cooperatively with others to get something accomplished, or even just playing with peers. Those social skills, of course, are critical once a child starts spending most of his or her time with other children, and they remain critical right through the school years. They are skills learned first at home, largely according to the manner in which parents deal with their children's displays of frustration, inattention, or "orneriness."

When Brett needed to tidy up the playroom, for instance, his mom simply required that he follow her instructions. When he threw a tantrum, she insisted again that he just get down to work. Brett would have been better served at that moment—and started along the path toward self-regulation of both his emotions and his behaviors—by some parental soothing and the offer of a helping hand to get things going.

Brett the preschooler

About two years later, we saw Brett again, this time for our preschooler peer quartet session. Like Derek, Brett was joined in our playroom by three other four-year-old boys.

From the get-go, Brett was friendly and ready for some fun. Indeed, he appeared to have leadership qualities, getting the group involved in a little game and giving directions. Some minutes into the free play, however, he noticed that one of the other boys, "average" Danny, had picked up a particularly spectacular toy spaceship, which Brett at once decided he had to have. Brett walked up to Danny and demanded that he hand the thing over; Danny refused. Now Brett's short fuse began to burn! As Danny moved away, he followed, grabbing for the spaceship and shoving the other boy. Behind the one-way mirror, we held our collective breath, wondering if we'd have to intervene to prevent a real blow-up. But the other children were starting to talk about a new game, and things simmered down.

As is often the case when young children are surrounded by seemingly limitless opportunities for play, the foursome had some difficulty coming to an agreement about what they would do next. Eventually it was resolved that they'd pretend to be the characters in a popular television series. Since it was Brett's suggestion and he got to play the role he wanted, all was well—for a time.

At some point the boys began to engage in rough-and-tumble play, a common yet important form of activity (and one that boys, in particular, often keep up right through their preteen years). This kind of being-together is developmentally meaningful because it tells us that children, at quite an early age, can distinguish between *literal* and *nonliteral meanings*. Roughhousing only *suggests* the literal meaning of aggression, through little jabs and pokes and wrestling-type moves, some growling, perhaps a few harsh words. It's the kind of play that often worries parents, but most young children realize that these behaviors do not, in fact, really mean what they seem to mean. They may even tell Mom or Dad, "It's just pretend!"

For Brett, however, the foursome's rough-and-tumble play moved swiftly into the real thing. Soon he was throwing four-year-old punches and had one of the other boys in tears. One of our assistants entered the playroom at this juncture to remind the kids that they were to get along nicely, but the damage had been done. For the remainder of the free-play segment, the other three boys stayed at a distance from Brett. When it was time for the "my last birthday party" speeches, Brett's peers looked at him impassively while he told his story. He seemed to be out of the loop.

A month later, Brett returned to the lab with his mother for the pre-schooler/parent session.

The parent visit

On this visit, Brett and his mother went through the same sequence of activities that we described for Derek and his mom—free play, clean-up, and Lego house building.

Brett's mother took matters in hand from the start, picking out toys, once confiscating an object she didn't want her son to play with, and calling him back to where she was sitting whenever he started roaming. It was almost as if she were expecting her child to misbehave and had resolved to head him off at the pass. After the play period, clean-up went much as it had gone during Brett's toddler visit, with his mother instructing him to do as he was told.

The twosome then got down to building the Lego model, which, as you will recall, required the parent to guide her youngster along in the task. When Brett, like Derek, appeared to be having a good deal of difficulty getting started, his mother didn't touch the blocks herself (as per our request); she simply watched her son, told him to "go ahead," and at one point, when he made a move, remarked, "That's not going to work."

Finally, after the Lego task was more or less done, Brett and his mother were offered a snack, an interlude during which we usually try to put everyone at ease. What happened on this occasion, however, was particularly telling about this parent and child. As Brett reached for an animal cracker, he inadvertently knocked over his glass of juice, making a mess on the table. His mom responded swiftly and impulsively, asking Brett in a most angry tone, though without ever raising her voice, if he was "just trying to make trouble." Rather than recognizing the spill as an accident, in other words, she appeared to see it as an intentional bit of mischief. To us, it was a scary moment.

What we learned about Brett the preschooler

- Brett lacked impulse control and the ability to "read" social situations with accuracy.

  Brett had no trouble jumping into the social swing of things with his peers. When all was going his way—when he decided what games they would play, and when he acted the role he wanted—he got along well with the three other youngsters in his group; like many uninhibited kids, he was outgoing and highly sociable. But when the scene changed—when he was unable to take possession of a toy, for example, or when the boys began to mix it up in rough-and-tumble play—this preschooler started to behave in ways that his peers found disagreeable.

  Why did he misunderstand his peers' intentions? Perhaps Brett carries with him an internal working model that others don't like him, that he is usually rejected, or that others could be expected to be unreliable or hostile. Perhaps he had learned to be suspicious of others' motives; after all, his own mother interpreted his accidental action—spilling his juice and making a mess—as something he did on purpose, to "make trouble." Thus, when the intentions of others carried with them reasonable doubt ("Do these kids really want to fight with me and inflict harm?"), Brett assumed the negative and responded aggressively and inappropriately.

And his peers didn't like it. A child may forgive an act of aggression if it comes from someone he likes and is friends with; a long-standing relationship can override the one-time occurrence, which is chalked up to being out of character. Among these strangers who didn't know him, however, Brett's behavior marked him for rejection and dislike.

- Brett's mom, like some mothers of aggressive youngsters, acted in a highly controlling and harsh manner toward her child.

Unlike Derek's mother, another overcontrolling parent, Brett's mom was consistently negatively controlling and hostile toward her son, even in situations in which Brett should have been pretty much free to do as he wished. She seemed to come equipped with a fixed notion of her child as being oppositional, or with a working memory of troublesome interactions in her relationship with him.

Our own research, and that of others, has suggested that many parents of aggressive children act erratically toward their youngsters, sometimes ignoring or even rewarding undesirable behaviors and at other times punishing desirable ones. Their attempts to assert control are inconsistent both in *whether* they occur and in whether they are positive or negative. Such inconsistency in turn interferes with a child's ability to identify rules and expectations, and has the net effect of exacerbating rather than diminishing externalizing problems such as aggressiveness toward peers.

Brett's mother let us know through her questionnaire responses that she viewed her son as being "difficult" and defiant, and that he "got into scrapes" with other children. She was not happy about that. It made *her* angry, and she believed that the best way to raise her child and to curb his undesirable behaviors was to punish him in some way that would make him learn swiftly that aggression does not pay.

Parents of aggressive preschoolers (unlike those of withdrawn children) do tend to feel confident that they can improve their children's behaviors in this manner. A few years later, however, the picture often changes. Despite their efforts, their children become naughtier, not nicer, and now another parental belief system kicks in, one that attributes a child's acting-up behaviors to *internal, dispositional* causes—the "He was born that way" argument. Mom or Dad may then adopt a laissez-faire or permissive attitude: "I give up, I've tried everything, and nothing works. I'm at my wits' end. This kid's on his own." Other parents, alternatively, may continue to react punitively and harshly, coming down hard on their children until they "come to their senses." These two contrasting parenting styles, research has shown, are associated with the same sort of child behavior.

What parents should know

- Demands that he go along with a parent's request may make things worse for the uninhibited and emotionally dysregulated child.

    As had been the case a couple of years earlier, Brett the preschooler, it seemed, was not getting much parental support in our playroom—no help accomplishing the clean-up, no useful hints on which pieces he might try where in building his Lego house, no smiles of encouragement. By demanding compliance from her "defiant" son rather than encouraging his participation and offering guidance when he was faced with problems to solve, Brett's mother was pretty much leaving him on his own to learn how to overcome his emotional dysregulation. In turn, his lack of control was leading him to act impulsively, aggressively, and irresponsibly toward other children.

- Impulsive children need help in learning how to think first and act later.

    Kids like Brett—not only in elementary school but in middle and high school as well—have at least three cognitive disadvantages. First, they are not as able as nonaggressive children to appreciate the thoughts and feelings of others—a key to social competence. Second, when they wish to be in control and other kids won't let them be, they react negatively or inappropriately and at once, without first considering consequences or possible alternative solutions to these interpersonal dilemmas. And third, they have difficulty understanding the *intentions* of others (as when Brett failed to recognize that the roughhousing was "just-pretend" behavior).

    However, if their parents are able to provide structure and regulation within social and task-oriented experiences, give them opportunities to practice their own regulation, and encourage them to understand others' perspectives, Brett and children like him *can* develop the ability to face situations and peers in an appropriately controlled manner.

The better path

By this point you may be thinking that there's a little bit of Derek or something of Brett in your son or daughter. It's certainly possible; as I indicated at the beginning of this chapter, these two youngsters represent the far ends of a continuum, and not every basically shy or basically uninhibited child will display such behaviors consistently, extravagantly, and in all situations. Still, you're probably wondering if there's anything you can do to help your somewhat timid or moderately aggressive youngster onto a more comfortable track with her peers. In chapters 9 and 10 we'll look at some especially useful strategies along those lines, but for now the short answer is yes, there's a great deal you can do!

The two mothers who have been under the microscope over the previous pages both loved their children. But each needed to learn to respond somewhat differently to her child's nature. The fact is, even small changes in parental actions or reactions can make life among his peers better for the *moving-against* or the *moving-away-from* child.

Here is the *single most important finding* in our work and in much other research conducted in recent years:

Children whose temperaments and behaviors cause them difficulty can, over time, become much more comfortable in their world and find a lot more fun in it.

Deep inside, the child may remain the same; his physiological or temperamental "markers" may remain stable. But undesirable behaviors are not inevitable. Biology matters, but biology, quite simply, is not destiny.

A Derek may always have high *moving-away-from* or avoidance tendencies, but if he can learn to cope with his social anxieties and insecurities, he may not stand out as unusually reticent in any way. He may be able to get out, introduce himself to others, take part in activities or join groups, make friends, and do just fine when engaging with his peers. In fact, because naturally inhibited kids are so sensitive, they tend to be empathetic, a characteristic that others appreciate.

A Brett may always have high *moving-against* or approach tendencies, but if he can regulate and control his overreactive emotions, learn to interpret others' intentions with more accuracy, and assemble a broader array of strategies to solve the problems that *all* kids run into, then the outcome may be a positive one. And because naturally uninhibited kids tend to be gregarious and outgoing, they have much to offer that peers admire.

My coworkers and I would argue, too, that at some point along the way, finding a best friend may also help Derek or Brett move onto that happier, more adaptive path. The *best* best friend for each will probably be someone who isn't just like him. If Derek befriends another Derek, chances are they'll have an affectionate relationship and explore their universe together, but it won't be a very extended universe. And if Brett hooks up with another Brett, the two of them will tend to promote and encourage the negative behaviors that keep them out of sync with most of their peers. But if Derek and Brett pair themselves off with best friends who are socially competent, good things may happen.

Chapter 4

The Heart of Parenting

What the Mothers and Fathers of Well-Liked Children Are Doing Right

Just as we now have many clues about what tends to make a child rejected, we are coming to understand a great deal, too, about what causes a child to become well liked—*and* how his or her parents may contribute to that happy outcome. The connection is clear. According to much research, youngsters who develop fine friendships throughout their school years and get along well in their peer groups invariably have parents who think about and interact with their children in particular ways.

These are the moms and dads, for one thing, who foster their children's social competence through direct and always appropriate involvement in their lives with their friends—by setting up playdates when they're young; keeping track, later on, of where they're going and whom they're with; and acting as listeners and sometime advisers as their sons and daughters enjoy or struggle with the ups and downs of friendships and peer groups.

But intriguing studies of children from toddlerhood through adolescence suggest that how kids act with their peers is also a reflection of other kinds of input from their parents, including how good they've been at helping their children feel generally secure about themselves; how their families go about reaching joint decisions; and even what kinds of friendships the parents themselves have.

From research into these various direct and indirect currents of influence, we have come up with a blueprint of the effective parent, which shows what the mothers and fathers of well-liked children are doing right. Here's a brief outline:

Take away the right lessons from your own past.

Of course, we parents all lived through our own childhoods, and quite often, a father's or mother's conviction that it's important for a child to have friends, and to learn how to make them, stems from memories of his or her own long-ago experiences—memories that may be good, bad, or ugly.

A mother who recalls herself as a lonely or shy child, or who remembers growing up in a neighborhood with few other kids, may decide to put extra effort into helping her son or daughter develop the kind of satisfying peer experiences that she missed. And studies show that a "good" father—a dad who is warm, nurturing, and involved in his children's daily lives—may have enjoyed a close relationship with his own dad, and grown up with a model of fatherhood that he emulates. Conversely, his father may have been distant and unemotional, and so he himself may be determined *not* to be that way with his own children. Parents who want their children to have a happier time of it than they themselves did tend to be well tuned in to their kids' social lives and what they can do to aid them.

Unfortunately, it's also the case that many adults who had unsupportive parents may, in their attempts to make sure that things turn out better for their own children, become overbearing and controlling. In a strange way, they repeat their parents' mistakes, despite having as their goal the development of socially skilled and content sons and daughters. And so life is not quite so simple; not every parent learns his or her parenting lessons well. The basic point is that it's not enough to *wish* the best for one's child; one also has to *know* what's best for him and work toward that through active, sympathetic, sensitive, and responsive means.

Be a source of felt security.

To return to our discussion of attachment theory and what it might tell us about a child's social development, the story goes like this:

When an infant's mother is warm, sensitive, clued in, and caringly responsive to her youngster's signals, that child takes in a reassuring message: "My parent is someone I can rely on, someone I can trust. Therefore, people in general can be relied on and trusted. Plus, I myself apparently am good at eliciting nice reactions from other people, so I must be worthy of receiving them."

Very early on, in other words, this young, secure child has learned what to expect in social situations: It's both pleasant and worthwhile to be around people. Thus, attachment researchers believe, the seeds are sown in infancy that will enable a child to initiate and maintain close one-on-one relationships in the future, including enduring friendships.

Over the past twenty-five years, a good deal of research has supported this notion that the quality of the earliest parent-child attachment relationship is a predictor of later success in the social world. But what about the insecurely attached child, the youngster who may not have acquired an *internal working model* that he or she is lovable and loved, and that others can be counted on to respond to him or her in positive ways?

The reasons for an insecure attachment may vary and may not necessarily reflect uncaring parenting. Perhaps this was the mother's third or fourth child, and she found that sticking to a strict schedule of nap-time, mealtime, and bedtime was necessary in order to keep chaos at a minimum, even though the routine didn't mesh well with this youngster's difficult or hyperarousable temperament. Or maybe a family member got sick or lost his or her job, or some other distressing but temporary happening created family strains that distracted and distanced the child's mother.

In a lab scenario like the Strange Situation, that youngster might exhibit behavior suggestive of an insecure attachment—or conversely might not if, for example, his father was from the start affectionately and appropriately responsive. Although the majority of babies—more than 60 percent, according to some studies—develop the same type of attachment relationship with both parents, some youngsters who fail to develop secure ties with one will succeed in doing so with the other, and thus gain the sense of self-worth and positive expectations about relationships in general that such connection encourages.

One other point puts this matter of early attachment in a broader perspective: There's little clear evidence that any child's attachment profile at age one or two guarantees a clear, trouble-free, sunny future (or the opposite) as far as relationships go. A revealing study of that broad arc from toddlerhood on tracked a number of individuals who as infants had either secure or insecure attachments to their mothers, following them right through their early school years and adolescence and into adulthood. Did they grow up to be well adjusted, popular, happily married, and so on, or the reverse? Only about one fourth of the participants, it turned out, had *persistently* good or *persistently* bad interpersonal relationships across time. Concluded the researcher, "Secure attachment to the mother does not make one invulnerable to later problems, and socioemotional difficulties and poor early relations with the mother do not doom a person to a life of loneliness, poor relationships, or psychopathology."

In thinking about the internal working model of social connections, and about what any child really needs in order to develop a good such model, it is a great deal more fruitful, as I mentioned earlier, to appreciate the notion of *felt security.* You cannot return to your child's infancy in order to do things differently. But you can always help him or her feel more secure.

Felt security, a central concept in child psychology, has to do with whether or not an individual is generally comfortable in her own skin, across situations and over time, as well as whether or not the world seems to her basically an intriguing, reliable, and friendly place that she is quite capable of navigating. Part of my own work with children and young adolescents has concerned the possibility that felt security with parents transfers to, or is predictive of the nature of, a child's peer relationships: Does the way he or she feels about the primary, parent-child relationship generalize or move its way into other one-on-one relationships? The answer appears to be yes. Parents provide their children with a model of what human connections are like; when the model is one of reliability, empathy, affection, and trust, a child is likely to establish peer relationships that reflect that earlier one.

Parental willingness is the key here: When a parent senses that things are not what they should be with a child, he or she must be motivated to attempt to improve the picture, and that effort begins with an absolute and unstinting willingness to take into account the child's perspective on life in the moment. For a child, that's the root of felt security—the knowledge that there's someone out there who will listen, understand, and help.

Encourage exploration.

Here's what happens when children are secure in their relationships with Mom and Dad: They feel good enough about themselves to investigate what the world looks like at a safe distance from their loved ones.

Exploration continues throughout a child's growing years. It's how she makes sense of her universe. And it's a process that begins with the concentrated effort to figure out the basic properties of novel objects or unfamiliar people. Once a child answers that object- or person-driven question—"What is it/she all about?"—then she can go on to address this self-derived question: "What can I do with this thing or person?"

Consider Maggie, a three-year-old in one of our studies, who at one point during a session was given a click-up, click-down ballpoint pen. She looked at it carefully, discovered the clicker part, clicked it over and over, and then tested out the pen's scribbling capabilities on a pad of paper when the clicker was up and when it was down. Taking a break from those efforts, she sat back in her chair, pointed the pen at the ceiling, and waved it back and forth over her head, perhaps pretending it was a magic wand, or perhaps "writing" on the sky.

A short time later, we placed a Plexiglas box with a hinged lid in the middle of the table Maggie was sitting at. Inside was a purple plastic pony, a toy that we knew Maggie really wanted. The box was just out of reach, but not for long: After a few moments of staring yearningly at the purple pony, Maggie leaned over and used the ballpoint pen to flip open the lid and then drag the box closer to her chair. Success!

This young child explored and figured out what the pen could do. Then she figured out what *she* could do with *the pen*, which included achieving an immediate personal goal—that is, getting her hands on that toy.

The same kind of exploration goes on in social company. Two unfamiliar toddlers come together, look at each other, poke each other, and glance over at their moms and then back at each other, scoping each other out. This is the dance of social relationships, recalling Anna's song to the king's children in *The King and I*: "Getting to Know You." First: What is this person all about? Second: What can I do with her? She looks a lot like me, she seems friendly, and she's playing with that ball over there.

Hmmmm . . . the ball rolled over here . . . how about if I roll it back to her?

Without exploration, a young child cannot move on to play creatively and comfortably. And play, of course, leads to a child's first taste of peer exchanges.

Do encourage your young child, right from the get-go and as far as safety and common sense will allow, to venture forth into her world and learn the lessons it has to teach. And then recognize that as she gets older, in all likelihood your youngster will keep right on venturing forth and exploring, sometimes to your dismay.

In a long-range study that my colleagues and I conducted, one of the most interesting findings was this one: The *most popular* fourth and fifth graders were the kids most likely to smoke cigarettes or drink beer in ninth grade. We know that well-liked children, the ones who are leading the pack, are often a bit on the cutting edge of things, like these youngsters; they take pride in pushing the envelope of acceptability, engaging in risky behaviors at earlier ages than most kids, and generally demonstrating to their peers (and to their parents) that they are grown-up now and can make their own decisions. In this case, the same children who early on experimented with objects and people, who at least partly in that way built up the social competence that made them popular, were by their first year of high school ready to step up to explore the "adult" world of cigarettes and alcohol.

Were they genuinely more grown-up because of it? Certainly not. Were they on the road to trouble? Studies suggest that the answer is no. Popular kids who are doing well in their worlds, who have good friends and supportive parents, may take risks, but they are not likely to slide down a slippery slope because of them. They comprise a very different population than the youngsters who we know are most apt to *abuse* alcohol and drugs—the children who feel unhappy with their lot in life and rejected by their peers.

The point is, children need to explore, and parents need to allow exploration to happen—within limits. If your toddler daughter wants to explore the properties of a wooden mixing spoon and a plastic measuring cup by banging the one on the other, she's probably doing just fine on her own. But when she decides to climb up on a chair and explore the inside of the bathroom medicine cabinet, you'll clearly need to put a stop to her investigation. Similarly, if your young teen wishes to explore the reaction he gets by dyeing a green streak in his hair, you'll probably be wise to say little and let him reach his own conclusions. Other kinds of adolescent exploration, however, just as surely call for greater parental involvement (more on this later).

Be appropriately in control—in an appropriately warm way.

In the last chapter, I described the lab sessions in which our preschoolers Derek and Brett and their mothers went about certain tasks we had assigned them. We were interested in observing, among other things, how the parents helped or hindered their children: Was Mom bossy and in charge of all the action, expecting her child to follow her instructions, or, at the opposite extreme, did she offer next to nothing by way of supervision and expressed rules and expectations? Was Mom warm and empathetic in her efforts to influence her child's behavior, or, just the opposite, either visibly angry and harsh or emotionally flat and distant?

Psychologists sometimes chart those variables in a diagram in which a vertical line represents the continuum of the affective quality of parenting, and a horizontal line represents the degree of control in parenting. The four sectors that result define parenting styles we have come to associate with particular outcomes in children's social behaviors. The picture looks like this:

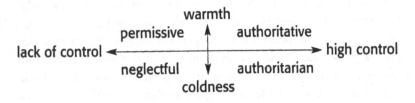

The parents who are getting it right fall somewhere in the sector we call *authoritative:* They demonstrate appropriate, thoughtful, and reasonable control by setting clear limits on a child's behaviors, while at the same time being warmly sympathetic to his wishes, feelings, capabilities, and point of view. In our lab visits, these are the mothers who recognize when a child is best left alone to explore and accomplish things, and when he might need supportive assistance to facilitate an effort.

In the context of family, these are the moms and dads who pay attention to what their kids are thinking and doing, and find ways to encourage independence while maintaining necessary parameters. They have a keen awareness of the need to balance *adult-centered parenting* with *child-centered parenting*. Adult-centered parenting is child-rearing from a mother's or father's perspective. The child whose dad is hell-bent on turning his unathletic son into a football star, despite the boy's expressed preference for more creative and sedentary activities, is on the receiving end of this kind of parenting, as is the child whose mother wants her to attend cheerleading classes when the girl herself would prefer to be on the soccer field. In both cases, parent and child may be on a highly visible collision course.

But the push-pull between adult-centered and child-centered parenting happens throughout your child's development. Sometimes, of course, you must be adult-centered and highly controlling for your child's sake. The youngster who thinks it's a neat idea to explore his territory by racing toward a street full of traffic, and the eleven-year-old who decides she doesn't want to go to school anymore, can't be allowed to make their own choices in those areas. In much of the business of life, however, being an authoritative parent means being child-centered.

Thus, when your four-year-old is struggling and becoming frustrated with a jigsaw puzzle, you might say, "What do you think would happen if you tried one of the pieces with a flat side?"

Or you might suggest to your nine-year-old, "OK, we've got three possibilities on tap for this weekend. We can go to the pool, or to the ball game, or to the movie. What do you think you'd like best? Let's talk it over."

And you might tell your fourteen-year-old, "Yes, you can go to the party, I like your friends, but you need to be home by ten. Let's figure out how to be sure you'll get back by that time."

And what much research indicates is this: The children of authoritative parents—mothers and fathers who demonstrate reasonable and reasoned control, along with warmth and support—are the kids who are the most socially competent. They're friendly and cooperative with their peers, they feel good about themselves and their abilities, and they take the feelings and perspectives of others into account.

We also know something about the costs to children of parents who react to and interact with their youngsters in less skillful ways.

Authoritarian ("Do what I say") parents are both cold, rejecting, or angry *and* highly controlling in a consistently and markedly adult-centered way. These moms and dads attempt to run the show; they demand compliance, allowing few opportunities for a child to explore, experiment, and make decisions. Especially for the uninhibited youngster, authoritarian parenting exacts severe penalties. Parents impose such a rigid structure and such high control that the child has little chance to learn to self-regulate; in addition, because Mom or Dad tends to punish noncompliance rather than encourage participation, the youngster has trouble seeing a task through to its successful completion. And much research traces the pathway from authoritarian parenting to child behaviors among peers:

Mothers who are disagreeable toward and controlling with their children tend to have children who are disagreeable and controlling around other children.

Parents who manipulate their children's behavior through commands, demands, threats, and other high-power, assertive techniques have children who try to manipulate their peers in the same way. And not so surprisingly, kids don't like other kids who are out of control, unpleasant, and bossy.

At the other extreme, the *permissive* ("Do what you want") or anything-goes parent is warmly agreeable to whatever notion a child comes up with ("Sure, if you think that's a good idea, go ahead—see you later!"), but provides little or nothing in the way of control, limits, or direction. While perhaps maintaining an atmosphere of acceptance and emotional closeness, these moms and dads nonetheless fail to provide their youngsters with structure. Again, for the uninhibited child, permissive parenting can be tremendously damaging—and it's a style that has been clearly linked to children's aggression and other socially unacceptable behaviors:

Mothers who set no limits and let their children get away with anything have children who think they can get away with anything in the peer group.

Neglectful parenting, characterized by low control and lack of emotion, is indifferent or uninvolved; these mothers and fathers are simply not there for their children. The children of such parents cannot help but feel insecure. They have no one to count on. It is unsurprising that such children bring their "felt insecurity" to the interactions with and relationships to peers.

All the suggestions I'll provide in the chapters to come, on how you can best aid and abet your child's social life from preschool through high school, really come down to the appropriate demonstration of control and warmth. Which means just this: Don't tell your child what to do and how to do it; instead, gather clues, keep open the lines of communication, volunteer opinions, bring up aspects of a situation that it would be wise for him or her to consider, and set reasonable limits. Don't offer suffocating, smothering expressions of affection, but do let your child know, through kindness, empathy, and understanding, that there's someone in the world who's crazy about him. This is what felt security is all about—your child's sense that his parents are appropriately in control, in an appropriately warm way.

Make it possible for your child to be in the company of other children.

Clearly, the more opportunities your youngster has to spend time with other children, the better and the faster he or she is likely to learn the social lessons that his or her peers have to teach.

Parents who are sensitive to that reality may, for one thing, choose to live in a particular community because it's full of young families. They may set up playgroups for their toddlers, enter their children in preschool programs, shepherd kids to birthday parties and sleepovers, and make their homes an inviting gathering place for their teens. By these efforts, they show their children that they believe friendships are good and that it's important and fun to be a social creature, at ease in the company of others.

One big payoff: The more active role a parent takes in providing or stimulating peer contact from an early age, the more socially competent the child will be. These youngsters, research shows, have a larger range of pals, spend more time playing in other kids' homes, and have the most trouble-free friendships. Even in the preteen years, kids develop closer, more stable, and higher-quality relationships when their parents *actively promote* their peer connections.

That said, *do not* overorganize those peer connections.

Allow children time to make their own fun.

Studies tell us that youngsters who get off to an early start, socially speaking—who attend qualitatively good child-care and preschool programs, for example—develop more sophisticated, adaptive kinds of play and interaction than kids who haven't had similar exposure; they're friendlier, and they make easier adjustments to kindergarten. But here's another piece of the picture: The youngsters who are *least* distressed about entering kindergarten, or "real school," who apparently have developed the best coping skills to get them through unfamiliar situations, are those who have had many opportunities for relaxed interactions with their agemates. Joining a group of kids on the swings at the park, in other words, may be a more effective social learning experience for a young child than attending formal toddler classes.

And as they grow through the years of middle childhood, when their parents are still instrumental in arranging their social schedules, children apparently continue to benefit enormously from the chance to enjoy casual, relatively free-ranging get-togethers with their peers. A study of children's participation in various community settings was particularly revealing in this regard. Two different types of activities were investigated, both involving kids from about seven to ten years of age—first, the structured, adult-run programs of Little League, Boy Scouts and Girl Scouts, and other formal organizations; and second, more informal kinds of recreation, such as visiting the neighborhood pool, the library, or the park with parents.

Interestingly, it appeared that even though the children who took part in structured programs obviously came into regular contact with their peers, they weren't necessarily better adjusted socially simply by virtue of being Little Leaguers or whatever. Unstructured activities, however—as when kids ran into other kids at the playground or the pool, for example, or organized their *own* games—apparently provided precisely the *kinds* of experiences that most enhanced children's social skills. Children who were more involved in these sorts of peer contacts, researchers found, developed better perspective-taking abilities and were more tolerant and accepting of others.

Kids' coming together for a pickup softball game in the empty lot down the street may be a thing of the past. Still, it's good to consider, at least, whether signing your child up for all manner of out-of-school classes and programs is really necessary, or even in his or her best interest. The benefits of peer-led, unstructured activities—the kind of do-it-yourself fun many of us remember from our own youth—are clear. When your child and his or her friends negotiate their own rules, choose up their own teams, argue about what's fair and what's foul, they're learning how to get along with one another.

Supervise your young child's interactions with friends and peers.

If children benefit from setting up their own fun, while they're still very young they also do best with a little support from Mom or Dad. When your youngster is playing with a friend or a small group of kids and is clearly doing fine on his own, a helping hand probably isn't needed. But when things aren't proceeding so smoothly, you will further your child's social competence by inserting yourself into the scene in certain skillfully unintrusive and timely ways.

A number of studies have been designed around this simple scenario: Put a child and mother in a setting with an unfamiliar child or children, and observe what Mom does to make it easier for her youngster to join forces with the other kid(s), and how she encourages the little group to "play nicely." Some parents watch from the sidelines or seemingly pay no attention; others take a more active role.

For example, in our lab we will bring a mother and child together with an unknown, same-aged child to participate in a session similar to the ones I have described, comprising free play along with some special tasks for the mom, such as getting the two children to construct a model out of blocks. We look at whether the mother displays adult-centered goals (for example, taking over the activity herself or trying to stop an ongoing game when the children are stalled or running into difficulties) or child-centered ones (asking the kids what they're doing, responding to their feelings, encouraging cooperation, and generally enhancing play initiated by the youngsters).

We consider, too, the means she uses to achieve those goals: Are they *high-power* strategies, such as direct commands ("Put that toy away now!") and psychologically negative comments ("You're being selfish")? Or are they moderate or *low-power* strategies, such as requests and suggestions ("Wouldn't you like to come over here where you'll have some more room?"), explanations ("If you push her, she might get hurt"), and positive evaluations ("Great job, guys!")?

Clear-cut outcomes are apparent: Young children (preschoolers) persist in their activities for *less* time and play in *less* cooperative ways when left entirely to their own devices. When Mom stays involved from a bit of a distance, and promotes child-centered goals through low-power strategies, the kids are more likely to stay engaged with each other in pleasant ways and have fun. In the next chapter, which describes critical social skills for preschoolers and kindergarteners, we'll take a closer look at the "indirect" kinds of parental supervision that, for example, promote a youngster's ability to join a group already at play—one of the toughest challenges for many kids. But generally speaking, these mothers seem to feel that what's good for the twosome or for the group is good for their child—which, of course, is just the attitude that children should usually bring to their own peer interactions, and a perspective they need to maintain right through-out their school years.

Explore the "whys" behind inappropriate social behaviors.

Studies consistently show that parents do play a role in helping their youngsters learn (or fail to learn) about the consequences of actions and why some actions are more desirable than others in the long run. There is a clear link between parenting and peer systems in this regard. The way a parent explains things to her child, in other words, is a predictor of that child's status among peers.

For example, mothers of first and fourth graders were asked what they'd do if they learned that their youngster had hurt another child's feelings by calling him or her names, grabbed a toy away, or taken something from a friend's house without asking. Popularity ratings had previously been assigned to the children in the study through classroom research.

Some parents said they would use an *inductive* disciplinary strategy, explaining to their child why calling another kid names or grabbing toys wasn't such a good idea:

"When you call Jimmy a stupid dumbhead, it hurts his feelings, and that makes him feel sad or angry, and he wants to do something to hurt you back."

"You can ask your friend in a nice voice to please let you use the toy, but when you just grab things, other kids don't like to play with you."

Here's what the findings indicated: The children of these parents were less bossy, demanding, or threatening with their peers—and more popular—than the children whose mothers employed *power-assertive* discipline—that is, threatening a child with punishment or giving him a verbal scolding.

The mother who suggests why asking nicely for a turn on the swings is a good tactic plants useful notions in her child's mind, or the seeds of social cognition: First, it's all right to pursue something you want, or to be assertive, as long as you do it in a friendly way. Second, another person is involved here, and the manner in which you achieve your goal will have repercussions in terms of how that person feels about you.

Oversee your older child's life with peers.

As your child grows older, your supervising and coaching should give way to overseeing his or her activities with friends. Psychologists call it *monitoring*—letting go while staying informed and connected, or being unintrusively involved.

Intrusive parents—mothers and fathers who insist on knowing chapter and verse of everything their child is up to, and who have a judgment to offer on his or her every decision—are especially troubling to preadolescents and teens. In contrast, involved parents—the ones who expect their children to tell them when they'll be home or to leave a note explaining where they are and with whom; who check in with their children after school with a phone call when they're at work; who get to know their kids' friends and maybe even those friends' parents—are reassuring and comforting to kids in the years when their attentions and emotions are increasingly absorbed by the peer group.

Most research has concerned the flip side of the coin—the consequences of relatively little, lax, or nonexistent parental monitoring. Such studies suggest that when parents don't keep track of their children, those children go off track in disturbing ways. Notably, the absence of monitoring is associated with peer difficulties. For example, researchers interviewed fourth-, seventh-, and tenth-grade boys and their mothers. The children supplied information about where they typically spent their time away from home, and how much they told their parents about what they were doing; the mothers, meanwhile, were asked how important they thought it was to be aware of their sons' activities. The children whose parents did little monitoring were the most likely to be delinquent and to have had contacts with police; in fact, the less monitoring there was, the more serious the aberrant behavior.

We believe that parental oversight and involvement may indeed be the *key* parenting factors in helping adolescents maintain good and stable peer friendships.

Help your child think through social problems.

One of the "functions" of peers is to serve as a barometer of what's socially acceptable and what's not. Your child picks up clues on how to act by watching what his or her agemates do, and then repeating or avoiding their behaviors.

A six-year-old, let's say, observes that every morning at school, a classmate gives her best friend a bear hug and lifts her off the ground, and that the friend responds to this greeting with a laugh and a look of pleasure. The six-year-old concludes this is an action that is well received, so she tries it with her own best friend. If her friend is not one to appreciate a bear hug and a twirl, the six-year-old may be not rewarded and reinforced (with a laugh and a look of pleasure) but rather punished (with an angry look, a command to "Cut it out!," and a cold shoulder for the rest of the morning from her friend). She may be puzzled, or hurt, and she may well decide it's something she won't try again.

This simple exchange demonstrates some complex and absolutely critical aspects of social competence, including perspective-taking ("This classmate of mine is an individual with her own likes and dislikes") and recognizing consequences ("Doing something she doesn't like bodes ill for our friendship or for my reputation in the group"). Such awareness, we believe, is actually most actively promoted within the peer group—that is, child learning from child. But parents can absolutely help the process along, from very young ages on.

Parents who are good at doing this will prompt a youngster to think through and reason about a friendship issue or a social dilemma at a level *just beyond* his or her own capability. Such a mom or dad might say, "It seems that you and Becky always start fighting about who gets to play with the Little Mermaid doll. What do you think you can do about that the next time she comes over, so things will go better?" or "Who you invite to the sleepover is your decision. The girls you don't ask are going to know about the party, though, and they're probably going to be unhappy, or maybe angry. Think about how you're going to handle that."

Such parental questions and prompts—"What are all the things you can do . . . ?" and "What will happen if . . . ?"—are *distancing strategies* that can be enormously effective in getting a child to expand his or her repertoire and at least *think* about alternative solutions to a difficult situation. During adolescence, in fact, these kinds of parent-child conversations can go a long way toward helping a teen anticipate and plan how to handle peer temptations. Even when teens act as if they possessed all the answers, they can be surprisingly receptive to a parent's encouragement to think things through!

Be playful, be friendly, be emotionally expressive.

There's a dominant theme running through all we have said in this chapter so far: Children model their parents in many ways. Indeed, they seem almost to ingest the ideas, feelings, and attitudes of these most significant adults in their worlds, with either helpful or hindering consequences for their own social lives. We see one more demonstration of that current of influence in the fact that friendly, playful, expressive parents tend to have friendly, playful, expressive children. And those are children who draw others to them and are popular throughout the peer groups of childhood.

We know, for example, that parents who play with their children raise kids whom other children like to play with. In one lab study, mothers and fathers of three- to five-year-old children were encouraged to engage their youngsters in a little horseplay—tickling, tumbling, wrestling. The kids who were most liked by other children, according to teacher assessments and observations of peer-peer interactions, had parents who were actively, physically playful during these lab sessions, and verbally stimulating as well.

Children who regularly enjoyed pleasant, lengthy, playful interaction with their parents also adjusted to school more readily and easily than others. On entering kindergarten, they were found to be more considerate of their classmates and to have happier attitudes about where they were and what they were doing: They liked getting ready for school, they said; they liked being with other children; they didn't feel lonely. It's apparent that children learn "good" ways to play from such interactions with their parents—and discover that laughter and encouragement and having fun are forms of social communication that others understand and like.

A little playfulness doesn't hurt with adolescents, either. Some friendly, warm, joking exchanges in the midst of a lot of sullenness are good for everyone.

Studies have shown, too, that parents who *have* good friends themselves raise kids who *make* good friends. Mothers who describe their best friends as being available, supportive, and interesting, for instance, and who say they see those friends often, have children who enjoy especially close peer friendships.

And finally, parents who express their emotions in positive ways have emotionally expressive children. And those youngsters are more popular than kids who either show no feelings or are constricted in their displays of annoyance, happiness, or sadness. Parents who freely, comfortably, and appropriately display emotions in the home—being affectionate, showing appreciation and saying thanks when someone does something nice, getting mad and then getting over it—have children who know how appropriately to express both positive and negative feelings to their friends, and who think it's important to do so.

It may be that parents who are comfortable with their own emotions—who know that everyone has good days and bad days, feels sad sometimes and happy at other times—send their children a message that feelings are normal. Such parents also, we know, let their children understand that it's acceptable to be angry, but tell them, in effect: Even though you're angry, sometimes you may need to just go along with the program, and other times you can think your way through to solutions to the problem you're having. These parents' children, in turn, learn to "read" the facial expressions of their peers accurately and respond to them in an empathetic manner.

What I have referred to as a blueprint of the effective parent constitutes, really, an overview of the attitudes and actions with which a mother or father meets the challenge, and enjoys the pleasure, of raising a happy child who enjoys good friendships.

Clearly, some kinds of involvement in a child's social life need to shift over the years, as hands-on supervising gives way to more distant monitoring. A degree of control that is appropriate with a four-year-old isn't suitable for a ten- or twelve-year-old. Other attitudes and actions, however, are fitting for a child of any age: Every child always needs to sense that he or she is securely held within a parent's loving and sensitive attention and concern. Every child benefits from a parent's belief that friends are important, and that what happens in a youngster's social life has a great deal to do with his or her self-esteem and future success in the world.

In the next three chapters, we will "plug in" the blueprint across the stages of childhood, from toddlerhood to adolescence.

Part II

A Child's Friendships over Time

Chapter 5

Making First Friends

Children Age Two Through Five

Across the span of the years from toddlerhood to school age, most children get their first real taste of peer experiences. They make their first friends and learn about the pleasures and the sometimes harsh realities of life among groups of kids. They begin to appreciate that others have thoughts and feelings that are not just like their own, and that they had better pay attention to that if they want to be liked and to have fun.

It is during these years, typically, that parents are most directly involved in their youngsters' social lives—which of course means having many opportunities to help them build their repertoire of skills. It's also a time when moms and dads can really begin to discern a child's social style. As the parent of a two-to-five-year-old, you'll be aided in your good efforts by knowing what psychologists have come to understand about several developmental milestones of these years in a child's life, including learning to communicate and handle arguments with others. These points, as well as what different kinds of play mean for children and why they're important, are the subject of this chapter.

Now, too, that you have an appreciation of your child's temperament, and of the situations that he or she finds easy or difficult, the following picture of young children's social landscape will help you to determine *what* your youngster needs from you, *when* he or she needs it, and *why*.

The youngest friends

Sarah's mother described a scene that took place as she and a friend, Emily's mother, were heading home from the park, pushing their youngsters along in their respective strollers:

"The two kids were looking over at each other, looking away, giggling a little. Emily got the idea it would be fun to hold hands, so they did, which meant we had to keep the strollers moving at the same pace, side by side. If one of us pulled slightly ahead, the kids had to stretch to keep holding hands, and that was apparently very funny to them. Then they decided to kiss. First Sarah leaned out to try to reach Emily, then Emily leaned over to Sarah, both of them straining against the safety harnesses. Sometimes they managed to smush their faces together, which they thought was the most hysterical thing in the world.

"Next, Emily took a piece of bagel she had and tossed it in the direction of the other stroller. Then Sarah rummaged around, found her stuffed toy monkey, and threw it at Emily. It landed right in her lap, so she flung it back. Both of them kept laughing until all of sudden they got tired of that routine. So they settled back and watched the clouds or the birds or whatever."

Their interactions were so affectionate, said this mom, "that you'd think they were the best of friends. And they're only two."

Do Emily's and Sarah's behaviors signify anything more than the amusements of the moment? Do these two youngsters enjoy a relationship that could be called a friendship? To a certain extent, the answer is yes.

In fact, children begin connecting with each other socially at even younger ages. Psychologists used to believe that infants took little notice of one another, except perhaps to observe other babies in the same manner as they might a doll, a dog, or a tree—as interesting objects of no particular social significance. We now know, however, that they are in fact capable of much more complex and refined associations. Despite having a limited repertoire of responses, even a three- or four-month-old will indicate that she is quite aware of another baby—watching, making sounds, smiling, pointing a finger, and giving every appearance of being pleased and excited when the interest and actions are returned.

By the time that baby gets into her second year, the emerging ability to "socialize" becomes a great deal more sophisticated. From that point on children are able to maintain lengthier interactions and to engage in the kind of game with which those two stroller-bound youngsters entertained themselves. In particular, the kind of back-and-forth, "complementary" behaviors that Sarah and Emily took such pleasure in are increasingly evidenced during the second year. In this case each youngster coordinated her action with her playmate's: Each imitated what the friend was doing ("You reach over to me, then I'll reach over to you; you throw your bagel at me, I'll throw my stuffed monkey at you"), and each took a turn first watching what her partner was doing, then responding, then waiting to see what happened next.

Such reciprocity of imitation is the very beginning of cooperative interactions—the beginning, really, of a child's social life among her peers.

⑤ PARENT SKILL: Look for good friendship possibilities.

If you spend a morning at your toddler's preschool and watch the interactions among that small group of agemates, you may observe that your youngster and another child seem drawn to each other in a charming and special way. Or you may get a sense of which child or children your own son or daughter might get along best with, and thus which would be good to invite for a playdate. It won't take you long to figure out who in the group is sweet and quiet, who's a little bulldozer, who's a leader and who's a follower.

Even two- and three-year-olds express preferences for certain peers; even they have their likes and dislikes when it comes to other children. The ones a youngster will find most attractive are usually those who are like him in some noticeable way—the toddlers of the same age or sex, the ones who enjoy playing the same games or tend to act in a similar fashion. We call this phenomenon *behavioral homophyly.* And even by the tender age of three or four, children clearly understand that friendship is something unique. By their behaviors, they let us know that friends are different from nonfriends. Good pals are involved with each other. They engage in more play, and play in more complex ways. They look happier when they're together than when they're with others, and they are both more cooperative and more quarrelsome than they are with children they don't think of as special friends.

So toddler friendships do exist. And they should be valued and encouraged—through playdates and other social opportunities—because, for one thing, they are markers of good interpersonal relationships to come.

If your toddler and his playmate remain friends over the next two or three years, a period during which children's play becomes increasingly imaginative, they're likely to bring special strengths to their ongoing relationship. They will already have a bond based on trust, pleasure, and understanding, one that will enable them to share symbolic or nonliteral meanings more easily. When a child has a friendship history with a peer, in other words, he will pretend-play in richer and more cooperative ways than are possible with another, less familiar child. And pretend play is the learning ground for all manner of social skills.

Toddler and early-childhood conflicts

Three-year-olds Edward and Corey attend a preschool program in a neighborhood center three mornings a week. They are friends. Edward's mom describes her son as being "happy-go-lucky, up for anything"; Corey's mom says her son is "kind of a mellow, laid-back little boy."

During visiting day at the school, the two parents watch their children at the sand table, where Edward takes command, shoveling all the sand into one corner to form a mountain. Corey picks up a dump truck and begins adding sand to the mountain, until Edward snatches the truck away for his own use. Corey then finds a plastic measuring cup and starts scooping with that, at which point Edward decides he needs the measuring cup, too, and takes it. Corey watches for a while, then gives his friend a shove in order to reclaim the truck. The two boys get into a minor tussle, which ends when Edward's attention is drawn to something going on over at the hamster cage.

Later in the morning, the class is let loose to run around in the outside play area. Edward, as he often does, soon has several kids trailing after him in a little kickball game, and Corey runs over to join them; soon Edward and Corey split off to swing from the climbing bars.

Their mothers aren't so pleased about all this. Edward's mom says she doesn't like to see her son "being so bossy and acting mean" to his friend.

Corey's mother, meanwhile, wishes that her child weren't "such a pushover and a tag-along."

In fact, the interaction between the two boys this preschool morning isn't unusual for kids their ages. Edward may be a *moving-against* boy by nature, belonging somewhere on that continuum of behaviors that describes the uninhibited child. Corey may be more of a *moving-away-from* type, more cautious and inhibited. But their mothers need not conclude that what transpired between their sons was necessarily a sign of social deficiency on either's part. In thinking about their children's social styles, they should bear a few things in mind:

- Two-year-olds or three-year-olds who are engaged with each other, especially children who spend a good deal of time together, can move quickly from laughing to pushing.

  The one who starts the conflict isn't necessarily shunned by his little friend thereafter. And once the tussle ends, they quickly and readily return to their play.

- Young children are most likely not "mean" or cruel.

  Indeed, few toddlers can be said to have genuinely hostile intent, or the wish to hurt other kids. Much of Edward's scrappiness is instrumental—he wants the *thing* another child has, and so he takes it. For a toddler, as I noted earlier in the description of our lab sessions, part of defining the self, or separating it from others' selves, consists in territory and object possession. Edward's mom might actually consider her son's tendencies in this regard in a positive light, because such assertiveness is more often a predictor of later social competence than it is a sign of social deviance.

- Quieter, more reserved children aren't necessarily pushovers.

  Neither should Corey's mother assume that her youngster's relative reactivity is a sign of something amiss. What is notable about the argument between Edward and Corey at the sand table is that even though Edward was the initiator of the toy dispute, "laid-back" Corey was the one who continued it, giving his playmate a shove and precipitating a scuffle. He was, in effect, imitating the more assertive behaviors of his pal—and perhaps learning the useful lesson that being acquiescent isn't always going to get him what he wants.

- Sometimes the *best* best friend for a child is someone who isn't just like him.

    On the next day of preschool, Corey at once seeks Edward out. Such interactions have been noted in many studies of how very young children behave with one another, and of what seemingly draws them together. We know that children who demonstrate an ability to start games and otherwise stir up the action are found attractive by their peers. Our research shows that toddlers such as Edward, who tend to initiate conflicts, are also apt to be socially outgoing in general, and that's a quality that a "mellow" Corey likes as much as the next child.

    Still, if conflicts are part of the normal behavioral territory for kids this age, it is also the case that adult guidance can be useful—and sometimes crucial.

⑥ PARENT SKILL: Give kids some help when they have trouble sharing.

Most parents are understandably delighted to see their youngsters "getting along nicely." But what about when they're *not* getting along so nicely? Some believe that at such moments children should be left alone to solve the problems that arise when two individuals want the same thing, on the theory that it is from such peer-to-peer experiences that kids learn about give and take, negotiation, and compromise. And it's true that sometimes preschoolers *can* resolve disagreements on their own. At other times, however, what ensues is a sudden deterioration into grabbing, hitting, and tears, with one child coming out the loser, and Mom or Dad having to jump in to calm the storm and initiate discussions about sharing.

Certainly, your young child needs freedom to explore and learn what toys and playmates are all about. But when the definition of "me" is still "what's mine," notions of sharing or taking turns can be hard to swallow or even understand. The two-and-a-half-year-old who owns twenty stuffed bears will still resist relinquishing one to another child! In a series of lab studies involving preschoolers, not *one* toddler was observed to offer "his" or "her" toys to another, spontaneously and without prompting. When their moms were asked to intervene and urge their children to share, however, about two thirds of the children complied. Later on, those children were in turn offered toys by *their* new playmates, because an atmosphere conducive to a little friendly exchange had been established. We've seen in our lab that play sessions flow more smoothly when parents promote joint activity, but without taking over.

In your home, nonintrusive supervision might comprise various simple strategies such as the following:

• When arranging a playdate, set the stage a bit ahead of time.

Think of activities that call for your child and her friend to play together, and be sure there are two sets of the same materials on hand—for example, two boxes of crayons—if it would make an activity easier.

• Consider putting away your child's most favorite doll or toy.

If you know your son or daughter is especially attached to a certain plaything and will find it hard to relinquish it to a friend, take it out of the mix. Not everything has to be shared.

• Give the children a jump start if you see they're having difficulty getting things going, and insert yourself briefly into a bout of play that's disintegrating into friction.

If you say some thing like, "Judy can scoot the truck over to me, then I'll scoot it over to you, then you can send it back to Judy," the two children may settle down peaceably on their own.

• Keep reading the signals.

If playdates always seem to run smoothly for an hour and a half and then fall apart, take the hint: Maybe it's beyond your child's capabilities right now to spend two or three hours with a friend. A shorter playdate that ends on a cheerful note is better than a longer one that winds up poorly.

ⓖ **PARENT SKILL: Explain why being a generous playmate is a good idea.**

In our work with parents, we sometimes ask mothers what they'd think if their toddler threw a tantrum at a friend's birthday party, and how they might handle it. Often the response we get is along the lines of, "Well, I'd assume my daughter was probably overstimulated or was just having one of those rotten days. And I'd try to explain to her that she was making her friend unhappy." Similarly, we ask mothers what they'd do if their child was wrestling with a playmate over a toy, and the argument was getting out of hand. A typical reply is, "I'd take my kid aside, and I'd say, 'Let's talk about what's going on here. Is there any other way you can handle this? Do you think you should put that game away for a while?'" These parents are saying, in effect, "I'd try to understand how my child is feeling and why she is acting a particular way. And then I'd help her think of better ways to solve the problem."

That's good, child-centered parenting, but do those ideas actually translate into maternal behavior? Possibly not, if the child is really in no mood to be reasoned with, or if the mother is stressed to the limit after her own rotten day. In that case she might remove her youngster from the scene at once and head for home with no talk at all, or angrily order the child to his or her room. We're talking here not about persistently authoritarian parenting, but rather about the kind of short-fused and snappish reactions to a child's behaviors that all parents are prone to have from time to time. The heat of the moment produces a range of responses that don't always match how parents *tell* us they would react. And yet the fact that in a *cool* moment, these mothers were capable of coming up with essentially thoughtful, empathetic, and helpful reactions to their children's peer dilemmas points to a good level of parental competence. What may be missing on occasion is appropriate action.

All this will probably strike a familiar chord. Appropriate action—in the form, say, of a few reasoned and reasonable words—might be hard to summon up when children are fighting and somebody's crying, everyone's tired, and your nerves are more than a little frayed. Then you might be more inclined to settle the playmates down fast with cookies and a cartoon video than to talk about why it's nice to share, and so on.

But talking to your child about sharing and the like *after* the fact—when things are quiet—is also a supportive thing to do.

- Do talk with your child about the "whys" behind appropriate social behaviors.

  You might point out, for example, that sharing your youngster's toys makes his friend happy, and that the friend will be likely to do the same when your child goes to his house. These earliest lessons in perspective taking can have a large impact on a child's relationships when he reaches school age. If yours is a basically *uninhibited* toddler—a sociable and fearless youngster who seems to get into object conflicts with his friends—helping him understand the consequences of his actions is especially critical. This is how you channel your child's admirable assertiveness away from aggressive behaviors and toward social competence.

- Put into words the connection between something your child does and something another person feels.

This is a connection that a toddler may not instinctively grasp, so your help here is particularly important. You could say, for instance: "You know, when Freddy fell down and you laughed at him, I think that hurt his feelings," or "That was nice, the way you let Whit use your action figures. I know it was hard for you to let him play with them, but he looked really happy, and I could tell he was having fun."

There's an even bigger lesson coming across in all this. When a playmate is invited to your child's home and you gently support the friend's entitlement to toys and turns, you are conveying a good message: Not only is it nice to make a friend happy, but it's appropriate to be gracious to a guest. At this age, your child looks to you for guidance on principles of justice, fairness, and altruistic behavior—sharing, helping, caring. In the bigger scheme of things, after all, it's incumbent on us to favor the weak, the less mature, the smaller, and those with limited or temporary access to resources—in this case, the visitor rather than the host.

Language and gestures

Young children actually understand a great deal about communication. Even a baby will indicate that she wants the cup of juice by curving her index finger and pointing; when Mom or Dad says, "Oh, you want juice now," the process of teaching and learning language gets under way. In their social settings, children of preschool age recognize very clearly that they don't have all the words they need to get their wishes across, and so they embellish and extend their powers of communication by using gestures. In making themselves known in these ways, they often demonstrate remarkable ingenuity with friends and in peer groups; when they aren't getting through with talk, they'll *show* others what they mean, offering a gestural ad lib, as it were.

In addition, preschoolers are quite able to alter their speech to suit their audience. If you listen to a four-year-old talk to a two-year-old sibling or to a neighbor's toddler, you'll notice that he or she uses shorter sentences and simpler words than when speaking with a fellow four-year-old or an adult. In our own studies, we've found that about 60 percent of preschoolers' utterances are socially directed, comprehensible, and evocative of appropriate responses. By age four and a half to five, moreover, children are much more likely than their juniors by just a year to use questions and indirect requests—"Can I have a turn?," for example, or "I'd like to feed the hamster"—rather than direct commands or demands to convey their social wishes and express their material desires.

This is a major advance, not only in terms of language but also in intellectual awareness, for it indicates an understanding of nonliteral meanings. When Emma asks Allie, "Can you give me your Barbie doll?," Allie recognizes it as an indirect request rather than a simple question. Instead of just answering, "Yes," and then continuing to play with her Barbie, Allie perceives that her friend is asking if she can have the doll *now*—a wish that she may or may not choose to grant. Similarly, children can make requests disguised as statements: "That's a neat pencil" can actually mean, "I'd really like to have that pencil."

Indirect communication is less authoritarian than commands and direct requests, and that's why peers like it. (It's the means, in fact, that sensitive parents use to influence their children, as I explained in the previous chapter—through low-power strategies comprising requests, suggestions, and explanations.) Commands are ego-centered; typically they are not issued in a friendly tone, and other children most often view them as disrespectful, bossy, and haughty. So a child's ability to rephrase a command as an indirect request is a sign of his or her maturing social competence. It's a nicer, more pleasant way of expressing a goal.

⑥ PARENT SKILL: Help your child be a competent communicator; suggest words to use.

Even a very young child can begin to learn this fact of life: Grabbing something away from a friend is not the best way of getting it; asking is always better. But your preschooler may not have many words at his or her command, or may need some practice in expressing wishes as questions or indirect requests.

• Suggest some useful scripts.

You might say, for example, "If you want the dump truck, ask Ryan, 'Can I play with that now?'" or "When you want a turn, say to Jessie, 'I'd like to go on the swing now.'" In other situations, a more direct script may be called for: "I know Ted is doing a lot of hitting when he comes over to visit. If it happens again, you can say to him, 'If you're going to hit all the time, you have to go home early.'"

Your child may give these approaches a try, find himself no closer to getting the truck or the swing than before, and *then* make a grab for it; and the tussles with the friend may continue. But even so, you're helping foster his ability to be a competent communicator, and that'll be a critical skill for your child in a year or two.

Ⓖ **PARENT SKILL: Teach your youngster a few body-language basics.**

Studies show that well-liked children present the whole communication "package" in skillful ways. They speak fairly clearly; they know about the gestural ad lib; they've learned the right words to use, including words that might defuse a situation in which another child is behaving aggressively ("If you're going to hit, you have to go home"). They also understand something about socially competent body language.

• In addition to useful scripts, consider whether your child might need some simple lessons in physical communication, a talent that even a youngster with good verbal skills may not have developed.

Here's an example: Sitting in on her daughter's preschool group one morning, a mother noticed that her three-year-old had difficulty making herself heard: "Eileen would say something to another kid or when a little group was playing together, and a lot of the time she'd be looking in another direction or walking around aimlessly while in midsentence. She seemed to have trouble catching another child's attention." Over the next day or two, this parent realized that her child acted the same way at home, "except I know what she's saying, or else I get myself into position to hear her, rather than the other way around!" She rehearsed Eileen in a more effective communication style: "I told her we were going to practice body talk. I'd remind her that when she wanted to tell me something, she needed to come over to me, or at least point herself in my direction, and she needed to look at me and make sure that our eyes were meeting. She picked up the idea pretty quickly."

This is an invaluable lesson to convey, especially if your child tends to be shy and wary. We know that well-liked children seem to understand that when they have something to say, they need to be within arm's length of a peer and make eye contact with him. Your *inhibited* child may find such closeness and contact a bit uncomfortable at first, but with your encouragement and gentle reminders, she will be able to put these simple social skills into practice with increasing ease. And the earlier a child learns these skills, the better: One of the difficulties that can lead an older child to become *neglected,* or overlooked in peer groups, is the inability to attract the attention of others in an accepted manner.

Playtime, together and apart

For many years, psychologists believed not only that children's social interactions became more sophisticated and complex from toddlerhood to age five, but also that the typical play behaviors of two- and three-year-olds simply disappeared over time, to be replaced by other behaviors. A toddler amused herself in one way, it was thought, and a five-year-old played in a different manner altogether.

Much of what we knew about children's social participation stemmed from studies conducted in the 1930s and 1940s by Mildred Parten, a researcher at the University of Minnesota, who described six categories of social behavior, ordered developmentally: unoccupied, solitary, onlooker, parallel, associative, and cooperative. According to that perspective, we might expect two-year-old Johnny, for example, to devote himself almost exclusively to unoccupied behavior and solitary play, feeling content even in the presence of other children to bang on his xylophone or arrange his stuffed animals on his own. A little later, he would become more interested in social exchange and would spend more time watching others from a distance.

By about age three, Johnny would be ready for parallel play. He might sit next to Susie, lining up his blocks while she doodled with crayons—in close proximity, but each pursuing his or her own fun. After parallel play would come associative play: Johnny hands a block to Susie; she gives him some crayons. Eventually Johnny would be capable of cooperative play, engaging Susie, or several children, in clearly defined interactions, in which each child understands what is to be done (the *rules* of the game) and who is to do what when (the *roles* in playtime).

This notion of a gradually unfolding sequence of behaviors, each one abandoned in turn as a child matured, influenced professional thinking for decades. It is one that many parents still seem to subscribe to, among them the mother and father of five-year-old Stephen.

Along with all the other kids' moms and dads, they were invited guests at a Halloween party in their son's kindergarten classroom. The children had a costume parade and played some games, and parents and children walked through a "haunted house," really a tunnel made out of draped bedsheets and containing bowls of cooked spaghetti "brains" and the like. The organized fun was interspersed with free times, when the youngsters could do what they wanted.

Stephen's mother and father observed their son, eager, like most parents, to see their child in action in a group setting with other kids. What they saw bothered them. Stephen took part in all the games and appeared to have a good time, but during the free periods he returned to the craft table and continued working on a clothespin puppet he was making, pausing now and then to watch his classmates run around. Although he acted in no way distressed, either during the party or on the way home afterward, his parents thought he "seemed babyish compared to all the other kids, just playing on his own a lot."

What might we say of Stephen? Perhaps he is one of those children who prefer activities involving objects rather than other kids. Perhaps he wasn't in much of a Halloween party mood that day. And probably, even though his parents didn't register it, not *all* his classmates were continuously and thoroughly caught up in joint endeavors.

In recent years, researchers have discovered that the old notion of what constituted appropriately "mature" behavior for a child among peers was far too simplistic. We know from observations in preschools and day-care centers that children are likely to display the full range of behaviors described by Parten—from doing things on their own to watching what others are doing to playing together—and that even five-year-olds spend *much* of their time in solitary pursuits or playing alongside but not really *with* other children.

In occasionally taking stock of what the other kids were up to while simultaneously working on his stick puppet, Stephen seems to have been engaging in what I have termed *solitary-constructive* activity. True, he may have been acting much as he did when he was younger, but such behavior can serve an important developmental function. In order to join a group and make friends, a child must read what others are doing, approach them, and gain entry into an appealing activity. Stephen may thus have been observing accepted social strategies, storing up information gleaned from watching his peers.

In fact, having the ability to play comfortably and contentedly on his own, perhaps next to another youngster who is likewise playing on *his* or *her* own, may serve Stephen quite well. After all, a child needs to be near others in order to initiate interactions with them in a proper way.

⑥ PARENT SKILL: Observe, but don't rush to compare your child to other children.

It's when children are first in regular peer-group settings—in preschool or prekindergarten classes—that their parents typically become concerned about their social participation and whether they are "keeping up" with their agemates. Here it's important to remember the research findings I've just described: Children don't always wish to do things with others, but sometimes prefer to play alone; solitary or parallel play is normal throughout this age period.

If you can keep those points in mind, parents' visiting days and the like *can* provide excellent clue-gathering opportunities, helping you evaluate whether your child is having difficulties or whether her behaviors are basically par for the course. Ask yourself, for example:

- Does she engage in mostly unoccupied or nonconstructive behaviors, not exploring objects or making things with them?

- Does she appear extremely anxious, perhaps with episodes of nail biting, hair tugging, tearfulness, and so on?

- Does she fail to initiate conversations with others, and shy away if another child approaches her?

If the answer to all these questions is no—if your child seems reasonably content and involved, even from a distance—her solitary or "on her own" behavior is probably no cause for concern and should not be considered babyish, immature, or unfriendly. Average children often move back and forth between interacting with other kids and pursuing individual activities.

If you answered yes to some or all of the questions above, however—if your youngster does show indications of extreme wariness and reticence— she will need your sensitive support. We'll explore this topic more fully in chapter 9.

Pretend play

Toward the end of the preschool years, functional play—for example, climbing on the jungle gym—becomes less frequent, and more of children's time is taken up with constructive activities such as building castles, arranging doll families, feeding guinea pigs, or drawing the inevitable pictures of family members minus necks and torsos. And now, too, an intriguing, complex kind of social activity emerges—pretend play.

The mother of five-year-old Jessica described a game that her daughter and her best friend, Annie, like to play every time Annie comes over for a visit. "They call it the selling game," said this parent, "and I get a big kick out of listening to them. They've got all the inflections down just right!"

Here's how things go:

Jessica has prepared for Annie's arrival by arranging twenty or so objects carefully across her bed, all of which will be offered for sale. The objects comprise an interesting assortment—seashells, pieces of her mom's costume jewelry, an elaborate hat from a Barbie doll's outfit, some miniature wrapped chocolate candies, a plastic palomino pony, and so on. After Annie arrives, both girls get to work writing down numbers on Post-It notes. Each object gets a note in front of it—its suggested price. Annie wants to add some more items to the display, including a couple of Jessica's action figures that she apparently has had her eye on. Jessica says no dice, and since it's her room and her stuff, Annie doesn't mount much of a protest.

Once the display is set up to their satisfaction, they assume their roles. It's settled that Jessica will be the seller—the acknowledged star part—and Annie will be the customer. This agreement has taken a while to reach; it's finalized only when Jessica reminds Annie that she was the seller last time. Annie makes her friend promise that next time she can be the seller again.

The selling game gets under way. Annie carefully examines the items on display, picking them up, studying them, and making comments: "Oh, this is very gorgeous." "Hmmm, I don't know. . . ." "There's only one of these, don't you have the other one?"

Jessica all the while attempts to interest her customer in one item or another. "This is very unusual and special," she says, holding up a rhinestone pin. "Somebody else will buy it if you don't buy it."

Annie says it's too expensive; she doesn't have that much money. So Jessica calls out to the "manager," a person apparently off in a back room, to check the price: "Hey, Manny, how much for this pin?" She listens silently to manager Manny's silent reply, then reports to Annie that the price is the price, no reductions. The same thing happens with the next two objects Annie likes, a feather boa and a silk rose corsage.

Now both girls break character for a moment, as Annie argues that Jessica is supposed to change the price sometimes, that she's just trying to keep her from buying the nicest stuff, and that she's not being fair. The dispute is resolved when Jessica agrees that Annie can buy the boa, and Annie shakes some "money" toward her to make the purchase. The two girls keep the game going for the better part of an hour before deciding to watch *Toy Story II,* their favorite video.

The selling game is clearly a whole lot of fun for these two, but in a large sense, playing store also marks some giant steps forward in the development of social competence.

Most children this age will engage in pretend play when they're alone in their rooms—having their stuffed animals "talk" to one another, for example, or building secret caves out of pillows and blankets. Bring two children together, however, and pretend play becomes much more complex. While Jessica and Annie were having a fine time engaging in "as-if" behavior, pretending that their activities and imaginary people were the real thing was also helping them learn about social rules, roles, and scripts.

Each girl assumed a character's role and reviewed the understood rules of the game, which meant there needed to be cooperation between them, sometimes preceded by disagreement and negotiation. The ability to have such discussions at age four or five and to reach a resolution augurs well for such children in the future. When two kids can thrash matters out in this way—"You were the seller last time," "You're supposed to change the price"—they're essentially compelling each other to see things from a different perspective, letting each other know how they're feeling about last time, this time, and next time, and deciding whether or not it's permissible to change the rules of the game.

⑥ PARENT SKILL: Encourage your child's pretend play, but stay in the background.

Jessica's mother said she enjoys "being a fly on the wall and listening to these kids doing their selling number. But I leave them on their own." That's good advice for any parent whose child is engaged in pretend play: Provide opportunities for him or her to get together with a friend or friends, set the scene by supplying the requisite materials—and then disappear!

Of course, you'll still be on the premises, acting as a monitor and making sure that the flow of interaction is a positive one. When modest conflicts arise over possessions, roles, and rules, you'll do best to remain in the background. But if either (or any) of the children becomes visibly upset, if the play sounds as if it were turning hostile and the friends seem unable to calm down on their own, you'll need to come forward and help them along with some distancing strategies.

- Ask questions.
    Here are some examples: "How can we settle this?"
    "What do you think would happen if . . . ?"
    "Why do you think Annie is angry?"
    "Is there any other way you guys can . . . ?"
    By encouraging them to ponder some of these "whys" and "what-ifs," you'll prompt your child and her friend(s) to get beyond the flare-up, without either entering the pretend sphere yourself or telling the kids what to do.

For children, pretend play is a means of learning within the context of equals, a world of rules and roles that are flexible and can be altered in ways that the participants define for themselves. These wonderful growth experiences call for the *absence* of parental direction. And that is what play is all about. Indeed, psychologists define *play* as a voluntary, spontaneous, and enjoyable activity organized by children. If a grown-up specifies the rules and roles, it's no longer play.

Superheroes and horseplay

Rough-and-tumble interactions constitute another kind of pretend play—one that many boys, especially, enjoy and, as we have noted, will keep up right through their preteen years. This type of horsing around *looks* like fighting, but it's not, and even children as young as three can distinguish "real/meant" actions from "nonliteral/pretend" ones when it comes to aggression. Interestingly, in most cultures more boys than girls take part in what researchers call "challenging" behaviors, including boasting, taunting, and physical testing.

Some parents are disturbed, though, by what they see as simulated aggression. The mother of five-year-old Simon, for example, found the fantasy play her son enjoyed with his best friend bothersome: "I remember my little brother, as a kid, pretending to be Superman and running around in his blue and red cape, looking all ready to save the world! He was cute! With Simon and his friend, what they get up to seems very different. They have their plastic swords and sabers, and they're smashing them around. It's all about power and harming people."

Fantasy play involving superheroes can seem particularly alarming to parents, sensitive as we have become to the possible negative effects of "violent" games. Cartoon images that parents never took very seriously when *they* were children—the type in which a character falls off a cliff, is depicted as a flattened mass on the ground, then pops up and runs off—may be promoting, we're now told, unrealistic ideas about life and death.

But much of this kind of fantasy play is really a way of dealing with the normal fears and frustrations that come with being a small person in a large world. Many children get a kick out of such games, and most are quite able to step out of their pretend roles and resume being "me" in short order. As long as two preschoolers are playing cooperatively and having fun, and no damage is being done, the children's wish to playact as rough-and-ready heroes should give their parents no cause for concern.

⑥ **PARENT SKILL: Listen for rough-and-tumble play that seems to be turning mean and nasty.**

Again, when children are having a good time pretending to be super-heroes, your best role as a parent is that of background overseer. Two boys engaged in horseplay, however, can go over the top, and then one or the other may be heard yelling, "Hey, you hurt me! You did that on purpose!" Of course, children can't be permitted to harm each other, and if the roughhousing is clearly getting out of hand, you'll need to intervene and maybe settle things down with a snack or another kind of diversion. But here's something to watch for:

- If your son's rough-and-tumble behavior with others often seems to proceed from "pretend" to "meant," he will likely benefit from some help in learning to distinguish between fun and "the real thing." He needs to be reminded, in other words—because he has difficulty accurately reading the intentions of others—that his friend is only playing.

  When you intervene by saying, "You know, he didn't mean to upset you or to hurt you; this is just a game, and you mustn't hurt him," you provide that reminder.

- Sometimes, one youngster may actually be trying to "get to" the other by teasing him and goading him on. In such a situation you might enter the fray by asking, "What's going on?," listening to the arguments, and posing the playmates some problem-solving questions, such as "How do you think you can settle this?" or "Would it be a good idea for you two to do something else right now?"

Entering the group

When Jeremy's mother took her son to his first day at preschool, they were among the first to arrive. Although she had taken the time to give Jeremy a tour of the landscape the previous week, visiting the school so that it wouldn't seem like alien territory when he started class there, that first day was still tense.

"The teacher was getting her materials ready and gave us a very warm welcome," this parent remembered. "The only others in the room were three boys who seemed to know one another already and who were doing a construction thing at a table. And I watched Jeremy watching them with a solemn look on his face. You could see the wheels turning, like, 'Oh, man, I've got to go up to those guys, and I don't know if they're going to let me play or what!'" For Jeremy, she said, it was like "crossing the ring of fire—the age-old, how-to-break-the-ice problem! But he's brave. New situations aren't so easy for him, but generally he makes out fine."

Breaking the ice can be a tough challenge for kids of all ages. Some children push their way in, while others hover on the outskirts, making no positive moves to establish contact and simply waiting to be included— and thus usually staying out, unless some exceptionally kind and generous child in the group extends a welcoming gesture. But most kids learn a better way during these years. A slow and subtle maneuver, it's a little social exercise that simultaneously benefits the individual *and* the group.

The socially competent child, even as young as age four, will linger on the perimeter for a bit, trying to figure out, first, what the others are up to, and second, what he might say to them: "Can I play, too?" "What are you guys doing?" or, "I've got this truck here, maybe we could use that." Perhaps he is a naturally confident and friendly, *moving-toward* child who approaches others easily, or, alternatively, a brave little soul like Jeremy, who has discovered that it's worth making the effort to overcome the instinct to withdraw, because other kids will be accepting, and he can have fun with them. Almost certainly, such children have learned something about getting their foot in the door from their parents. In fact, much research has demonstrated that parenting is a *key* component in whether and how successfully a young child picks up group-entry skills.

Here's an example: In a study of the association between children's status in the peer group and maternal child-rearing behaviors, the psychologists Victoria Finnie and Alan Russell gathered a group of four-and-a-half-year-olds and their moms to find out whether and what kinds of parental instructions or advice were effective in helping a child cross that "ring of fire." Two youngsters, not close friends and neither popular nor unpopular, were brought into an empty classroom by a teacher and encouraged to play with a set of building blocks. Once the pair was involved with the blocks, the teacher left, and the target mother and her child came into the room. The mom had been told that the overall goal of the session was to get all three youngsters to play cooperatively.

A few parents let the children fend for themselves while they read a magazine or reorganized their handbags. Some got the already involved pair to start a new game that would include the new arrival. Other mothers, after observing the situation for a minute or two, took the measure of the first pair's activity and got a reading on how their own child was doing—did she look uncomfortable or seem not to know how to join the others? And then they took action, suggesting to their youngster how she might ease her way into the twosome's play. For example, if her child was hanging back, a mom might offer some verbal coaching ("Why don't you go over there? You could say hello and tell them your name"), prompting ("Maybe you could ask if you can play with them"), or enthusiasm ("That looks like fun!"). Once the three kids were involved, these parents generally continued to step in as they deemed necessary, always doing so in a way that encouraged all the children to enjoy themselves. Perhaps not surprisingly, the study found that these mothers' children were identified by teachers as being among the *best liked* in their classrooms.

The message is clear: A young child will benefit from a parent's sensitive help and intervention in this matter of entering a group. It is an essential skill for children to acquire, both because its absence is a predictor of peer rejection and because mastering of peer-group entry assuredly helps youngsters feel better about themselves and their own social competencies.

Group entry will remain an inescapable challenge throughout your child's school years (and beyond!), whether the group to be joined is two other boys playing stick hockey on the sidewalk or fifteen girls on the baseball team, whether it's four children assigned to work on a joint project or a threesome who always sit together at the back of the school bus. It is in groups that your child learns how to balance group goals with personal ones; when to speak up and when to listen; when it makes sense to go along with others and when it's right to strike off in another direction.

First, though, your son or daughter must learn *how* to enter a group.

When we observe kids at play in our lab studies, we note that it's almost always a bad idea for one child to disrupt or radically alter a group activity that is already under way. This can happen, for example, when a newcomer assumes that the group isn't functioning properly, decides that its members aren't playing the game "right," or feels he should be included because he knows a better way. This child *may* in fact have something useful or enjoyable to contribute to what's going on, but his assumptions are egocentric and will quickly get him pegged as obnoxious. When children are playing well together and another child interrupts them by abruptly inserting himself into the game or attempting to peel off one or two members, such behavior will be seen as overly assertive, out of step, and rude. In my childhood, individuals who acted that way were termed "buttin-skys" and "know-it-alls." No one liked those kids then, and no one likes them now, even though they may not necessarily be aggressive, anxious, or whatever.

Easing into and becoming a member of an ongoing group in a manner that peers find acceptable will allow a child to achieve personal social goals, which may be to have fun and even to redirect group activities along different lines. A youngster can, in other words, be assertive, so long as he or she hasn't first been intrusive.

ⓖ **PARENT SKILL: Teach your child to watch, listen, move closer, and then ease in.**

Watch, listen, move close, ease in—the well-liked child comes to understand that this is the best sequence to follow if he wants to join a group. During the preschool years, you have a golden opportunity to help your child acquire these critical social skills.

• Once again, pick up the clues; observe your youngster at the playground or the park, or sit in for a day at the beginning of the school year (as many mothers and fathers are now encouraged or even required to do, serving as parent aides). See how your child acts.

One parent observed her seven-year-old son at the park as he watched two other boys stand on the tire swing and rock it dizzily back and forth. Eager to join them, her son stood up on the adjoining swing and tried to get that one rocking in the same way. The other two paid no attention to what he was doing. The mother recognized this behavior as being typical of her son: "Mark will go up to some kids who are having fun, and then start doing what they're doing. Usually he just gets ignored."

Running next to or "acting like" other kids generally isn't a good group-entry strategy. Mark's parent thought he had the first part right:

"Watch and see what the others are doing, and know that if you want to join them, you should probably do the same thing. Mark just needed to take it to the next step." She encouraged him to move closer to the group, stand next to its members for a little while and watch, and then talk: "I told him just to say, 'Can I play?' or 'That looks like fun, can I try it?' He's started doing this, and sometimes it works well for him." Mark is likely to take a few leaps forward in confidence once his new skills start paying off.

- If your child is either on the inhibited side (inclined to hover on the outskirts of the group) or just the opposite (tending to barrel right in), he or she needs to learn the better approach that Mark's parent promoted: First, observe what the group is doing, by watching, listening, and getting the lay of the land; then ask to join the activity, or present yourself in such a way that the others will think it'd be fun, useful, or interesting to have you join them.

From toddlerhood to age five, your child learns his or her first lessons in the social ways of the world. If all goes well, by the end of this period a youngster will know something about

- why it's good to share and do things with others;
- how to attract the attention of peers in positive ways;
- how to negotiate and compromise; and
- how to join groups.

The beginning of "real" school opens a whole new phase of development, one that may be characterized for your child both by the formation of intensely loyal friendships and by the presence of intense peer pressures. This stage in a child's life is the subject of the next chapter.

Chapter 6

The New Look of Friendship

Children Age Six Through Twelve

As your child gets older, the groups he or she is part of grow larger, social nuances become trickier, and adult supervision wanes. Other factors also come into play: Whereas early in middle childhood your son may have wanted to have nothing to do with girls, for example (and vice versa), by preadolescence that picture will be changing.

If all goes well, your youngster will learn skills during this phase that will help him or her cope with the social challenges that are an inevitable part of these years. Finding a "network"—a small group of kids who offer one another support, acceptance, and comradeship—and figuring out how to deal with the sometimes brutal teasing that peers so often inflict are two crucial requirements.

Across the years of middle childhood, too, a child will begin to tell a different story about what a friend is, and why he or she likes some peers and dislikes others.

What makes a friend a friend

Michael, an outgoing and chatty first grader, says his best friend is Owen, who attends the same school as he does and lives in the next apartment building. When asked what he likes about Owen, Michael describes the great time they had together the previous afternoon: "He got a Razor scooter for his birthday. It's so neat, but my mom won't let me get one yet. Owen lets me ride his sometimes. We have to stay in this park next to my house and we have to wear helmets. Yesterday I had my skates on and we were racing each other around. I was exhausted!" Asked if he has other friends besides Owen, Michael replies, "Of course! Practically everybody's friends with me."

Seventh grader Hugh, another outgoing and chatty fellow, reports that his best friend for the past couple of years has been Will, a boy he met on the first day of middle school. The good thing about Will, he says, is that "he'll always help you out, and he'll stick by you. He does really well in school without even studying, and he's helped me a lot of times with my homework. Also, he doesn't go along with people just to be popular or whatever, which is the way I am myself, I think." Will can occasionally seem remote or standoffish, Hugh says: "He went to music camp last summer, and I didn't see him for, like, a month. Our first day back at school, I went up to him, and he said, 'Hey, how's it going?'—sort of a remark you'd make to someone you didn't know very well. But that's just the way he is. It takes him a while to warm up. People don't always understand that about Will." Hugh has a small group of other friends, he says, "mostly guys who are as crazy about basketball as me."

The responses given by seven-year-old Michael and thirteen-year-old Hugh are representative of their respective ages and stages of development.

First and second graders' accounts of the children they like and don't like reflect the concrete and the here-and-now: A friend is a playmate, a kid it's fun to do things with; nonfriends are those who are difficult or not much fun to be around. During this reward-cost stage, a youngster conceives of a friend as someone who lives nearby or is otherwise readily available, has desirable toys, and enjoys the same games and activities. Since that description probably encompasses a fairly large number of peers, a child of this age typically reports having lots of good friends. Even so, the most important factor in defining a friendship is how satisfying the relationship is personally.

Starting around age ten or eleven, more abstract notions emerge. A friend begins to be defined that way "because he sticks up for me," or "because we share values," or "because we think the same things are important." Later still, on the verge of adolescence, a child's concept of a friend generally includes an element of empathy: Friends are expected to make active attempts to understand each other, and be willing to reveal their thoughts and talk about personal issues. By this stage, emotional connections have strengthened; displays of concern, tact, and patience are possible; and a friend's idiosyncrasy may be explained as "just the way he is." Feelings and intentions, besides the things they do when they hang out together, are often what bind friends or drive them apart.

And all the while, throughout middle childhood, children are studying their peers intently, sizing them up, and measuring themselves against them.

"Where do I rank?" ("Who am I?")

Psychologists know that by age six or seven (though I myself believe it actually starts much earlier), children begin to engage in *social comparison.* Whereas for the younger child, defining the self is mostly about territory and object possession, the first, second, or third grader starts to notice that other kids do certain things as well as, better than, or less well than he does, and accordingly marks himself on particular skills or traits within this universe of known others: "Jill is a better reader than I am, but I can add better," a seven-year-old might remark, or "Jason can run faster than I can. I make nicer drawings than Kevin."

This marking process continues into adolescence (or beyond: Quite a few of us keep right on making social comparisons well into adulthood). And it becomes more intense, more emotional, and more important as children measure themselves less against an ideal standard and more against the classmates they see around them every day.

This is partly how a child pieces together a picture of herself, of who she really *is.* And for many children, the picture has to do not only with who is the better reader or the faster runner, but also with who has more friends. Thus, during the later elementary-school grades and in middle school, your child may suffer newly sharp pangs of insecurity about her relative social position ("Am I popular? If I hang out with this kid, are those kids going to make fun of me?").

Because the popularity hierarchy is a main organizational feature of life at this age, even average children who are generally doing well and have some friends can become acutely sensitive to their relative status. Very few, it seems, are unaffected by the shifting sands of peer acceptance: In one study of eleven-year-olds, about one third of the children questioned reported having lost a friend or having been chosen last for a team or other activity—*within the previous month.*

Where he or she ranks in the group is likely to be much on your child's mind during these years, even as his or her relationships become deeper and richer.

The "best" best friend

Preadolescence, according to Harry Stack Sullivan, often called the father of American psychiatry, is "spectacularly marked . . . by the appearance of a new type of interest in another person." This same-sex youngster becomes a child's very closest friend, with whom she enjoys a kind of relationship she has not previously experienced, not even with a parent. Sullivan noted, "All of you who have children are sure that your children love you. . . . But if you will look very closely at one of your children when he finally finds a chum . . . you will discover something very different in the relationship—namely, that your child begins to develop a real sensitivity to what matters to another person. And this is not in the sense of 'what should I do to get what I want,' but instead 'what should I do to contribute to the happiness or to support the prestige and feeling of worthwhileness of my chum.'"

Finding that special friend, Sullivan believed, could prove to be the salvation of all manner of children who experienced difficulty in their social lives. It might provide a corrective or a helping hand for unhappily isolated children, unpopular teacher's pets, and youngsters "who will not grow up," as well as "those who, because of illness or social handicaps or what not, have hung behind" their peers throughout the earlier years of childhood.

Children themselves often recognize and describe such friendships as being qualitatively different from their connections with others. Becoming close friends with her classmate Olivia at the beginning of fourth grade, said Kate, "was the best thing that ever happened to me so far. I knew everything there was to know about Olivia, and she knew everything about me. Before her, I used to feel sort of different from other kids. It was the first time I felt normal and just completely happy."

The two girls "were in each other's pockets," said Kate's mother, and "at one or another's house after school most days all that year." The friendship remained intense throughout the summer, when both girls attended the same day camp. Weekends found them at their computers, putting out an illustrated newspaper that reported family outings, the habits of their pets, reviews of TV shows and clothing fashions, and poems written in limerick style that humorously portrayed their siblings or various classmates.

While they clearly had fun together, they also "seemed older than they were," said Kate's mother: "Sometimes they'd just talk quietly and seriously for long stretches. They dug up some old LPs of mine from my college days, an album called *Folk Songs from Around the World,* and I'd see the two of them lying head to head on the rug in Kate's room, eyes closed, listening to those records over and over." When Olivia's cat got sick and had to be put to sleep, Kate, her mom said, "was as upset as Olivia was. She put together a love package, she called it, with Olivia's favorite snacks and a bead bracelet she'd made, to cheer her up."

Midway through their fifth-grade year, however, the friendship was shaken when Olivia became friendly with another classmate, a new girl named Sophie. Relations between Kate and Olivia grew somewhat strained. They still talked and met outside of school, but often when Kate wanted to line something up for an afternoon or a Saturday, Olivia was noncommittal and looked uncomfortable; apparently she already had plans with Sophie, though she didn't say so.

For a while, her mother said, Kate "was wounded. I think she felt terribly betrayed, and she was violently jealous of this other girl." Eventually the wound healed; Kate and Olivia, now in seventh grade, remained pals, though some of the old intensity between them was gone.

ⓖ PARENT SKILL: Take your child's best best friendship seriously.

Many psychologists support Sullivan's notions that it is in a "chumship" that most children first acquire a sense of true intimacy and trust outside their family circle, and that a youngster's ability to have such a relationship is an important aspect of growing up. For one thing, they believe, a child learns lessons there that he will apply later, in the cross-sex relationships that develop during adolescence.

Not *all* children, it should be noted, will connect with a "chum" during these years. If your child has not experienced such a passionate friendship, there's not necessarily any great cause for concern. But if your child *is* lucky enough to have a best best friend, you need to appreciate that the relationship is intense, emotional, and very important to her. Your youngster's feelings about it should be taken seriously, even if you yourself are well aware that she will have new friends in her life next year and the year after that.

When Kate felt so wounded and betrayed, her parent talked to her about how it was natural and good to have different friends, how Olivia's wish to spend some time with Sophie didn't mean she was abandoning Kate—but "all to little avail, I'm afraid," said Kate's mother.

In fact, Kate may well have been taking in her mother's words of wisdom, even though they didn't appear to make her feel much better. In her reactions, Kate was typical of children this age, who see a close friendship as an exclusive relationship: "If you're my friend, you can't be hers, too," seems to be the prevailing sentiment. Although youngsters learn a great deal over their middle-childhood years about the give-and-take of friendship, and about how relationships can survive fights and disagreements, it's usually not until later, in adolescence, that they begin to find it easier to accept that a best friend can have *other* friends as well.

Pairs and packs: face-to-face and side-by-side peer connections

Girls in particular, we know, are prone to form such same-sex friendships, and to start doing so at younger ages than boys. The intensity of such chumships, in fact, may be the reason girls have closer, more intimate relationships with just a few others and spend more time together in pairs or small groups. Boys, in contrast, tend to hang out in "packs."

Even two-year-olds, our studies show, prefer to be with same-sex peers; still, Johnny and Jane might call each other friends in preschool and enjoy playing together. After about age seven, however, gender segregation tends to be almost absolute. For some years, boys will stick with boys, and girls with girls. Along the way, they will begin to show noticeably different patterns in the nature of their friendships.

Much has been written about these separate cultures, with most research seeming to indicate that what a girl seeks from her friends and how she interacts with them are not the same for a boy and *his* friends. Girls' interactions satisfy social or *communal* needs, or focus on achieving closeness and connection through the sharing of thoughts, emotions, and understanding. Girls, in other words, like to *talk*—about their happy times and their miseries, about the people they know and their feelings about them. Keenly attuned to the social environment, they build friendship networks through the cultivation of personal relationships. (This is not to suggest that girls' friendships are invariably smooth, comforting, and affectionate: During these years and into high school, when so many children are jockeying for position and peer acceptance, both sexes are fully capable of displaying the hostile and hurtful behaviors that can make life awful for those on the receiving end.)

Boys' interactions, conversely, serve to promote and solidify individualistic or *agentic* needs for action, control, excitement, personal achievement or one-upmanship, and so on. Boys tend to come together in competitive hierarchies, each determined through participation in activities that challenge the individual to prove his mettle in comparison to his peers'.

Girls typically have "face-to-face" friendships, psychologists conclude, while boys have "side-by-side" ones. What might be best, according to much professional thinking, is a little of each. In order to derive the maximum benefit from peer experiences, preadolescents need to connect with others through both face-to-face and side-by-side activities.

The findings of one study were particularly telling about gender differences. Researchers asked fifth and sixth graders to keep a diary for a week, in which each child was to write down three things he or she had done each day with friends or other peers (no sibling interactions were to be included).

Taking up most of their time, the kids reported, was the act of "conversing"—apparently referring to gabbing with others throughout the day. Other frequent pastimes included "acting silly," watching TV or listening to music, playing sports, and shopping, among some two dozen activities in all. When the children were separately asked which activity was the most *important* to them, all of the boys ranked playing sports at the top of their list. Although the girls spent about as many hours engaged in noncontact sports (for example, swimming) as the boys, they said talking to friends was what mattered most to them. They often called one another on the phone; the boys did not.

Such differences may go a long way toward explaining why boys' friendships tend, as a rule, to be unlike girls'. Separate kinds of activities, the researchers inferred, had separate psychological functions. Listening to music with friends, talking on the phone, and the like "provide opportunities for socializing and enhancing relationships, but not so much for the identification of unique aspects of the self." Those unique aspects of the self—among them, demonstrations of leadership, strength, or toughness—were, the investigators suggested, better promoted through competitive activities. At the same time, however, "boys' greater investment in team sports and their lesser interest in some of the relationship- and nurturance-promoting activities . . . may inhibit the development of skills for establishing intimacy."

From these conclusions, we can advance some broad speculations: Taking part in a competitive activity might be good for your daughter; learning to share his thoughts and feelings with greater ease might be good for your son.

⑥ **PARENT SKILL: Encourage your son to talk.**

Perhaps because they have little experience in doing it, or maybe because their male friends discourage it, most boys consider it a sign of weakness to engage in any kind of intimate disclosure—from talking about feelings of unhappiness or anxiety to seeking help with, or understanding about, a problem. We know from our own work, including interviews conducted with the youngsters in our current Friendship Study, that the middle schooler or preadolescent boy who's fortunate enough to have one very close friend may share some of his woes with his buddy. Mostly, however, boys keep to themselves and suffer in silence—which suggests some sensitive ways for you to think about and interact with your child:

- Appreciate the fact that while your son may have plenty of friends, he may not be opening up to them about things that are on his mind.

He may in fact have a great deal on his mind, and with some encouragement, he'll probably feel relieved to tell you about it.

• Spend some relaxed, parent-child hanging-out time together.

Launching a frontal attack on your son's emotional life—"What are you thinking about?" "Is anything worrying you?"—may very well get you no more than a "Nothing" or a "No." A more indirect approach may be called for here: Wash the car or unpack the groceries together, got to a ball game, talk a little about your day, and suddenly he may casually tell you about events that have nothing to do with the car or the ball game.

• Discover when it is that your child usually feels most in the mood to talk.

Many children, both boys and girls, are relatively more expressive at certain times of the day. If you read the signals, you may realize that when he's tired and ready for bed, or on Sunday evenings when he's mentally gearing up for another week at school, your child gets talkative. Make yourself available at those times, and be ready to listen.

• Learn from his friends.

Children of this age—and adolescents, too—sometimes find it easier to talk to their *friends'* parents than to their own. Especially if your son is a quiet, sensitive type, his more gregarious friends may be better sources of information about their classroom life. By welcoming them into your home and being a pleasant but unintrusive presence, you may learn a lot about what's gone on during your child's day, without putting the heat on him.

Children and sports

The mother of eleven-year-old Paul was concerned: "Sports are a very big deal in the school Paul has just started attending. Everybody's on these teams. And Paul is a completely unathletic kid, happiest in front of his computer. I'm afraid he's not going to fit in with most of the other boys he's around all day."

Most parents *do* want to see their children fit in; when a youngster seems to be at odds with the prevailing culture, they worry. And maybe Paul's mother had reason to be apprehensive about the environment her son was entering.

We know this about children and sports: Most boys long to be athletically gifted; such talent is a clear social advantage throughout the elementary- and middle-school years, when physically well coordinated and athletic boys tend to be most admired by their peers. (In high school, the emphasis often shifts, depending partly on school or even classroom norms.) And boys and girls both—though in some communities more than others—see participating in sports as a way of achieving acceptance and popularity. They're doing more of it than ever: According to one survey, nine-to-twelve-year-olds are now playing sports for an average of five hours a week—an increase of 50 percent over twenty years ago!

⑥ PARENT SKILL: If your son isn't following the pack, try to ascertain whether or not he's bothered by it.

Certainly, it's important for you, as a parent, to know if the school setting your son is in places disproportionate value on an area of accomplishment or endeavor that is just not one of his strengths. If it does, you may want to ensure that he at least has opportunities elsewhere to meet others who share his interests. A critical question to consider in this regard is, What's important to my child, and why?

Eleven-year-year-old Paul, for example, may look around at his peers, engage in some social comparison, and perceive that he's worse than practically every other boy in school at soccer, basketball, and every other conceivable sport. That awareness will not make him feel bad about himself, however, if he places more value on getting top grades or being a computer whiz. Such a reaction is by no means uncommon; some youngsters seem to care less than others about "fitting in." And Paul may be more object-centered than people-centered, constructively happy in front of his computer and developing expertise there that will serve him well later on.

Conversely, Paul's realization that he's poor at sports relative to most other boys *may* make him feel inept or inadequate. Seeing himself as unadmired and perhaps unworthy, he may be more comfortable shying away from those he believes would judge him as incompetent. If he opts to spend the bulk of his time at the computer because it lets him avoid other kids, he may become expert with regard to objects, while remaining woefully *in*expert with regard to peers and anything social or sociable.

To sort out where *your* son stands, do a little information gathering.

- You'll learn a great deal about what's important to your child by simply asking him.

   If the apparent sports madness at his school is causing you to worry about your "unathletic" child, it's perfectly reasonable for you to say, "I know you're not too interested in sports. But it sounds like most of the kids in your class are going out for teams, and I was wondering if that bothered you. Is there a lot of pressure at school to be on a team?" Listen to what he has to say.

- You can learn even more about your son's discomfort, or lack of it, by picking up the clues.

   Ask yourself, Does he have a friend or two with whom he clearly enjoys spending time? Do they typically engage in constructive activities together? Is he responsive to social approaches from other kids? Does he seem happily involved in his nonsporting interests?

   If the answer to such questions is yes, the "problem" may be more in your imagination than in your son's reality. If, however, you sense that he's hiding behind his computer because he harbors feelings of social inadequacy, then sensitive parenting might involve nudging him gently onto a wider path.

Competitive endeavors: Peer pressure or parent pressure?

The father of eleven-year-old Tony noted that his son and his best friend spend hours playing a computer game that, to him, "hardly seems to make any sense. And they can't get enough of it." This parent was concerned about his child's "obsession" and felt that he and his friend should instead be "doing something that will have a payoff later on. All that energy could be put to some better use than playing these dopey games."

Many children around Tony's age develop similar obsessions. The fantasy scenarios that younger children often amuse themselves with—for instance, the five-year-olds' "selling game"—typify a kind of spontaneous, unstructured, and pretend play that rapidly begins to disappear across middle childhood. By early adolescence, it is almost entirely absent from children's interactions, replaced by games with or without formal rules, such as the one that made so little sense to Tony's father.

Part of the fascination of these games lies in the need to remember or master an intricate body of information, which the ten-to-twelve-year-old has typically developed the mental ability to do. Contradicting the long-held belief that a child's brain was fully mature neurologically by the time he or she was a few years old, recent studies have shown that parts of the brain keep evolving well past adolescence, with a surge in growth around age ten to twelve. Tony and his friend are probably thinking in more complex ways than they could just a year or two ago, and they may be delighting in flexing mental muscles newly at their command. Part of the attraction, too, may be the fun of pursuing something that their parents don't "get."

Maybe it *would* be more productive for Tony and his buddy to spend at least some of their free time in activities that would connect them to the broader world. In talking about a later "payoff," however, Tony's father may have been entertaining a notion not in his son's best interests. As it happens, Tony is a serious swimmer. Until recently, he regularly took part in meets, but then he decided he'd had enough of competitive swimming for now, much to his parents' dismay. Tony's father, in particular, was envisioning college scholarships to come.

Many kids who get caught up in sports during these years, boys *and* girls, love it. But some don't. For a significant number of preadolescents, participation in team or competitive sports is motivated not by the desire to have fun, but rather by the need to satisfy their parents and their parents' goals.

In talking to mothers and fathers, I've come to realize that many assume that the playing field is a natural socializer, the arena in which kids learn about teamwork, winning, and losing. That assumption isn't entirely wrong. While peer-led games, as I have noted, may be even more apt to teach those lessons, participation in organized sports can certainly provide youngsters with excellent opportunities to figure out what they're good at and how they can achieve their personal best while at the same time helping others along.

To cite one example: Leaders become increasingly visible among groups of children of this age, both boys and girls. One may emerge as the task or instrumental leader, the outstanding player, acknowledged by all as the fastest or the highest scorer, the one who gets the job done. The emotional leader, in contrast, may not be a top performer, but he or she will nonetheless assume the role of captain, whether or not so designated by the coach. This is the youngster who keeps everyone's spirits up, who offers a pat on the back or a kind word to the teammate who made a bad shot, who gives the group an encouraging pep talk when things are going badly. Children may discover wonderful strengths they never knew they had by playing team sports.

Some parents, unfortunately, become intensely invested in their children's athletic expertise and achievements. Tony's father may have been one of these, and Tony himself may have responded to the pressure by calling a halt to the kind of swimming he'd been doing.

⑥ PARENT SKILL: Let your child decide whether taking part in a sport or other competitive activity is truly important.

The eleven- or twelve-year-old who states one day, "I'm not going to practice; I'm not doing that anymore," probably has a good reason for digging in his heels. The activity may have lost its appeal, or it may be eroding the child's sense of self-worth; perhaps it's satisfying someone *else's* goals, but not the youngster's own. In any case, his wishes should be respected.

Remember that during these years your child is developing an image of herself as inferior to, equal to, or superior to her peers in various areas. The child who recognizes that as an outfielder, she is not as skilled as someone else (or as *everyone* else), but who has been persuaded by her parents' ambitions that being "better than" in sports matters a great deal, may be in danger of developing strong and negative perceptions of herself. And even for the youngster who does well, peer comparisons can be dismaying.

Research tells us that children with exceptional skills in a particular area—be it sports or another competitive activity—may actually develop distorted notions of their own worth due to the composition of the peer groups within which they draw their comparisons. The eleven- or twelve-year-old who is an excellent figure skater, for example, may be spending large blocks of time with nine other same-age experts, and in that group of ten, she may be only the eighth-best skater. Thus, even if all ten rank among the best in the state, number eight may consider herself inadequate in comparison to her immediate peers. When children involved in competitive activities measure themselves by the standards of a small elite, rather than by broader cultural standards, they often come away feeling not very good about themselves at all.

Even for the best of the best, after all, college sports scholarships are hard to come by. And if truth be told, fewer than one percent of budding athletes makes it to the "pros."

The points I want to make here are these: When a parent has to force a child to participate in an activity, that child is going to suffer. Too great an emphasis on skills and performance may in fact inhibit a youngster's ability to form positive relationships and true friendships. And finally, being on a team is hardly vital to the development of social competence; children are inevitably getting together on their own during these years, in their own ways.

The tight little world of cliques

"In elementary school, you didn't have to hang around with one bunch of kids," said twelve-year-old Greg. "You were just friends with whoever you wanted to be friends with. Now you've gotta have your group, or you're sort of nowhere."

This sixth grader was referring to the prevalence and importance of a social unit that dominates the social scenes of middle childhood: the clique, a voluntary, friendship-based group of, usually, from three to nine members of the same sex. We don't know much about the cliques of third and fourth graders, other than that some children do form or join them; the assumption has long been that such networks are more meaningful in later childhood. Indeed, by the beginning of middle school, almost all children acknowledge belonging to a clique, within which, they indicate, most of their socializing takes place. The pattern continues into early high school.

Clique membership is sometimes fluid; some kids may leave, and others enter. Those who leave may do so because they have come to realize that they have different interests or want to move in other directions; they may have already begun to establish friendships elsewhere. In other instances, more painfully, a once "in" clique member may find herself abruptly "out," due to nothing more than the capricious manner in which such status can shift among children of this age. Here's an example:

The second half of sixth grade, said Cara, now a high school senior, "was a nightmare." She had been part of a tight knot of six girls who called themselves the Lunch Bunch because they liked to commandeer one of the cafeteria tables for their exclusive use. Every evening, the girls spent hours talking on the phone together; all belonged to their school's handbell chorus, a distinction regarded by most of their classmates as both elite and highly admirable.

Midway through the year, the members of Cara's class went on an all-day field trip to a local park preserve, where they went through a series of exercises designed to promote cooperation and teamwork. It was during one of these challenges that Cara made what she considered, in retrospect, to be her fatal mistake. Faced with a hand-over-hand climb on a rope ladder stretched over a small stream, Val, one of the two acknowledged leaders of the Lunch Bunch, couldn't make it across in several tries. An amused Cara poked fun at her—"in a good-natured way, I thought."

But Val and Sylvie, the clique's coleader, turned on Cara after that, and the other members followed suit. Cara was ousted for the next couple of months: "They'd all race down to the cafeteria without waiting for me. When I got to the table, they'd be talking, and they wouldn't include me. If I said something, they'd all stare at me and then start talking again themselves. And then a little later, Sylvie would say, 'Cara, you're being such a little clam today, don't you want to say something?'"

Eventually the Bunch sent Cara a note. She recalled, "It was in computer class. Sylvie printed out this message, crumpled it up, and threw it at my head. The note said, 'This is a peace offering. Take it or leave it.'" Cara had mixed feelings. The class was large enough, she said, "that there were kids who were kind of floaters, not really hooked up with any one group. I tried to talk to those kids more, and that worked out OK. But I really felt very hurt by what had happened with my friends, and I felt awful, too, when I wasn't part of the Bunch, because it really was so great to be with them." Although the peace offering had been delivered in a less-than-pleasant manner, she decided to take it, not leave it, and began spending her time with the Lunch Bunch once again.

When a child is wrestling with both puberty and school transitions—

entering middle school or junior high and encountering a new set of routines and expectations—the clique can be a port in the storm. Studies of children in middle childhood (and beyond) show that being part of a tight-knit group of friends who are by and large prosocial in their behaviors and attitudes increases a young person's sense of psychological well-being, helps her cope with stresses, and does much to abate her feelings of loneliness.

⑥ PARENT SKILL: If your child is abandoned by a clique of friends, be sympathetic.

As Cara found out, the flip side of membership in a "great" clique can be the "nightmare" of an unceremonious ouster. Being dumped hits a child hard, and parents—apt as we adults are to take a broader worldview of such passing social upheavals, and to be aware that life does go on—may not always fully appreciate the depth of the pain it can cause. While there may be little parents can do to eliminate that pain, they need to take seriously the fact that it exists, and to bolster their youngster's sense of *felt security*—that is, his confidence that there are loving people around who aren't going to fail him.

- Simply listening—with appropriate expressions of empathy and understanding, and without a lot of interpretations and judgments—and tuning in to his point of view may be the best gifts you can offer a child who's been getting the brush-off from peers he thought were friends.

- Armed with a few details, you'll be in a good position to pose questions or make suggestions that will encourage your youngster to take a broader view of the whole unhappy situation.

You might say, for instance, "Do you think maybe your friend didn't understand why you said that? Did you do something that hurt her feelings?" or "What are these girls really like? How do you feel about them now, after what happened?" or "I know you want to make your own decisions about your friends, but maybe it would be a good idea for you to spend more time with some other kids for a while—maybe set up some things to do with somebody else."

Such parental involvement, first and most important, lets your child know that *somebody* is trying to understand. Then, too, a youngster who's full of hurt and feeling betrayed will likely be having a hard time seeing the forest for the trees; bringing up and giving him or her a chance to talk about and think through even seemingly obvious possibilities—"Did your friend not realize you were kidding?"—can help a lot.

Gossip, gossip, gossip

Clique members love to gossip, as do most children during the middle- and late-childhood years. Girls gossip with their close friends; boys, it seems, tend to gossip with other boys who *aren't* their particular friends, as a way of finding common ground. Parents often regard gossip—or any talk about someone who isn't there—as a fairly negative or hostile activity. In fact, it may not be; sometimes it's driven by perfectly benign motives.

You may overhear your daughter gossiping, for example, about the connections among her peers—who's friends with whom, which kids can't stand each other, which girl was seen holding hands with which boy, who passed a note to whom in math class, and so on. Generally such discussions are not strongly pejorative; the talk may actually be humorous, good-natured, even kind, much of it concerned with what's likeable or admirable about other individuals. Gossip of this kind seems to serve the function of helping children to consolidate or define the separate social maps of their peer groups.

Other talk, however, is a great deal nastier. At this age, kids sometimes use gossip to confirm their membership in cliques and other same-sex groups, and to define the core attitudes, beliefs, and behaviors that determine inclusion or exclusion. Talking negatively about someone who isn't there may be a way of ensuring that that child *remains* excluded. Such gossip thus becomes an in-group, out-group expression, strengthening both positive feelings about insiders and negative ones about outsiders—or about anyone who has moved from the one category to the other for whatever reason. This kind of tale-telling, or relational aggression, may be motivated by jealousy or by a child's or a clique's wish to spread rumors about someone as a way of harming him.

ⓖ **PARENT SKILL: Help your child to step back and take a broader view of malicious talk.**

Gossip may upset its intended victim or target, or it may not. We've learned from our studies that children who become aware that they're the subject of such talk do consider who's been doing the talking, and draw their own conclusions. The child who enjoys a sense of felt security in his or her world, who has friends, and who doesn't regard the gossipers very highly in the first place typically will not be terribly emotionally bruised or battered.

If your child is having a bumpier time of it, however—perhaps because the transition into a new school has been especially stressful, or because she is a basically *inhibited* child who's keenly sensitive to perceived slights—and you're hearing statements along the lines of "Everybody was talking about me," some supportive perspective-taking might be a good idea.

• Ask information-gathering questions.

For example, you might say, "Do you know what it was that she said?" or "Was there something you did that led up to this?" or "Did you overhear them talking, or did somebody tell you that?" or "Is that girl a nice kid? Is she someone you like?" And so on.

It's tempting to rush to soothe an upset child with assurances that those gossiping kids are "just mean." They may in fact be relationally aggressive peers; your child may indeed need your empathetic appreciation of a genuinely unpleasant situation. But it's also possible that nothing quite so terrible is going on at all. One of the difficulties an overly sensitive child can struggle with is the conviction that most other people are thinking about her, most of the time. If a group of classmates are talking and burst out laughing just as she walks by, such a child will likely conclude that the joke is at her expense.

If your child is oversensitive, she needs to understand that not everyone has strong opinions about her.

Everyday teasing

Christopher remembered exactly when and where he first realized that his small size might make him an object of ridicule. "My first day in first grade," he said, "all the kids were supposed to sit on these two little benches that were facing each other. A kid sitting on the bench across from me pointed at me and said, 'Look, his feet don't touch the ground. He's a midget!' This guy and some others started calling me Midget off and on, whenever they thought about it. Once they wanted me to climb up into my cubby, this little space where you could keep your coat and stuff. They said it was my midget hole. Like a jerk, I guess, I climbed in there and curled up and smiled at them. I couldn't think of anything else to do. I hated being called Midget, but maybe I thought that was my thing, being little and cute."

Maria, then a third grader, was likewise subjected to teasing: "My mother took me to a local barber shop, where my dad went, because haircuts there were really cheap, and we needed to save money. But I don't think this barber knew what he was doing. I wanted to have long bangs, like most of the girls had, and they came out all short and completely crooked. I looked really dumb."

In school the following day, four girls in Maria's class, a tight and highly exclusionary group, stared at her throughout the morning and giggled among themselves. While Maria was getting ready for gym later that day, the four approached her: "One of them said, 'Maria, we wanted to ask you something, OK? We think it's cute the way your bangs stick straight out from your head. What we wanted to know is, how do you get them to do that? Do you put gel on, or do you just not wash your hair and let it get all greasy?'"

Twelve-year-old Samantha remembered being on the school bus one day when her skin had broken out: "One kid kept looking at me, and then she said in a loud voice to the whole front of the bus, 'Hey, everybody, let's play I Spy.' She started, and said, 'I spy something red.' Everybody kept guessing but nobody got it, so finally she pointed at me and she said, 'It's Samantha's humongous red zit!'"

These children's experiences—still painful for them to talk about years later!—are revealing. As a parent, you should be aware that:

- Teasing—which is an attempt to make another child feel ashamed or humiliated or just lousy—happens all the time and throughout the school years among children, even when they're quite young.

- Especially in middle and late childhood, children's developing sense of self may cause them to become suddenly and acutely sensitive to what other people are saying about them—and to suffer agonies of embarrassment over meanspirited teasing.

- During these years, the nature of aggressive display changes, becoming less physical and more verbal.

    Kids who are annoyed with or envious of a peer, or who hope to demonstrate dominance over him or her, may toss out insults in a show of power. Other teasing, however, may be motivated not by genuinely hostile feelings but rather by a momentary desire, on the part of the teaser, to stand out by showing off his or her presumed cleverness.

- Especially for boys in groups, teasing is also a way of communicating.

    Physical jostling—the shove or elbow to the ribs, essentially a continuation of the rough-and-tumble behaviors that began in young childhood—is frequent among boys in middle childhood. So is razzing or verbal teasing, typically expressed through very open, unsubtle putdowns, as in, "Hey, Charlie, my sister can throw better than you can. When she gets home from kindergarten later, maybe she can give you some lessons."

- Few children are immune to teasing: In surveys, almost all of those questioned reported having been teased by peers within the previous month!

⑥ **PARENT SKILL: Tell your child to counter teasing with humor and a couple of other useful tools.**

Psychologists believe that learning how to handle teasing is one of the social skills that are most critical for children of this age. It's a skill, too, that can be practiced. In particular, both the *inhibited*, on-the-shy-side child and the *uninhibited*, quick-to-anger youngster should learn a few simple ways to cope with everyday ribbing.

- Suggest that your child face down the teasing.

    Being on the receiving end of hurtful comments often causes children to blush, look down or away, and slump a little. Reacting the opposite way—a strategy you can suggest to your youngster by saying, for example, "You know, if somebody's teasing you, it often works best to just stand up straight and look that person in the eye"—can take some wind out of a teaser's sail. One sixth grader advised other teasees, "Just stare right at the kid and just suck it up. Act like you don't care. Don't give him the satisfaction of seeing you're upset."

- A sense of humor helps.

    Throughout these middle-childhood years and into adolescence, children who can't take a joke tend to be unpopular. Many withdrawn and aggressive kids fall into this category; if your youngster is among them, you may want to gently suggest to him or her that when it comes to teasing, it's often best to just laugh and shrug it off.

- Sometimes, agreeing with a teaser can stop her in her tracks.

    When Maria told her mother about the scene before gym class that afternoon, her mom said, "If that happens tomorrow, why don't you say something like, 'I know, my hair looks really stupid, doesn't it?' And then just smile and walk away."

- Occasionally, a direct verbal confrontation can put a stop to teasing.

    For this approach to work, a child must express his feelings in a serious and determined tone: "I don't like it when you make fun of the way I look. It makes me feel really crummy. I really want you to stop." Pleading, as in "Please don't do that," will only make things worse; what's needed is a more direct "Cut it out."

Again, almost all children come in for their share of ribbing. But teasing that is persistent over time, and persistently mean, is something else again.

When teasing turns to tormenting

Two stories, two eleven-year-olds:

In a small private school, a group of fifth-grade girls repeatedly teased Elena, a child who is, said her mother, "sort of naturally nervous and jumpy. She's always been upset by loud noises, strong smells, sensory extremes. When she was very little, for example, she'd cry miserably and twist away if a gust of wind blew in her face. Her pediatrician once told me that Elena had what he called 'soft' neurological signs that might explain this supersensitivity." One of her classmates came to recognize that it was easy to startle Elena, and from that point on she and two friends delighted in doing so. Said Elena's mom, "They'd try to spook her whenever they could. They'd hide behind the door after dismissal, for example, then jump out at her and start screeching." Elena usually responded to these displays of aggression by tearing up and otherwise looking miserable.

At a Parents in Action meeting, Elena's mother brought up the fact that her daughter was upset about the actions of several of her classmates, and immediately another mother said that her child, too, was unhappy about what she referred to as mean behavior. The parents of the other girls, as it happened, were also at the meeting, and their response both surprised and dismayed Elena's mother. "This other parent and I gave some examples of how these girls acted, and we were polite and not accusatory," she said, "but the parents basically laughed it off. They said something like, 'All kids this age do this sort of thing.'"

The meeting facilitator got the parents of the clique members to agree to talk to their children about the need to "be friendly" and "not hurt other kids' feelings." Fortunately, said Elena's mother, the school year was almost over.

Now Alan's story, told by his father:

When Alan, now a high school senior, was eleven, he was picked on mercilessly over a stretch of several months by a classmate and that boy's friends.

Among the youngest in his grade, Alan was somewhat immature socially, but he was a skilled athlete and an outstanding ice hockey player. His tormentor was another hockey player, but not nearly as skilled as Alan. Alan said nothing to his parents or anyone else about what was going on. Over a period of weeks, however, it became clear to his mom and dad that all was not well with their son: He often looked worried and glum and was reluctant to leave for school in the morning. One evening, finally, they questioned him, and he confided in them.

Lenny, the bully, was in the habit of waiting for Alan outside the classroom with his two pals, then walking with him down the hall in a chatty, seemingly friendly manner. As the boys climbed the stairs, however, Lenny would give Alan a shoulder shove hard enough to knock him down. During recess breaks, Lenny, aided and abetted by his cronies, would watch for opportunities to smash Alan into the fence surrounding the school yard. Alan's response to this abuse was to try to stay out of Lenny's way as much as possible and to make sure he was with a couple of friends whenever he left the locker room. Lenny was difficult to escape, though, and the situation had now reached the point where Alan was hiding in the boys' washroom during recess every day.

Believing that his son had done everything in his power to avoid the harassment, Alan's father took action: He called the school principal and asked if it might be possible for the boys to meet with a counselor who could encourage them to talk things out. He was clear about the need for such intervention, explaining to the principal that Alan was unhappy about going to school and was doing poorly in his studies for the first time ever. Later, Alan reported to his father on the outcome of his phone call: Summoning the two boys to his office, the principal had said, "When you kids see each other in the hall or the lockers, just ignore each other. Do not make eye contact, do not talk, just keep walking."

The "just-pass-each-other-by" solution didn't work for long. After a week or two, the bullying started again. Alan's father made another appeal to the principal, who was unresponsive. "What would happen," Alan's dad asked the man, "if I advised my son to find this boy on his own outside of school and take care of business? I certainly wouldn't approve of my giving my son that advice or of his taking that action, and I imagine you wouldn't approve, either." The principal's response took Alan's father aback: So long as such a confrontation did not occur on school property, he indicated, it wasn't his concern.

With no resolution in sight, his son still being hounded, Alan's father called Lenny's parents, explained the problem in general terms, and asked for their help. But they made it clear that they were basically proud of their child—he had lots of friends, they said, and was a decent student. "Boys are boys," said Lenny's father. "They'll work it out themselves." Like the mothers of Elena's classmates, these parents saw the entire situation as a nonissue. And Alan, for his part, was horrified by what he regarded as his father's meddling in his business and treating him like a baby.

In the end, the problem was resolved on the ice. Alan's father suggested to his son one evening that during the next game, Alan could convey a message, fair and square, to his tormentor: You are not to bother me again. And Alan, an expert player who had the benefit of years of hockey training, threw Lenny a ferocious and painful, though perfectly legal, body check. Lenny never bullied him again, in school or anywhere else. It was, quite simply, the end of the story.

Bullies and victims: a behavioral profile

These children's experiences, and their parents' concerns and responses, illustrate aspects of this unhappy phenomenon that all parents, and other adults in children's lives, need to understand.

Recent studies concerning bullying and victimization point to a few general truths:

- Bullying is just plain meanspirited.

    Bullies don't act the way they do to obtain access to activities or things; their goal is precisely to inflict pain and misery on others. We tend to think of bullying as *physical* abuse (typified by punching, shoving, and the like), but hurting another *relationally*—by spreading rumors about that person or getting others to exclude him; by preying on his sensitivity; by teasing and humiliating him—is also a kind of bullying, one that is in fact far more common than the physical assault.

- Bullying looks pretty much the same throughout childhood.

    The main difference between the third-grade bully and the sixth-grade one is that the eleven-year-old is expected to *know* better. By later middle childhood, youngsters have acquired a level of social-cognitive maturity that allows them to better understand what the world feels like to the victim of bullying, and to appreciate the consequences, both for the victim and for the instigator, of mean behavior. Bullying by a ten- or eleven-year-old, then (and certainly that inflicted by an even older child), is considered far less acceptable and far crueler than the same behavior coming from a younger child.

- Such interactions are invariably demonstrations of power and dominance.

    Bullies may be bigger and stronger than others, and they almost always have the power advantage of a small cohort of henchmen. One payoff for the bully, then, is that he or she commands the respect and admiration of a group of followers.

- While all children get teased occasionally, a few become singled out for regular and persistent tormenting over time.

Although the spur may be some physical anomaly or out-of-the-norm behavior—the victim may be very short or very tall, for example, overweight or puny, too slow, too studious, or a stutterer, or have a funny-looking haircut or a pimple—what keeps the teasing going in certain cases is some deeper characteristic of the child who's being teased or bullied.

For example, we know that most boys accept some jostling and ribbing as being par for the course. One youngster in a group, however, may have particularly thin skin. Perhaps he is one of the physical "babies"—boys who are less developed than their peers, and for whom the onset of adolescence can be especially hard. Any group of eleven-to-thirteen-year-olds will include some little kids among some suddenly very big ones; differences in musculature, bodily hair, and other hallmarks of adolescence are impossible to ignore in locker rooms and on sports fields. In such settings, the early-maturing boys tend to be stronger, tougher, and more confident than the later-maturing ones, and often lord their unmistakable prowess over them. Or perhaps the thin-skinned youngster is a sensitive or shy child who is not as comfortable socially as the majority of his peers.

When this child is the subject of teasing, he takes it seriously and personally; his reaction to the elbow in the ribs may be wariness or an instinctive cowering. Over time, others' awareness of his responses is codified into a shared group knowledge: This is a kid who's fun to torment. Early in a school year, or when a team is first being selected or other specialized and informal groups are getting started—that is, before the classmates or teammates actually know much about one another—the teasing that goes on is not typically very pointed or meanspirited. (And on a team, interestingly, even over time, the easy mark may in fact be supported by his teammates in play situations.) But as the members of the group spend more time together, reputations emerge, and thin-skinned children who react sensitively to teasing can find themselves in trouble.

- Bullying notably takes place in the *absence* of anger.

Bullies often harbor no particular ill will toward or past grudges against their victims. In their own minds, they may feel they're simply "messing with" some clearly vulnerable individual—a child caught without the immediate support of others, perhaps, or one who over a period of time has revealed himself or herself to be sensitive and easy to "get." Bullies feel little remorse, distress, or anxiety over their behavior and have little sense of the negative consequences that could ensue.

- While bullying is an aggressive act, bullies don't *always* come from the ranks of aggressive kids.

    The bully is unlikely to take on another child one on one, as aggressive children will do, or to direct hostile actions at anyone who "crosses" her—or even crosses her path the "wrong way"—without regard to that other child's relative power or to the setting they're in. Bullying behavior is something of a social event, carried out in the company of the leader's supportive pals or henchmen. Without witnesses, there's little fun to be had or satisfaction to be taken in harming another person—and the pleasure of *publicly* wielding power is the name of the bully's game.

- The term *victim* conjures up a negative image of a helpless or inept individual. That's an erroneous impression.

    The fact that a child is being bullied does not mean he or she is physically or psychologically weak. Neither Elena nor Alan had any great difficulty getting along in the broader social world. A popular or socially competent kid can be targeted, too.

    Recently, thanks largely to the work of the Norwegian psychologist Daniel Olweus, we've learned that in some cases bullies and their victims *do* maintain what might be called legitimate (albeit abusive), ongoing relationships with each other. A vulnerable child may simply long to be in the company of a stronger one, despite that individual's rough behavior. Or perhaps the association seems to confer a measure of status: This is a kid whom many others respect or fear, the victim may think, and he is befriending me, so I'll pay the costs of being around him. The bully/victim pairing—essentially a "friendship" defined by power—evolves over time. It's an alarming dynamic wherever it appears: Such relationships may predict future abusive or dysfunctional connections.

    Bully/victim relationships, fortunately, are rare. Typically, victimized children are anything *but* willing participants in their own bullying; they do not "bring it on themselves" and are not "asking for it." It's critical that parents and teachers understand this.

- Other parents—and teachers—may not place much weight on incidents of teasing or bullying.

  Thankfully, school personnel have become greatly more sensitive on the issue of peer conflicts over the seven or so years since Alan's father failed to get through to his son's principal. Enormous changes have taken place in many adults' awareness of and attitudes about such behavior, which is now generally recognized as a clear and present danger—as well it should be. But still . . .

  Although studies invariably show that most bullying happens in school, suggesting that it should be treated as a school problem, individual acts almost always occur out of sight of teachers, coaches, and other supervising adults.

  Kids know what's going on but are reluctant to talk about it.

  And the "boys will be boys" mentality still prevails in many communities, as well as in the attitudes of some parents.

- Children who are targeted by bullies are often loath to tell their parents what they're experiencing.

  Elena told her mother about being bullied, and Alan told his parents, too, but only after they asked him specific questions about what was going on with him. Many other children, however—perhaps most—say little or nothing about such repeated tormenting, remaining silent because such episodes are deeply embarrassing and humiliating for them, because they think their getting bullied means that something is wrong with them, or because they believe they should handle the problem on their own.

  If your child is a target, understanding what bullying is all about and how children experience it will enable you to take appropriate parental actions. Escaping from such a situation isn't easy for any child, and your son or daughter may not be able to manage it without your support and guidance.

⊚ PARENT SKILL: Read the signals.

Your child may not be telling you or anyone else what's going on, but some signs can be a clear indication that all is not well:

- He's reluctant to leave for school and makes excuses about why he should be allowed to stay home.

- She complains about early-morning stomachaches or headaches.

- He is quieter than usual, and looks worried.

- Her school clothes or belongings are dirtied, damaged, or otherwise not-quite-right-looking.

- His grades are slipping.

- The wariness you took for back-to-school jitters has persisted or even intensified over the course of the term.

⊚ PARENT SKILL: Encourage your child to talk to you.

When you suspect from these or other clues that your child is being victimized, bring the subject up with her. Say you've gotten the feeling that something is going on, and you'd like to hear about it.

Sometimes a parent's recollections of his own ugly childhood experiences can open the flood gates. Peter's father, for example, described to his twelve-year-old son the months-long stretch when he was repeatedly picked on by three classmates: "It almost always happened in exactly the same way, which made me feel extremely foolish and gullible. This one kid would start talking to me out in the yard where we lined up before school started, and the other two would race by, grab my schoolbag, and heave it over the fence. All my stuff got scattered around, I'd be late getting into class, and I'd get a demerit. At the end of school every day, my stomach would start churning, because I always tried to be the first out the door so I could run home before these guys caught up with me. I told Peter I could still remember that boy's name!" Peter, looking relieved, responded by telling his dad his own story.

ⓖ **PARENT SKILL: Work with your child to plan a course
     of action.**

Although there is no one-answer-fits-all solution for the parents of a
child who is being bullied—or persistently and painfully teased—certain
responses are, we know, categorically *un*helpful. Recommending retaliation in kind (as fathers often do with sons), or suggesting that Mom or
Dad will immediately step in and fix the situation, will not make a child
feel efficacious or any less at the mercy of what's going on. What's more
likely to ease a bad situation is a reasoned and reasonable approach—one
that begins with an understanding of the child's perspective and personal
history, including such factors as temperament and personality, and how
easy or difficult it has been all along for him or her to make friends or fit
into peer groups.

- If your child comes by his or her sensitivity "honestly"—if you know,
  for example, that being in a group of children has always made your son
  or daughter feel vulnerable or discomfited—efforts to involve him or
  her in out-of-school activities (as well as some other strategies I'll suggest in chapter 9) may help enormously.

- Gather information and offer suggestions.

  Ask your child:
  "What exactly is happening? Do you know why?"
  "How do you know these kids, and how do you feel about them? Do
  you seek out their company? Are you trying to be friends with them?"
  "Can you simply avoid this individual or group?"
  "Have you tried to talk it out with the kid who's bothering you?"
  "Can you discuss the problem with your coach or teacher?"
  "Can you find out if your school has student mediation, so you and this
  kid can sit down with another classmate who's not directly involved and
  talk about what's been going on?"
  "Do you want me to get in touch with your teacher or principal?"
  Many children who are going through the unhappy experience of being
  targeted, but who feel secure at home and have friends, can be encouraged
  to deal with the situation on their own—which is exactly what most will
  want to do anyway. But if your child's attempts to work things out have

been unsuccessful, he or she is enduring a kind of misery that calls for further action on your part.

⑥ PARENT SKILL: If necessary, intervene.

Mean attacks demand attention because they're seldom resolved without constructive confrontation—generally some combination of discussion, perspective taking, conflict resolution, and apology, which a bully and his victim are unlikely to accomplish on their own. Intervention might include the following tactics:

- If possible, call the other child's parents and give a short, factual explanation of what you've heard from your child. Try not to sound judgmental. Ask if they have any thoughts on how your children might work their problem out.

- Speak to your child's teacher or coach, again offering a short, factual explanation of the situation as your child has described it to you. If you've picked up any signals that it's affecting your youngster's school work or desire to go to school, share those concerns. Reach some concrete agreement to stay in touch with this other responsible adult in your child's life—plan to talk by phone, say, in a week's time, at which point you'll compare notes.

⑥ PARENT SKILL: Don't tolerate bullying behavior.

If you suspect that your child is on the other side of the bully/victim dynamic—if he precipitates fights, ridicules other kids, and seems oblivious to the fact that such behaviors cause others pain; if teachers have reported bullying incidents, or other parents have called you—*do not* chalk it up to a passing stage or to "boyish" behavior.

The truth is, boys *should not* be boys through bullying. And neither should cruel behavior in girls be excused as something "all kids do." Putdowns and insults are not uncommon during these middle-childhood years, but really nasty teasing, mocking, and intimidation should not be permitted. Engaging in such behaviors isn't good for the child who's doing it, however many friends she may have and however well things may seem to be going for her; it's simply not how competent social beings act, and over time the bully can become depressed or lonely, rejected by those she truly wants to be with.

I've noted that the bully doesn't always come out of the ranks of highly aggressive children, even though his *behaviors* are aggressive, and meant to hurt another. The difference is that the bully is not *reactively* but rather *proactively* aggressive—in other words, coolly out looking to inflict pain. Such a child might well benefit from many of the strategies outlined in chapter 10, aimed at parents seeking to help the uninhibited, aggressive youngster. The parents of a bullying son might, for instance, encourage him to think about the consequences of his actions; reinforce his positive behaviors; explain why apologizing to someone he's hurt would be the right thing to do; stay in touch with his teachers; try to promote a more pleasant and respectful parent-child relationship; and finally, consider getting professional help if the situation begins to seem out of control at school and at home. To these I would add:

- Talk to your bullying son or daughter about a specific incident you've learned of, and try to find out why he or she targeted a particular child.

  You might start off the discussion by saying, "I'm very concerned about what happened and about your behavior. Please describe the situation to me and tell me why you were picking on this kid."

  If you know that your child is not typically a mean or aggressive youngster, focus on why he or she was bullying another and who else was involved. An average child, when in a small group of peers, may on rare occasions feel either emboldened or pressured to go along with an act of victimization, or to behave in some other way he or she wouldn't otherwise consider behaving—a way that he or she in fact thinks is wrong. It's not like this child; he or she knows better and is capable of feeling remorseful.

  If you see your child in that description, talk with him or her a bit about such feelings, and about how the larger group is likely to perceive his or her bullying behavior.

- Consider whether your child should be encouraged to broaden his horizons through out-of-school activities that will ensure contact with different kinds of peers.

  In some schools, unfortunately, the prevailing atmosphere is one of extreme and hostile cliquishness, with kids who don't fit the norms being targeted for humiliation. If your child makes fun of others because they're "different," try to get him involved in an extracurricular activity that will require cooperation with a less homogeneous mix of kids. Lessons learned through real experience can be a great deal more powerful than talk about respecting the differences among people.

Many of our studies of children's friendships take account of the various relationships in a child's life—parents, friends, siblings, and so on—and what each means to him or her. Here's what we have learned: At age ten or so, children view their parents as their mainstays—their chief sources of help, comfort, hope, and strength. By the time they're about thirteen, they report that their friends are just as supportive of them as their parents. Three years later, they say they derive even *more* support from friends.

In this chapter I've described the connections and behaviors that are typical of middle childhood. Very briefly, they are:

- truly loving a best friend;
- joining a clique;
- teasing and gossiping; and
- mapping the contours of the social landscape.

For children aged six through twelve, these milestones seem to be part and parcel of the ongoing processes of psychological separation from parents and establishment of self. The pace of "separation and individuation" will quicken during the teen years, when peers come into bold relief and parents fade into the background—though without ever disappearing entirely, as we shall see.

Chapter 7

The Sea-Change Years

Children Age Thirteen Through Sixteen

Teenagers want to be with other teenagers.

It should come as no surprise to you, if you're living with an adolescent, that during a typical week—even aside from the hours kids are in school together—high school students spend more than twice as much time with their friends as they do with their parents. They *depend* on their friends to lend a sympathetic ear and offer emotional support when they're faced with dilemmas about relationships, school, siblings, or life in general. Indeed, intimacy and self-revelation—including the long, emotionally laden discussions that many teens, especially girls, engage in—are perhaps the most significant hallmarks of adolescent friendships, representing a major developmental change from younger years.

Although belonging to a group still helps your teen to feel good about himself or herself and to cope with many stresses, the tight clique world of the middle-school years is now on the wane. Kids begin to "degroup," forming ties to a greater number of more broadly defined cliques. Same-sex groups merge into mixed-sex ones. Reputation-based crowds draw the social map in high school.

During these years, inevitably, your relationship with your child will undergo a sea change—*in some respects*. The daughter who used to have no problem with a parent's requests or suggestions now bristles at any hint that her mom or dad is "trying to run my life." But as she struggles both to separate from and to stay connected to her family, as peers increasingly influence her emotional health and happiness, your adolescent needs, and wants, a new kind of support from her parents, as we'll explore in this chapter.

The two systems: Is it parents versus peers?

In a widely read study of American adolescents, the psychologists Mihaly Csikszentmihalyi and Reed Larson equipped seventy-five children with beepers, contacted them at random times throughout the day, and recorded their on-the-spot accounts of what they were doing and how they felt about it. On "Quality of Experience" charts, the researchers rated the teenagers' responses in categories designated Affect, Activation, Cognitive Efficiency, and Motivation. It turned out that when he or she was with friends—to a markedly greater degree than at any other time (with family, in classes, or at home alone)—the adolescent was in fine fettle and form, feeling happy, cheerful, sociable, alert, active, involved, excited, and clear.

"One way or another," wrote Csikszentmihalyi and Larson, "most adolescents succeeded in having a better time with their friends than they had anywhere else." Only in the area of cognitive efficiency was the picture a negative one: In the company of peers, the teen had greater difficulty concentrating and controlling his or her actions—the very news a parent most hates to hear. Moreover, much of that "better time" with friends, by adolescents' own accounts, involved being silly, noisy, rowdy, and spontaneous—in other words, just plain goofing around.

No one would question that over these early-teen years, children spend increasing time with, and increasingly *wish* to spend time with, their peers. To a hugely greater extent than in middle childhood, peer interaction takes place without adult guidance and control or even observation. Such developments inevitably prompt the notion of two separate worlds, family and friends.

The father of one fifteen-year-old described the difference between his son's demeanor when he was with his parents and the way he acted when he was with his friends: "When he's alone with us, Noah is in general apathetic, nonverbal—a lump. Then his buddies come over, and there's a miraculous transformation: Noah talks, he smiles, he laughs, he cracks jokes. He's like two different people."

The mother of a thirteen-year-old described her daughter's phone conversations with friends: "Suddenly we're not supposed to hear any of this. If I walk into Holly's room when she's on the phone, she stops and watches me until I leave. She has a life going on with her friends that she makes clear I'm not supposed to horn in on."

If you're the parent of a young teen, one or both of these descriptions may sound familiar.

As the presence of peers in your child's life and the influence they exert come into sharp focus during adolescence, you may start to develop a "them versus us" attitude and feel curious or anxious about that "other world," which in some regards seems so unlike your own. In fact, the belief that adolescence inevitably involves a child's turning against family as he or she moves toward friends is one with a solid history in psychoanalytic theory. Although my own work with young people and most recent research into adolescent friendships and groups belie these notions, I know they're still festering at the back of many parents' minds.

One classic argument, advanced by psycholoanalytic theorists such as Anna Freud and P. Blos, goes as follows:

In early childhood, sometime around age four or five, the child becomes attached to the parent of the opposite sex and hostile toward the same-sex parent. Since it's frightening (to the child) for Johnny to wish his father would disappear so he could have his mother all to himself, or for Jenny to view Mom as a rival for Dad's affections, the youngster subconsciously sets up defenses against those uncomfortable feelings. When puberty arrives with its powerful hormonal changes, the defenses fall, and the child seeks a safe retreat from newly resurfaced sexual and aggressive drives toward his or her parents. Faced with this (in Blos's words) "intrapsychic turmoil," the young teen finds refuge among friends.

So friends, if all goes well, are crucial to the adolescent's move toward ending dependency on his parents and becoming something other than just their child—because in addition to providing a safety valve for uncomfortable erotic feelings toward family members, peers offer the kind of security, feedback, and validation that the teen no longer derives or can accept from his parents. Among peers, the adolescent comes into his own as an individual, on the way to becoming a member of the adult world.

Disengaging from parents and identifying with peers can, however (according to these arguments), have their price: If her friends behave in ways that the adolescent has been taught are wrong, she will follow them anyway. This theory holds, in fact, that peers and adults typically maintain opposing sets of values—and that the teen must ultimately choose peers over parents, and embrace the norms and rules of her agemates. So separate are the two worlds of parents and peers, these theorists suggested, that the young person is only barely connected to adult society during these years.

Teens and their parents: the real story

Now for the good news: Contemporary, nonpsychoanalytically oriented thinking suggests that the transition to adolescence is nowhere near as problematic for parents (or children) as traditional psychoanalytic theory posited.

It's true that in these years, parents may no longer command center stage in some ways; as we have seen, between age thirteen and age sixteen, adolescents begin to name friends—not parents—as their main sources of support. Faced with a problem, Holly might rather get on the phone with her girlfriend than walk into the kitchen and talk things over with her mother. And Noah, who communicates with his parents in monosyllables, comes to life with his pals. As they work hard at defining themselves as different from their parents and most other over-thirties, as they become increasingly allegiant to their peer group and push for greater autonomy, young adolescents almost inevitably get into conflicts with their moms and dads over much of the business of daily life. From a parent's perspective, it may seem at times that children find it impossible to hold the two systems—child/parent and child/peer—in balance simultaneously.

But the notion of intrapsychic turmoil that blows a child out of the family nest and into the wholly separate world of his peers does not seem to hold up to the empirical scrutiny of researchers. It's something of a myth that with the onset of adolescence every child will abruptly and inevitably enter a period of Sturm und Drang that will be a test of endurance for his mom and dad. The research data simply are not there to support the claims that most kids go through major hardships at this stage of their lives, and that most parents can't cope. Nor do teens themselves seem to feel that their parents have turned into aliens. In one national poll of children between the ages of thirteen and seventeen, for example, more than 50 percent of the respondents stated that they got along with their parents "very well," and almost all of the rest said "fairly well." Two thirds of these adolescents thought their parents were "in touch with what life is like" for teens today.

Even more important, and absolutely reassuring, is that when hardships arise, most teens *do* turn to their parents for support. Even then—*especially* then—young people need and benefit from parental attention. In a series of interviews that my colleagues and I conducted with children through the first year of high school, the most socially adaptive teens—the ones who had good friends, satisfying hobbies or interests, and high hopes for the future—told us that in times of need, they could count on their parents for emotional support. The message was: I really need my friends around to feel good about myself in general, but when it gets tough to make it through the day, I need my mom and dad more.

Although they may *see* a lot less of their parents, adolescents continue to rely on them, not only for guidance but also for support in their friendships and activities.

Getting together

Having fun, of course, is part of the shape of friendship during these years, and a shared taste in music or enthusiasm for sports is a way for kids to connect. But older children are also drawn into friendships with those of their peers who have similar attitudes or philosophical opinions (Is abortion right or wrong? Does this country need stricter gun-control laws?). Interestingly, in our observational studies of very young children, it's not at all difficult to predict with a fair degree of accuracy which ones will eventually become friends in the classroom: Those who play the same games and like the same toys are the most likely to bond. By the teen years, however, the factors that lead children to become friends are far more complicated. Adolescent relationships are marked not only by similar preferences but also by commonly held thoughts and opinions on whatever it is that matters most to a particular twosome.

To get that far, a child this age needs a specific social skill: the ability to extend a relationship beyond the boundaries of classroom and school. While most kids meet their friends in school, it is in nonschool settings that those friendships really "take," or become especially and uniquely close.

To be well liked, adolescents—much more so than younger children—must be able to strike up conversations, offer interesting comments, follow up on casual social suggestions, call friends and arrange to get together with them, adjust to changes in plans with equanimity, and so on. Most teens typically do not experience great difficulties in getting things going with their peers, but some have a harder time of it.

(6) PARENT SKILL: Encourage your reticent teen to take the initiative.

Retiring, watching-from-the-sidelines youngsters of all ages—what we call *moving-away-from* children—need to become more comfortable about initiating social interactions, but it's especially important for young teens, for whom social discomfort can be a painful disadvantage. Such adolescents can make real strides in this area if they can somehow relax a bit and start behaving a little more boldly—perhaps by adopting an attitude of "nothing ventured, nothing gained" regarding social overtures.

One parent realized that while her daughter, Lynne, seemed to get along well with her new junior high classmates, she was often at loose ends after school and on Saturday afternoons. Lynne's mom sensed that she felt a little lonely or left out. Once or twice, she suggested to her daughter that she give this classmate or that one a call, but Lynne shrugged off her suggestions with, "Yeah, maybe I will." So Lynne's mother decided to take it a step further: "I had met a couple of nice girls in her class at the school fair and a couple of other functions, and I mentioned these kids. I asked her if there was some reason she felt uncomfortable about calling them."

Lynne replied that she didn't think she knew them well enough; she wouldn't know what to ask them to do, she said, or even *how* she'd ask them. "So we had a little rehearsal," said this mother. "She would think up a particular thing she'd like to do with Kim—maybe go shopping for a CD she wants. Then she'd think of calling her and what she'd say: 'Hi, I was going to go to Tower Records tomorrow afternoon, do you want to come with me?' And I asked her what was the worst thing that could happen." Her daughter laughed and answered, "She could say, 'You dork, don't ever call me again.'" Deciding that the worst probably wasn't going to happen, Lynne agreed that the phone call was worth a try.

Revealing the self

During these years, your child is not only is spending more time talking with friends, but also talking to them with a new degree of emotional intimacy.

The addition of an element of self-disclosure—frankness and spontaneity, the ability and the willingness to discuss thoughts and feelings and to share personal information, including problems and possible solutions—is considered the most striking difference between childhood and adolescent friendships.

Research on the characteristics of adolescent relationships shows that teenage girls talk to their friends more than teenage boys do (as is the case, too, with younger children). And girls are also more likely and more eager to engage in lengthy psychological discussions. When faced with stress or worries, girls look to their friends for advice and comfort. Teenage boys also turn to friends for psychological support, but they find it through distraction and escape—by *doing* things, that is, rather than *talking about* problems. Some studies, in fact, suggest that a teenage boy may find it easier to be on emotionally intimate terms with his parents than with his closest male buddy.

Philip, an articulate and perceptive fourteen-year-old, noted that the boys he spent time with at school never talked to one another about what was bothering them; he never knew, he said, whether anything *was* bothering them. Philip described himself and his avenues of support this way: "I'm actually considered one of the cool kids in class. I can put on an easygoing kind of style, so I get along with most people. The guys I know, they'd help you out if you ran out of money or something. But basically, they'll just scorn you or look at you like you're a wuss if you act depressed. I've spent almost one year now with these guys, and some of them I consider my friends—we get together after school—but nobody I'd call a great friend, in the sense that I'd tell him my problems."

Philip was finding things difficult at home, largely because of animosity between his parents, who were divorcing, so he was glad to have one friend he could open up with, his classmate Laura: "Aside from my sister, Laura is the only one I really talk to. We don't spend a lot of time together in school, but we started e-mailing at night and now I call her when something's really hassling me." Girls, Philip thought, "don't mind getting emotional. They don't consider you a poor specimen if you sound like you want to cry. Also, they listen better."

For the typical teenager—the boy who has a friend or two he's comfortable confiding in, the girl who turns to her friends with comparative ease—a peer is someone to talk to without experiencing anxiety, embarrassment, or guilt. Invested as they are in shedding family dependencies and loosening their ties to their parents, kids are often reluctant to drag Mom or Dad in to help with their internal and external conflicts.

In adolescence as in adulthood, the number of people with whom such an element of trust and comfort can be established is not large. Interestingly, adolescents who say they have *many* friends describe their friendships as *less* rewarding and supportive than do teens who have fewer friends. The comment of an eighth grader in one study underscored the trend toward fewer and better: He wasn't seeing so much of one former pal anymore, he said, because that boy "is trying to single out his friends now. At the beginning of the year, he was friends with almost everybody because he wanted to be friends over the school year with a lot of kids. Now he's singling out best friends."

Teens who develop real competency in the social skills we've just reviewed—boys and girls who are good at initiating activities and working at relationships, who can open up and let friends get to know them—are teens who feel happy about themselves. They tend to be more sociable and less anxious or depressed than those of their peers who are involved in less intimate friendships.

They also tend to be better at managing conflicts.

During these years, children gain a more mature awareness of how two people can have opposite opinions or feelings about a particular issue or situation and manage to reason their way to some kind of compromise or mutual understanding. Where the younger child might get in a fight with a friend, walk away from an argument, and end the relationship (or capitulate for the sake of preserving it), the teenager values himself, his friend, *and* their relationship enough to express opinions or feelings openly, talk them through respectfully, and, if necessary, agree to disagree.

That's a lesson he may have learned at home.

Conflict resolution: at home, with friends

In school-supported, student-mediated discussions—a forum increasingly common in high schools nationwide—classmates learn about social cooperation by talking out problems or differences among themselves. In such settings, adolescents display varying strengths: Some are able to convey their feelings, discuss issues, and negotiate with their peers in a highly successful way, for example, while others are at a loss. What researchers are finding is that the good communication and negotiating skills of the most successful kids seem to have been encouraged and honed within their families.

In several intriguing studies, psychologists discovered clear-cut connections among how adolescents talk to their parents, how their parents talk to them, and how they communicate with friends. In particular, the researchers were interested in the interplay between two key components of social competence, *individuality* and *connectedness.* How good were teenagers, they wondered, at expressing and achieving personal goals while simultaneously respecting the thoughts, feelings, or wishes of others? And how did they go about reconciling the two?

Here's what they found: When an adolescent's individuality *and* connectedness were strongly evident and well balanced within the family, he or she exhibited the same qualities among friends.

In one experiment, parents and their teenagers were assigned a cooperative task similar to one we use in our Friendship Study: Plan a daily itinerary, they were instructed, for an imaginary two-week family vacation on an unlimited budget. The researchers videotaped the family discussions and later tallied the number of times the teenagers asserted their individuality (by disagreeing with a parent's idea or putting forward their own preferences) and expressed connectedness (by acknowledging another point of view or a good suggestion, or working toward a happy compromise). Subsequently, each teen was paired with his or her best friend in a school setting, and the two were asked to plan their ideal weekend, with the stipulation of parental permission to do whatever they wanted and, again, limitless funds.

There was a lot more disagreeing between the pairs of teens than between the teens and their parents—not surprisingly, since peer relationships are by nature more egalitarian than parent-child relationships, and arguing with a best friend is considerably less stressful than arguing with Mom or Dad. Significantly, however, the adolescents' relative skill at stating their case clearly to their best friends, listening to the friends' arguments, and working out mutually satisfactory plans could be predicted by what went on in the earlier exercise involving their parents.

During the family-vacation-planning assignment, for example, one set of parents asked their daughter where she thought they should go—and then essentially ignored (albeit in a pleasant enough way) any suggestion she made that didn't fit in with their own agenda. Later, working out the imaginary weekend with her friend, the teenager seemed to repeat that pattern, sloughing off or putting down her friend's ideas and not talking about ways they might incorporate some of them into a joint plan.

Another family engaged in a very different kind of discussion. Talking over possibilities for their fantasy vacation, the parents and their daughter came up with the idea of taking a weeklong rafting trip down a western river, through canyons and gorges. Once the plan was on the table, however, the daughter began to have second thoughts about whether she'd really enjoy such an expedition. Here, in part, is how the conversation went from that point:

DAUGHTER: Well, could we take, like, a shorter trip?

FATHER: Yeah, you can take shorter trips.

DAUGHTER: How long are those?

FATHER: I think they have just day trips . . . one-day trips. Would you like to do that?

DAUGHTER: Yeah, I guess.

FATHER: That might be best the first time. . . .

DAUGHTER: 'Cause I haven't ever been in a raft.

FATHER: Six days is a lot of time on the river.

DAUGHTER: Maybe five would be OK.

FATHER: OK.

Dad, in this case, listened to what his child had to say, and responded to her ideas, including her reservations—which the daughter in turn clearly felt free to voice. In the later meeting, this teen entered into a lively discussion with *her friend*, with each expressing her own and hearing out the other's thoughts, and both then hashing out a final decision that incorporated some of what each wanted.

⑥ **PARENT SKILL: Allow your teen a good deal of say in family decisions, while you model a respectful way to listen and reach compromises.**

Studies such as the one I've just described lend weight to the argument at the core of sensitive parenting: If you act in a certain way with your child, that's likely to be the way your child acts with his friends. Pay attention to what your teen has to say, expect him to pay attention to what you have to say, and those skills will be taken into his peer world.

Of course, family decisions may not be the only things your child has a lot to say about. During adolescence, many kids form strong opinions about and even take absolute positions on all manner of issues, from why marijuana should or should not be legalized, to the evils of capitalism, to which movies are great and which are stupid. And it can surely be irritating to hear your fifteen-year-old "expert" suggest by his tone of voice that he has insights you couldn't possibly conceive of. But if you pull rank—by saying something like, "Well, when you've had a little more experience of the world, then I'll ask for your opinion"—you will alienate him in an instant.

It's not that difficult to show respect for your teen's ideas while making your own known. You might say, for example, "I appreciate your point of view. It's not the way I see it, but I can understand that we have different thoughts about this." By responding in this way, you'll provide a model that will serve your child well during these years, when ideas and values are such an important part of friendships, and differences of opinion are both inevitable and necessary for growth.

Branching out: the decline of possessiveness and jealousy

The mother of sixteen-year-old Mandy talked about her daughter's relationship with her longtime best friend, Liz, and how it recently seemed to have shifted into another gear. Liz had connected early in the school year with a new classmate named Gabi, and when Gabi suggested that she might be able to pick up some extra spending money by working a couple of afternoons a week at the small diner her family owned, Liz was delighted. As Gabi and Liz began to spend more time in each other's company after school and to share waitressing-related jokes and experiences, the bond between them grew—a bond that Mandy wasn't a part of, though all three girls were often together. From time to time, Mandy talked to her mom about Liz and Gabi.

"What's interesting to me," this mother said, "is that clearly Mandy has a lot of opinions about what's going on. She knows Liz very well, of course, and she loves Liz. She doesn't know Gabi very well, and she's vaguely disapproving of her. Gabi is very smart, but she doesn't take her work seriously, according to my daughter—she likes to party, and she's a flirt. At the same time, Mandy thinks being friends with this kid is sort of *good* for Liz. Gabi's very fun-loving, she says, and Liz is kind of loosening up and being more outgoing."

There was something both admirable and a little poignant, said Mandy's mother, about her daughter's reactions: "I think Mandy misses the old Liz. But there isn't a lot of jealousy or anger. She seems to be weighing various things in her mind—what Liz needs to do, or in any case *is* doing, how she needs to accept it. She feels if she acts resentful, she'll turn Liz off altogether. And she herself is spreading her own wings, with new people." Her daughter, she said, seemed "suddenly more gracious about her friends."

Mandy's emotions, and the way she handled them, typify another leap forward in how teenagers understand the meaning of friendship. For kids a couple of years younger, at the age of tight twosomes, friendships are exclusive, and the presence of a third party arouses possessiveness—indeed, it can readily push friends into conflict. During adolescence, however, children begin to recognize that it's good to grant friends the freedom to develop relationships with others, even emotionally intense and involving relationships—good for the sake of individual growth and good for the strength of the initial friendship.

And just as friends allow each other a greater degree of independence in these years, peer groups are also becoming more relaxed.

From cliques to crowds: "degrouping" in the peer group

Five young people told five different stories about how kids in their schools got together:

One day about halfway through eighth grade, Janet, now in her last year of high school, elected to sit in the cafeteria with two girls who always stuck to themselves. "They were considered sort of outcasts," said Janet, "and the kids I hung out with generally didn't have anything to do with them. But I got to know one of them when we were assigned a science project together, and I actually got to like her. Also, she was giving me some help with biology." Her brief association with the outcasts, however, "meant the kids I used to eat with started making fun of me. Now, as I'm leaving high school, people seem a whole lot nicer to each other."

Adam, a sophomore, attends an academically prestigious private high school that enrolls only about thirty students in each grade. There are no hard-and-fast cliques in his school, Adam said—"just basically the really smart kids and the relative goof-offs. Also a small bunch who seriously fool around with drugs. But everybody knows everybody. There aren't, for example, kids I wouldn't talk to or spend time with."

Devon is a junior at a midwestern high school, one of slightly under thirty-five hundred students in the school as a whole. "There are tons of cliques," she said, "but there isn't one in-group. Some kids stick together because they're all in band or theater. Some kids are the outlaws. Most of the kids I know hang out in groups, and you know who all the other groups are. I don't actually consider myself part of any one. I prefer to kind of move around with different people."

Isaac, a college freshman, recalled of his large suburban high school, "The idea that there were a bunch of druggies and a bunch of brains and a bunch of girl scouts—that was all kind of a myth. You can't always type a kid by his crowd. The wildest party man was also the smartest guy in my class. Some of the worst kids in terms of spreading lies and rumors were the cheerleaders, supposedly the 'good-school-spirit' types."

Belle, another college freshman, said, "By the end of high school, you're not really in your tight little gang anymore. A lot of kids have paired off, a lot haven't. But if your girlfriend was seeing a guy, maybe you'd do things with them and another boy—somebody you weren't dating, just a friend."

In recounting their experiences, these young people highlighted some realities of adolescent social life in schools:

• Cliques, which came to the fore during the middle-school years, are still very much in evidence.

   Especially during the earlier teenage years, in eighth, ninth, and tenth grades, when "belonging" is important to the young adolescent's sense of self, cliques can be exclusionary and hurtful. Later, intergroup or between-clique antagonism fades; kids seem to be nicer.

- Cliques may be a defining feature of the social map, or they may not.

  The power and importance of cliques depend on various factors, not least the size of the school and its prevailing environment. Some researchers suggest, reasonably enough, that very large schools with depersonalized and complex routines virtually compel young adolescents to band together in these ways.

- Not surprisingly, how important a child believes it is to be part of a group will determine how he or she feels about being accepted or rejected.

  Some teens are fairly autonomous individuals who have other things going on in their lives. Some are satisfied with having one or two friends; others have the confidence to move among and be accepted by several different cliques.

- As kids get older, they tend to "de-group."

  Research suggests that in general, fewer children belong to one particular clique as the teen years pass, and a greater proportion have ties to multiple groups, to none at all, or to other kids who "float" among several cliques. Various studies have documented the decline in the number and significance of cliques through the years of high school, a process that researchers call *de-grouping*. After the first year of high school, teens typically begin spending less time in same-sex groups and more in mixed-sex and predominantly opposite-sex groups. By their junior and senior years, many kids no longer identify themselves as belonging to any group at all—a reflection, no doubt, of their evolving sense of self.

- "The crowd," according to many studies, is the significant development of these years.

  Whereas a clique generally comprises a small number of individuals linked by friendship, a crowd is a reputation-based collective of similarly stereotyped individuals. Kids are assigned to one crowd or another by the consensus of the grade or school population; though friendship-based subgroups may form within a crowd, its members aren't necessarily good friends and may not even spend much time together.

Teens themselves are keenly aware of these crowds: Almost every ninth grader, for example, can name the major ones in his or her school. And where once upon a time American high school students might have pointed to the athletes or the cheerleaders, crowds in large urban and suburban schools today come in an amazing variety of forms. Even in the late 1980s, the psychologist Brad Brown could record nine different commonly used teen labels—"jocks, brains, eggheads, loners, burnouts, druggies, populars, nerds and greasers." A more recent newspaper account went further, listing "Abercrombies, alties, chicas, computer nerds, drama freaks, floaters, goody-goodies, goths, hip-hoppers, hippies, Homie G's, intellectuals, preppies, punks, raverz, stoners, techies, teen queens, and trendies." Nor is *this* tally exhaustive, as new crowds continually take shape.

Crowds are a highly visible feature of high school life for many adolescents, and a generally harmless means of social identification or separation. Of most concern to parents, of course, is the adolescent who seems drawn to "a bad crowd," a subject we will explore more fully in chapter 11. The critical thing about the bad crowd situation, however, and many other issues that can put teens and parents at loggerheads, is in what ways and in what areas mothers and fathers attempt to wield control.

Parental input: what an adolescent considers off-limits

As your child elects to spend increasing amounts of time with the friends, groups, and crowds of his or her world, you may find yourself *more* determined to exert control in other arenas, where you think you should still have the final say.

Remember the little diagram in chapter 4? It defined the *authoritative* parent—which is what *every* mother and father should aspire to be, with *any* child of *any* age—as one who exerts a consistent degree of reasoned and reasonable control in a warm manner. Being an appropriately, effectively, warmly authoritative parent is probably never more of a challenge than during a child's adolescence!

In many areas of daily life, teens yearn to be free. They want to be allowed—and believe they have a *right* to be allowed—to make their own choices concerning many matters of significance to them, from the clothes they wear, to their bedroom furnishings, to their friends, to what they will have for dinner. Younger children, of course, also often wish to decide such things for themselves, and can be hardheaded in their determination to do so. But since adolescents have more mobility, more freedom to come and go, and more money at their disposal than at any previous time in their young lives, just as they're turning further away from their parents and toward their peers, their insistence on having their own way can cause their moms and dads alarm, frustration, annoyance, or even anger. Parents may well find it difficult to remain warmly in control at such times, and what's more, they may fear that if their child refuses to heed them regarding some matters, their influence over him will be shaky in *all* matters. But that's not usually the case.

In fact, teenagers do think their parents are *right* to determine the rules and expectations relative to many of their behaviors. Mom and Dad are and should be, adolescents believe, "authority figures"—sometimes.

Much interesting research into what teens and their parents think on the subject of who should have the final say-so about what has been conducted by the psychologist Judith G. Smetana. In one study, children from fifth through twelfth grades—roughly, ten-through-seventeen-year-olds—and their parents were presented with a list of "transgressions," or actions/activities by a child that might be expected to cause friction within the family, and asked whether or not it would be OK for parents to establish rules about each one. The list was divided into four general categories:

First, *moral transgressions,* or behaviors having to do with the rights and welfare of others—stealing pocket money from parents; refusing to share with other children in the family things around the home that belonged to everyone; lying to parents; hitting siblings.

Second, *conventional* transgressions, or the failure to do things that either had been agreed upon or should be expected according to social conventions—not doing assigned chores; not informing parents of plans or whereabouts; not cleaning up after a party.

Third, *personal* transgressions, or matters that seemed to affect only the individual—sleeping late on a weekend; talking on the phone when no one else needed to use it; watching MTV.

And finally, *multifaceted* transgressions, or behaviors that the child might consider his or her territory but parents might find inappropriate, objectionable, or offensive—dressing in punk clothes; going out with friends instead of joining the family on a picnic; hanging out with a friend that parents don't approve of; not cleaning one's room.

The results showed that the children, both preadolescents *and* teenagers, were largely in agreement with their parents about *moral* and *conventional* infractions: Such matters, all said, should fall under parental jurisdiction. Whether they were ten or seventeen, in other words, youngsters believed that their parents were justified in establishing the rules and expectations regarding such things as lying, telling Mom and Dad about plans, and so on.

Not so surprisingly, parents' and children's points of view diverged when it came to the *personal* and *multifaceted* items, such as dressing "punk," opting to spend time with a friend rather than at a family gathering, and letting one's room turn to a shambles. Teens felt those choices, including the selection of friends whom parents didn't especially like, should be left entirely up to them, and Mom and Dad should butt out. Parents disagreed: Mothers, in particular, thought such behaviors should be subject to their control, or felt their adolescents should acquiesce to their wishes in these regards. Parents, it seemed, saw their children's "transgressions" in these areas as a clear threat to the family unit.

Other studies have echoed the two significant findings reported by Smetana:

- Contrary to popular reports and to the nagging fears of many teens' parents, kids *continue to believe* that Mom and Dad are the voice of authority, even the font of wisdom, in certain areas.

  Peers sway a child's decisions about which clothes to wear, which social activities to attend, how to spend discretionary money, and so on. But adolescents report that they are *most* influenced by their parents— and most likely to turn to them for guidance—in such matters as which college or future vocation to consider, as well as in the acceptance and expression of important values, or the right ways to live.

- Teens and parents argue mainly over those behaviors or events that adolescents see as their own turf.

  In fact, data show that when the parent-child relationship is essentially solid, strong, and loving, battles between parents and teens are few; when they do occur, they're usually over what one observer has termed "garbage and galoshes"—or the mundane bits and business of everyday life, such as taking out the trash or dressing warmly.

The lesson for parents is this: As adolescents begin to insist on having greater control over their lives, moms and dads need to adjust their own reasoning accordingly, and consider when and how it may be appropriate to yield control in those personal domains.

That starts with picking the right battles.

Picking your battles . . . and making your case

Child-raising guidebooks often advise the parents of toddlers that life will proceed with fewer tantrums and standoffs if their children are allowed to make their own choices about less important matters. If a three-year-old is permitted to decide whether to have cereal or toast on a given morning, so the thinking goes, or whether to wear the blue shirt or the yellow one, he or she will be more comfortable about accepting parental control over things that really matter. This is sound advice for the parent of an adolescent as well.

Picking the right battles clearly should include making a determined effort to avoid as much as possible the garbage-and-galoshes issues—those matters that your child considers to be within his or her personal domain and that, irksome though you may find them at the time, are of little importance in the long run. Other matters, however—things your teen may *wish* were within his or her personal sphere—call for a reasoned and sensitive approach on your part, as well as some competent skills.

Ⓖ **PARENT SKILL: Reflect on what you know about your child; no one rule applies to all.**

The mother of a sixteen-year-old daughter and a seventeen-year-old son outlined her thinking on curfews: "Our rule is, there isn't one rule. As a parent, you have to be firm without being arbitrary, and you have to know your child. My daughter has her head in the clouds half the time, while my son is a little professor, serious and responsible. And they're both lovely and adorable. You have to explore the context of each situation, weigh that against what you know about the kid, and decide what's reasonable right then." Her daughter usually gets specific curfews; with her son, she feels comfortable leaving things more flexible.

A thorough knowledge of the child, based on the experiences and impressions accumulated through years of living with him or her, should serve as the starting point from which a parent establishes rules that are not arbitrary, but sensible and appropriate.

⑤ PARENT SKILL: Offer a reasoned explanation of your point of view, or of why the rule must be the rule.

Adolescents often think their parents are "overreacting" when they express concerns or fears about their behaviors. If you supply supportive, relevant information for any argument you're making, your child is more likely to *hear* you and to understand where you're coming from.

The mother who talked about her dreamer daughter and little-professor son said that most negotiations in their household revolved around how and when the teens were allowed to use the car. Her son drove to and from particular activities and was always clear about where he was going and when he'd be back; her daughter, newly licensed, "wants to cruise aimlessly with her friends." This mother initiated a discussion with her daughter one afternoon "by raising with her some facts. There was a five-year study conducted on teenagers and cars. What they found was that the more kids there are in a car, the higher the possibility of a fatal accident. If a sixteen-year-old driver has a friend along with her, she's thirty-nine percent more likely to get in an accident and get killed than if she's alone. If she's got three or four kids in the car with her, that increases to a hundred eighty-two percent! The reason is not drinking, not drugs, but the distractions friends pose for an inexperienced driver."

Although her daughter was not persuaded that anything so awful was likely to happen to *her*, she did, her mother said, "understand why I must raise objections about some of what she wants to do with her friends, and she accepts my rules now about the car without the huge arguments."

⑤ **PARENT SKILL: Strengthen connectedness by demonstrating genuine interest in your youngster's decision.**

Your child's need to explore during these years may lead him or her down interesting paths, some of which you'll probably be inclined to dismiss out of hand as a bad idea. Don't do it: Trying to meet your teen halfway will not only prove your concern but also show that you acknowledge his or her wish for greater autonomy.

One fifteen-year-old announced her intention to become a vegetarian like her two best friends. Both of her parents disapproved and tried to talk her out of it, which only made her *more* determined. Stepping back from the contentious tone of their argument, her father spent an evening on the Internet informing himself about current medical thinking on the subject of vegetarianism, then contacted a nutritionist about menus—after which he asked his daughter to sit down with him and look over the material. "I just want to make sure you know how to eat properly and get a balanced diet," he told her. "Then we can see if maybe we should introduce some of these ideas into the way we *all* eat." She listened with interest and then said she thought it was "neat" that he had taken the time to track down information.

Almost certainly, this teen would have proceeded with her plan in any case. Her father's response indicated that he realized as much, and while he still wasn't entirely happy about it, he'd satisfied himself that it was safe and that his daughter would be making an informed decision. Like the mother who was concerned about her daughter's driving, he found that "having the backup of some facts and figures, and moving the discussion into neutral territory, helped."

⑤ **PARENT SKILL: Respectfully express your opinion— sometimes—on matters of physical appearance.**

Many of the things adolescents do (or wear) that go against their parents' grain fall in the murkier area of taste and style—murky because the way a child dresses, for example, really should be up to him or her, even if it drives a parent crazy. Yielding control in these matters, however, does not have to mean slipping into the *permissive* parenting mode, whose message

is, "Whatever you want to do, it's your decision." In fact, it's perfectly understandable, even fitting and proper, that parents, with their greater and
more realistic experience of the world, might want to offer some thoughts
now and then.

When fifteen-year-old Sally, for example, came home after spending a
night at a friend's house, her mother could hardly help noticing that "both
girls had dyed their hair jet black and were seeming very pleased with
themselves. And they looked terrible!" She didn't tell them as much right
then and there, but she felt it was appropriate to let her child know what
she thought: "If you don't give kids any feedback, it doesn't help them to
make better judgments about things. But you have to try to do it without
making your child feel like an idiot. Kids get embarrassed very easily at
this age." She told Sally later, after her friend had left, that she "personally
didn't think the black hair was becoming to her, but I understood she
wanted to experiment with another look." It was this parent's belief that,
"if you don't offer your opinion at all, it's uncaring."

Your offering an opinion or taking a stand within an atmosphere of respect strengthens your child's *felt security* even as it heightens your influence.
Teenagers who have a good relationship with their parents really do want
their approval regarding the choices they make. By contrast, teens who are
insecure in their child/parent relationship, who perceive their parents as un-
trusting, unsupportive, or insensitive, or who feel the need to demonstrate
"independence" without appreciating the interdependence of family members, are likely not to give a whit about what their parents think.

Monitoring: letting go while staying connected

Said one mother, "I read an article about teens, how they won't tell you
what you want to know, so you have to find out for yourself. This colum-
nist said to read their letters, break open their locked diaries, poke through
their wastebaskets, listen in on their telephone calls, follow their traces,
watch what they're doing on the computer. Has it really come to that?"

Certainly it should *not* come to that—not if you're tuned in to your
child and have no reasonable grounds for suspicion or anxiety concerning
her health and safety. Determined though the typical adolescent may be
to preserve her privacy, teens who have had the benefit of *authoritative*

parenting will most often consider it both appropriate and reassuring that their parents want to be kept informed about their schedules and plans.

Monitoring—which in its broadest sense means staying in touch, being aware of a child's activities with friends, and expressing opinions, concerns, or expectations about his choices—has been the subject of much research into the ways in which parents can affect their adolescents' lives. Many of the noteworthy results have pointed up the unhappy outcomes experienced by children who do *not* receive adequate monitoring from their parents. Conversely, we know that well-monitored adolescents not only tend to stay out of trouble, but also find it easier to resist peer pressure to get *into* it. What's more, studies show that teens whose parents know who their friends are and where they're hanging out actually have more intimate, enjoyable, and stable relationships with their peers.

⑥ PARENT SKILL: Welcome your teenager's friends into your home.

Simply being present—in a nonintrusive, nonsnoopy manner—when your child comes home from school can be a good way to monitor what's going on with her.

Three months after her daughter turned thirteen, the mother of now sixteen-year-old Amanda lost her job and began a consulting business out of her home. Amanda's becoming a teenager and her mother's becoming self-employed were unrelated events that in combination turned out to be a boon for each, this parent thought in retrospect. She recalled, "Some afternoons Amanda would come into my room where I was at my computer, sprawl on a chair, and tell me about something that had just happened. Other afternoons she'd walk straight to her bedroom, shut the door, put on her music, and get on the phone, and I wouldn't see her until dinnertime. Either way was all right. There was a new rhythm to our time together.

"I met a number of other kids, too. When she'd come home with one of her friends, I'd sometimes hear her say as they walked in through the living room, 'Go say hi to the resident mother.' A moment later, some kid would stick his or her head in the doorway to my bedroom/office and say, 'Hi, Mother.' This might be Chrissie with the purple hair and black lipstick, or Adam, who usually wore odd leather stuff. Sometimes 'Hi' was all I heard; other times they'd stay and talk for a minute.

"One day there were a couple of frames left in a disposable camera, so I knocked on Amanda's door and said I wanted to take a picture. There were Amanda, her best friend, Ali, and Adam, and they struck a pose. Looking at this photo later, I had to smile. The three of them are dressed in head-to-toe black. Adam is wearing a leather dog collar around his neck with spikes coming out of it. Ali has her arm languidly draped over my daughter's head. Nobody's smiling. And if you didn't know them, you'd think that was a sinister bunch! But the thing is, I *knew* these kids. And they were smart, funny, decent children."

Those afternoons, said Amanda's mother, showed her the power and the wisdom of "parental hanging around. You learn an awful lot!"

Just by being there and making it clear you're glad to see your child and his or her friends—welcoming them without crowding them and definitely without asking them a lot of questions—you can learn a great deal. And you'll find that if you don't act like a watchdog, your adolescent child really won't mind your presence in the home.

⑥ PARENT SKILL: Get involved at your child's school.

Of course, many parents can't be there when their kids get home from school, and here the good news is that being around or right on the premises is by no means critical to monitoring. Neither is it the only way to stay in touch with your child's life.

When Joseph, now an eleventh grader, entered high school, his mother found a way to be in the building fairly regularly. She explained, "A lot of parents think it's important to do school stuff when the kids are little. I think it's even more crucial to do that kind of thing when they're older, if you possibly can." The school published a parents' newsletter, a monthly mailing about activities, and this mom volunteered to oversee the process. Joseph's younger sister has just begun ninth grade, and their mother plans to continue her volunteer work: "My kids know I do this, and they think it's fine. I don't get in their way or in their face while they're at school; actually, I've rarely run into them."

For her, the benefits have been great: "I talk to the teachers, to the office secretaries, sometimes to other parents, and I really get an idea of the kids in Joseph's grade. I know what they're up to!" Among other things, she has learned that several parents allow children to drink beer at parties in their homes—apparently adopting the attitude, she said, "that they're going to get beer one way or another, so it's OK in their house. So without grilling my son, I know when to raise what issues. I can say, 'If you're going over to Ted's house tonight, remember, no beer!'" It's a form of monitoring, she said, "with a couple of degrees of separation, which makes it more pleasant for everybody."

⑤ PARENT SKILL: Remember that small demonstrations of caring and connectedness will mean a great deal to your child.

One of the findings that have come out of the National Longitudinal Study on Adolescent Health—a long-term project involving thousands of students, whose purpose is to uncover the factors in a child's life that will protect him or her from risk—is this: What teenagers most want and need to know and feel is that their parents are psychologically available to them. Being psychologically available involves, of course, listening to a child, trying to appreciate his or her perspective, and offering appropriate help. But it also means letting a child know that he or she is held by strong bonds that are expressed in myriad small ways, whether parents and child are together or not. In fact, psychologists believe that monitoring has little positive effect if it is not accompanied by the consistent message that a child is well and truly loved.

When we ask children what it is their parents do that makes them feel they're watched after, cared for, and truly loved, they often mention the little things: "My mom always calls me from her office in the afternoon, just to say hi." "My dad remembers when I've had a test that day and asks me how it went." "When my parents go out, they tell me where they're going and when they'll be home." Leaving a note on the refrigerator or a sandwich on the counter, remembering about something that's going on in a child's life—kids notice these small kindnesses, and appreciate them.

⑤ PARENT SKILL: Make it clear that your child's safety concerns you.

Even adolescents, impervious as they feel to danger, like knowing that their parents worry about them.

Sixteen-year-olds Stephanie and Grace, for example, have a little joke between themselves, one that has to do with their mothers. In Stephanie's school, some students buy lunches from a kind of steam table on wheels, a truck that appears in the area most days and sells hot meat sandwiches. Stephanie's mother didn't like the sound of that; she raised the possibility of salmonella poisoning and told her daughter she didn't want her eating from the truck. Grace attends another school. On the same block is a building under repair, from which a small patch of molding fell harmlessly to the ground one day. Every morning after that, Grace's mother reminded her daughter to walk on the other side of the street until the repairs were completed.

The girls rolled their eyes telling these stories. "The things parents can get into their heads!" they said. But they were smiling when they said it. And now when the two friends want to wish each other well—or just send the message, "So long, take care, see you tomorrow"—they have a code: "Don't eat off a truck," says Grace. "Don't let a building fall on you," says Stephanie.

From the end of middle school to the end of high school, children's friendships and peer relationships undergo dramatic shifts, which collectively truly do amount to a sea change. During these years, your child:

- spends most of his or her free time with peers;
- extends his or her relationships beyond the classroom and school;
- shares intimate thoughts and feelings with friends; and
- enjoys less possessive, more accepting friendships.

Toward the end of that stretch, most teens will be looking ahead to an even more dramatic segment of their lives, when they'll likely leave home for the first time and begin to prepare themselves for the adult world. These can be tumultuous years. They call for one additional parental response: empathy with what a child probably perceives as the struggles he or she has endured and the mountains that have had to be climbed.

A high school sophomore brought home his school yearbook one day and showed it to his father, who observed, "The graduating seniors each had a page to themselves that they could design however they wanted, and one after another, they acknowledged their parents. This is what these kids wrote, direct quotes: 'Thank you for strengthening me to brave what lay ahead.'. . .'Your love and support have gotten me through.'. . .'Thank you for giving me strength, courage, and faith to survive.'. . .'I wouldn't be where I am today if it were not for you.'. . .'I could not have done this without you.' This is heartfelt! Still, you have to wonder: 'Brave' what? 'Gotten through' what? 'Survived' what? Reaching the age of eighteen? High school? These were, generally speaking, regular kids from regular families."

Teenagers often view their lives as the stuff of melodrama. Often they'll reminisce, ruefully, about their younger selves, amazed at where they've been, how far they've come, and that they've made it through at all. "I think it's a good idea," said this parent, "to agree with your kid that he has it rough, that life is difficult. Even though you know this child has had the benefit of hot dinners, driving lessons, a pile of Gap clothes, orthodontia, a couple of besotted parents. This self-dramatization, it's really a sweet thing, because if they don't feel full of themselves now, then when?"

Over these last chapters, we have considered the characteristics of a typical child's relationships and groups from preschool to high school. Happily, our studies show that most children are, socially speaking, thoroughly typical: They get along with their peers and feel accepted, have friends, take some hard knocks along the way, and learn some useful lessons from them. They generally find in their friendships rich veins of enjoyment and support.

Some children have more trouble. In the following section, we'll take a look at what parents should understand and what they can do when things don't seem to be going right for their child.

Part III

In or Out?
Longing to Belong

Chapter 8

Popularity

What It Means for the Child Who Has It
and for the Child Who Doesn't

When e-mailing became the hot thing among twelve-year-old Melanie's classmates, Melanie's mom found herself caught up in her daughter's online social life: "Melanie had a handful of kids on her buddy list. She told me some of the girls in her class had forty or fifty names on theirs. This was the way these kids made contact in the evening, and I'd see that Melanie often wasn't at the computer, or she'd be on and off in five minutes. It started to bother me a lot that my daughter wasn't very popular." She came up with a bunch of names *herself*—mostly the children of her coworkers—and suggested that Melanie might want to fatten up her buddy list with these additions. Melanie ignored her advice.

This parent's emotions may sound all too recognizable to you. When a child seems to have lots of friends and be involved in many social activities, when his or her buddy list is full of names, parents are pleased. When things are otherwise, however, they become concerned, and in fact may be even *more* likely to feel unhappy about their child's apparent unpopularity than the child himself or herself. And then it's all too easy for mothers and fathers to act in ways that are not terribly supportive of, and may even be damaging to, a child who's dealing with his or her own concerns about being popular or unpopular.

Popularity defined: decency versus dominance

To put "popularity" into a usefully broad context, and to help you start thinking about what it really signifies or doesn't signify to your child, here are several points to keep in mind at the outset:

- Popularity is not a characteristic that belongs to the individual. It's a phenomenon or a reputation bestowed on a child by his or her peers.

- A child may be deemed popular by the group for various reasons.

A particular youngster may be rightly perceived by most of his or her classmates as a kind, empathetic, altruistic person who's also fun to be with. He or she is easy to like. We might call this *popularity-as-decency.*

However, if you ask a child or a group of children, "Who's popular in your school?" you may be given the names of several classmates who seem to have achieved their reputations for reasons that have little to do with kindness, empathy, or concern for others. A peer may be considered popular because she's pretty or wears great clothes, because he's captain of a team or has a pierced eyebrow—or because he or she wields power, perhaps even in ways that make life unpleasant for some classmates. This we might term *popularity-as-dominance.*

- Psychologists are interested in popularity-as-decency.

In our studies, we ask children not "Who's popular?" but rather, "Who's helpful?" "Who gets into fights?" "Who's a leader in your class?" "Who wants to be alone a lot?" "Whom do you most enjoy spending time with, and whom do you least enjoy spending time with?" We want to know, in other words, who is perceived as genuinely likable, and who isn't. The picture that emerges is derived solely from social behaviors and reflects social competence.

- A child's likability (or more specifically, *un*likability) within the peer group is predictive of a number of outcomes in life.

In the broadest sense, popularity-as-dominance (though some children may wish to achieve it) does not loom terribly large in the big scheme of things, and that's a perspective that parents can encourage their sons or daughters to adopt. Popularity-as-decency, by contrast, matters a great deal. By and large, the kids who don't get along well in their peer groups are the ones most apt to run into difficulties, whether academic, social, or relating to feelings about the self.

Gaining an awareness and understanding of these different profiles may help you feel less worried and more relaxed, thus less inclined to jump in with suggestions, opinions, and interpretations that might actually make your child more uncomfortable about his or her social status. It will also put you in a better position to see your child clearly and to consider what sort of parental support, if any, truly would be in his or her best interests.

"Who's popular?": what kids say

In her acclaimed book for preadolescents and teens, *Growing Up Feeling Good,* the educator Ellen Rosenberg reports the responses of a number of sixth, seventh, and eighth graders, both boys and girls, who were asked for their thoughts on their peer groups. A popular kid, they said, was one or more of the following: a good athlete; good-looking; well developed; the brother or sister of someone popular; liked by most people; the owner of a certain electronic game or other possession; rich; a good dresser; a good student; fun to be with; a nice person; honest, dependable, and reliable; a good friend; skinny; friends with someone very popular; going out with someone popular.

In a long-term study of third-to-sixth graders (eight-to-twelve-year-olds) in one community, the sociologists Patricia A. Adler and Peter Adler identified several factors that marked a child for popularity. Through interviews with children, parents, and teachers, they determined that the most popular *boys* were usually the best athletes and also exhibited "coolness"—they wore certain clothes, for example, and had particular kinds of haircuts.

Especially among older boys, "toughness" and a sassy attitude were much admired. The most popular boys sometimes defied their teachers, often argued about existing rules, and had to be disciplined more frequently than other boys. Many of these youngsters were the cut-ups of the class, boys who attracted favorable attention from peers for their clownish behaviors. Popular boys also demonstrated what the researchers called savoir faire, or good social skills with both adults and other kids. Some used that quality, however, to control their peers—excluding classmates they didn't want included in their activities, for example, or establishing and then abruptly changing the rules of desired behavior in order to flummox their would-be followers. By the time they reached fifth or sixth grade, the most popular boys were interacting with girls and sometimes "going" with them. In general, even the more academically capable boys preferred to hold back in class, not wishing to be pegged as "brainy-brains."

As for *girls,* the Adlers found that perhaps the most significant determinant of high status in the group related to family—in particular, how much money a girl's parents had, and how free she was to spend it. "Rich" girls—those who had their own computers, TVs, and phones; dressed in the latest fashions; took up skiing and horseback riding; and went on costly and exotic vacations—were popular girls. The parents of these youngsters also tended to allow them a large degree of freedom, which the girls took as license to participate in "fast" activities—to the admiration of their more restricted or less daring peers.

Popular girls were precocious about boys, too, often calling them on the phone and asking them silly questions—which the boys found both embarrassing and exciting. These girls formed highly exclusionary cliques, passed notes in class, and gossiped about the out-of-it kids; other girls considered them "snobby," while acknowledging their high status. Said one teacher, "Their conflicts aren't over play as much as jealousy. Like who asked whom over to her house and who's friends with whom. There is some kind of a deep-running nastiness there."

Popularity, according to these revealing accounts by middle- or upper-middle-class youngsters, largely reflects dominance in the pack, and we know that such hierarchies can be assessed and measured even among groups of children as young as three or four. Dominance has to do with being able to lord it over others, or to demonstrate power relative to others, or to convince others to do what one wants. Who will dominate is determined, to a large extent, by the environment: Status depends on what the neighborhood values and admires. These judgments of who "has it" and who doesn't are especially commonplace during the years of later elementary school, middle school, and early junior high—when children are ferociously engaged in enhancing their relative position among peers, when self-esteem may be based largely on social comparisons, and when boys and girls both have yet to develop the sturdier sense of self and more mature appreciation of human nature that typically come about in later adolescence.

When asked, "Who are the popular kids?," the high-status children know and name one another. The lower-status child will name them as well, recognizing the classmates who possess envied characteristics or who wield a power this child aspires to or fears; they may be the peers who seem to be growing up faster, who have the liberty, wherewithal, confidence, or bravado to engage in risky behaviors, who are exploring and experimenting in ways that seem exciting and fun. Significantly, they are often not children whom the lower-status youngster counts as friends, or even *wants* as friends. He or she may not even *like* them all that much.

Certainly from middle school on, a nomenclature is well in place; the popular kids—whatever may have vaulted them into their high-status position—are noticeable to everyone else. The relative *importance* attached to that status, however, varies with the individual. If what determines student-perceived popularity depends to some degree on the prevailing school culture (or even the community culture), what a particular child *thinks* about it makes the difference in how he or she feels and even what he or she does.

The in-crowd: wishing to be popular

Many children in our studies have told us that they don't feel popular; in fact, they say they're *un*popular. When we explore with them the personal significance of that perception, most indicate that it's not a big deal; it's just the way things are, they say, and anyway, they have their friends. Others, however, make it clear that popularity *does* matter to them, that anyone who isn't in the dominant group in school is a "loser," and that they're experiencing various degrees of unhappiness over their exclusion. And when a child longs for status, the struggle to attain it—or, once it's been attained, the effort to *main*tain it—can produce problems.

Typically, the nature of peer groups evolves from middle school to the end of high school. Same-sex cliques, which demand a high degree of conformity from their members, predominate and shape the social organization of a school or class through the early teens. By later adolescence, the boundaries of those groups are more permeable, as membership in them waxes and wanes, the behaviors that define them become less fixed in stone, and older adolescents in general display kinder, gentler feelings toward all their peers. "In" and "out" matter less.

Teenagers who consider it *very important* to be in a popular crowd, though, seem not to enjoy that passage toward heightened individuality and acceptance. In their study of age differences in peer groups, the psychologists Leslie A. Gavin and Wyndol Furman asked children ranging from preadolescence to late adolescence to rate how much they valued being in a popular crowd. In addition, the researchers sought to determine the nature of the groups the students were part of by asking how much arguing went on, for example, and how often kids were apt to "talk behind the back of other people." Children were also questioned about how much these unpleasant behaviors bothered them personally, and how welcoming the group was to others.

The responses generally followed the predicted and familiar arc of social development as grades went on—*except* for those adolescents who said they really wanted to be part of the popular crowd. These teens described their groups as hostile toward outsiders, rigid in terms of who could join, and characterized by hierarchies and a need to follow the leaders. They seemingly demonstrated, in other words, more of the clique-driven attitudes and behaviors of younger children. "The advantages of competing for popularity appear to be very important for these students," the researchers concluded. "In turn, they were willing to experience the stress that competition may entail, including giving and receiving a good deal of antagonism." These may be adolescents who, for one reason or another, feel relatively insecure in themselves, who have been unable to form sustaining and more independent friendships, and who rely on clique solidarity to foster a sense of personal identity.

These several observations about popularity-as-dominance suggest some pointers for parents:

⑥ PARENT SKILL: Consider whether your child's seemingly
   underactive social life is a matter of concern to him or her.

Like Melanie's mother, who felt compelled to line up e-mail buddies for her daughter, many parents may wish to insert themselves into domains that really belong to their children.

Even assuming that their child is generally "unpopular"—as measured by the paucity of invitations received from classmates, or the fact that the phone isn't tied up in the evenings—parents need first to consider carefully whether that state of affairs is truly troubling the child. If she seems reasonably happy and content with life, apparently enjoys school (or at least shows no aversion to going there), has a couple of reliable friends, and expresses no deep distress over her relative status in the peer group, it's probably not a big issue.

In that case, it's wise for parents to say little about their concern, to refrain from picking at their own emotional scab by asking a lot of questions about who's going to what social event and so on, and simply to stay tuned in to their child and remain ready to be empathetic and warmly responsive if she does start to seem unhappy.

We've often had mothers tell us, "My child has always been a one-on-one type, always singling out one other child to pal around with. He's never been part of a big, happy gang of kids." To which I would say: If your child finds one other child to befriend, and the pair clearly have fun together and enjoy each other's company and are supportive companions, good for him. Stop worrying. Not every child needs to be part of a big, happy gang. Not every child needs many friends; for some, one or two will do.

⑥ PARENT SKILL: If your child clearly and futilely is longing to belong to the popular group, encourage a little perspective-taking.

Few kids will tell their parents in so many words, "I'm not popular, and it's making me miserable." But it's likely to be very clear to any attentive parent when a child is deeply bothered by a lack of acceptance: Maybe she's often gloomy or sad, or he's moody or angry around the house, or she seems to be turning herself inside out to fit in with the "in" crowd.

It's a good idea to keep in mind the developmental passages of these years, and the fact that as time goes on, your child's growing sense of self will ideally enable him or her to care less about being "in" or "out." If all the popular girls in third or fourth grade are wearing a certain style of sneaker or taking gymnastic lessons, and your daughter is clamoring for the same because it's the cool thing, then it might be appropriate for you to do what you can to help her fit in, provided that the family budget will allow such an expenditure. If, however, your young adolescent is clearly desperate to belong to a popular crowd that isn't welcoming her into its midst, and if she seems to feel like a loser because of that rejection, then you would do well to raise the subject with her.

Children really do want to and will talk about their frustrations, disappointments, and unhappiness in these matters when and if they perceive that their parents want to and will listen.

One informed suggestion here: Advice or observations derived from a parent's perspective, accurate though they may be—for instance, "You won't even remember these kids' names in a few years, just forget about them"—are likely to fall on deaf ears, and to both turn a child off and shake his sense of felt security. Questions and points to think about derived from *the child's* perspective, in contrast, are likely to help him get sorted out, feel better supported, reflect on the difference between having relationships and being popular, and see his place in the universe in a somewhat brighter light. Try asking, for example:

"What are these kids like? Do you feel OK about the way they act?"

"Are you comfortable being around them? Are they people you'd really like to have as friends?"

"Have you thought about joining one of the teams or the after-school clubs, if that's what some of these kids do?"

"Do you think maybe you're trying too hard to get in with the popular kids? Is there another group you could spend some time with?"

⑥ PARENT SKILL: If your child is in with the "in" kids, and they're not so nice, encourage a move in another direction.

Being part of the popular group can begin to be discomfiting to the child who secretly doesn't like a lot of what's going on within it, but feels somewhat stuck—a situation described by thirteen-year-old Polly. When her family moved to a new city, she entered a school in which she knew no one. An outgoing individual, eager to find a niche for herself, she became ensconced in a group she had quickly identified as the popular girls: "After school we go to a coffee shop a couple of blocks away, and we all sit in two booths and drink coffee or tea. It's like you're not supposed to drink soda anymore. We're on what they call this junior committee for a parents' group that arranges dances at a private club. We're supposed to get to know kids from other schools who can be invited to these things."

By the end of the year, Polly felt she was paying a price for being part of her set: "It's almost like our job is to be popular, and to act like we're better than everybody else. I know that some other kids see me as just a snob. I sort of have to prove that I'm really a nice person and I'm friendly. But it's hard to get another reputation."

Your "in" child may have a fine time with her group of friends because they're basically good kids; alternatively, she may come to decide it's not for her after all. The preteen or young adolescent who has had the benefit all along of sensitive parenting; who has experienced at least one or two good friendships in her life; and whose internal working model of relationships is based on kindness and support, will likely come away unscathed from throwing in her lot with the dominant kings and queens of the school. It's all part and parcel of exploring the social universe. But she may benefit, as well, from having a parental sounding board.

Polly, for example, told her mother some of what was happening, confiding that the girls in her crowd were quite critical of others and sometimes mean. A classmate had recently been appointed to the junior dance committee, but the other girls had decided they didn't like her, and so they had gone about their planning without telling her. Polly felt this was both unfair and just plain wrong. "The only reason is," she told her mom, "they think she's nerdy. And she's really nice." "Should you take a stand about this somehow?" her mom asked, and Polly replied that she was thinking of simply turning up at the group's next scheduled meeting with the new girl in tow. "How would the others react?" her mother wondered. Polly thought they'd pretend to be glad the new girl was there, and she predicted that after that they might try to keep *her* out of things, too, but she said she was going to do it anyway. "Well, from what you've told me," said her mom, "I think you've got the right idea. Good for you."

"Who's a decent kid?": what researchers look at

Reviewing that list of traits by which sixth, seventh, and eighth graders described their popular classmates, we may note, interestingly, that children *themselves* offer an intriguingly mixed bag of impressions about their high-status peers. The popular kid may be nice or skinny; may be reliable or "built"; may be fun to be with or rich; may be emotionally supportive or have great stuff. Children (though not *all* children all the time!) seem to recognize the two different profiles of popularity.

On the one hand, they credit the highly visible aspects that are important at their age and/or valued in their particular schools and communities; they acknowledge that yes, some kids are admired and do acquire status mainly because of what they own or how they look or whom they know. On the other hand, they also point to the less superficial and more internal, psychological characteristics that make a peer stand out: Kids can be popular because they're nice, kind, helpful, and fun—in a word, likable.

In recent years, a great deal of research into peer cultures has focused on precisely those characterological aspects. Psychologists have been interested in the personal qualities that attract others to a child in positive ways, as distinguished from the more ephemeral characteristics that peers may admire for the moment. The results of such studies are consistent from one to the next: Even among preadolescents and young teens—kids who are keenly aware of in-groups and out-groups and the troublesome aspect of popularity-as-dominance—it is those humane and decent peers who are truly embraced.

Children who are liked, we know, most often tend to act in particular ways.

Children who are not so well liked, or are outright disliked, tend to act in other particular ways.

Mapping popularity: five categories

In studies of popularity, researchers typically ask each child in a classroom to name the three kids he or she likes the most and the three he or she likes the least. The youngsters are then mapped according to the five categories I described in chapter 2: Kids who score high in both preference and impact—in other words, those who are nominated often by most of their peers and are liked by most—are classified as *popular*. The children who fall somewhere in the middle on both preference and impact are *average*. *Neglected* children are those who rarely show up on anyone's lists, while *controversial* kids get many positive and negative votes—they stand out in the group and are both liked and disliked. Those who receive many nominations in the "don't like" category are called *rejected*.

These classifications have been a standard feature in the developmental literature for years and are sometimes used by professionals who work directly with children, families, and schools in formulating intervention or counseling programs.

Parents, of course, typically are not likely to think of their sons or daughters in terms of the classifications we use in our studies. But there is something to be gained by knowing a little bit about what they mean, and about the nature of the child who falls within one or another category. Especially if you're feeling reasonably concerned about your child's behavior with friends—or even unreasonably worried about your "unpopular" son or daughter—the following exploration may help you refine the picture of your child's social life.

At the same time, I want to stress that labels, for the most part, should not be taken *too* much to heart. For one thing, they don't always stick. True, many popular children and rejected children tend to remain that way, but many others change their status over time. In particular, we know that *most* children who occupy the classifications of neglected and controversial do *not* stay in the same category, even over relatively short periods—for example, within a single school year.

So, useful though these terms may be for certain research purposes, widespread though they are in the literature and in "What's going on with our kids?" accounts in the popular press, and revealing though they indeed can be for the parent who wants to support his or her child, it's important to remember this simple fact: Many labels lack precise meaning.

With this caveat in mind, let's examine what it is that researchers have shown about the connection between how a child behaves and what peers think and feel about him or her.

Well liked and well-enough liked: the popular and the average child

Just what are the personal attributes that children find likable about a classmate? First, it must be said—after all—that appearances *do* count: From preschool through high school, children respond favorably to their most physically attractive agemates.

Having a name that other kids like, some research shows, is a leg up as well.

Children also apparently like boys who play the way they think boys *should* play: In one of our own studies, ten-year-old boys who frequently played in ways that were more typical of girls were rejected not only by male but also by female peers. (Girls get a bit of a break in this regard, it seems: The ones who played more typically like boys were neither popular nor rejected.)

Most of all, however, study after study has shown that well-liked children are kids whom other kids find it pleasant to be around, because they act in the following specific ways:

- When entering a new peer situation, they size up what's going on, consider the common frame of reference, and fit themselves into the ongoing activity.

- No pushovers, they are assertive without being hostile.

- In a group, they do not draw excessive attention to themselves by, for example, talking overbearingly about their own hopes, dreams, goals, or wishes.

- They speak clearly and make themselves understood.

- They share their things.

- They're kind and quick to help others.

- They're not egocentric; they can understand and appreciate their peers' thoughts, intentions, and emotions.

- They initiate interactions with others and respond pleasantly to others' pleasant approaches.

- When in leadership positions, they are not domineering; rather, they behave in much the same way that their parents do with *them*—that is, they exert warm, generous, and compassionate control.

In addition, well-liked children possess two other important qualities:

- They have a sense of humor.

- They have the ability to make and keep friends.

In our studies, *the majority of children* we see fit somewhere into this picture. A small proportion—perhaps one in five or six—we label *popular;* these are the children I referred to earlier as the genuine stars of the world of childhood. Practically everyone who knows them finds them extremely likable. Next, a large percentage of children are what we call *average.* Not quite the stars or the leaders, these are the kids who behave in acceptable ways, get along with others to an acceptable degree, and feel mostly content with their social lot in life.

How well-liked children get that way—as I've been suggesting throughout this book—is no great mystery. They may come into the world with basically sunny temperaments that predispose them to meet new people and situations with a minimum of difficulty. Probably they have in their lives a primary caregiver who provides security, control, and supervision, along with encouragement to explore the world on their own terms. And almost certainly they continue to develop all along those skills that enable them to make friends and to mix comfortably in groups.

In other words, such children develop social competence—which may be defined, again, as the ability to achieve personal goals in social interaction while simultaneously maintaining positive relationships with others, over time and across situations.

In any school or grade, then, it's likely that a small number of kids are extraordinarily popular and a large number could be said to be popular enough. Of concern are the youngsters who fall into the categories described below—children of *neglected, controversial,* and *rejected* status.

Under the radar: the neglected child

Neglected is a term that can have different meanings, as may be seen in the stories of Jordan, a fifth grader, and Amy, in third grade.

In one-on-one conversation, Jordan comes across as a polite child with both a sweet nature and a serious demeanor; he looks thoughtful, a boy who takes things in. His mother described him as "an old soul, from the time he was a little kid, and sort of precocious in his understanding of the world. His kindergarten teacher once remarked to me that sometimes she'd make a little joke, a pun or play on words, and Jordan would be the only one who got it."

Jordan makes good grades in school; his passions, however, lie with his many hobbies. Currently he is, in his mother's word, "crazed" about magic; he spends much of his allowance on books and equipment related to that enthusiasm, and most of his weekend time practicing magic tricks. His partners in this (as in some of his other endeavors over the years) are Wally, his best pal from the time they were four-year-olds in preschool together, and Richard, the son of his father's business partner, who is a year and a half younger than the other two but can be found many afternoons or early evenings at Jordan's house. The three boys attend different schools, but the friendships remain strong, and they talk to and see one another frequently.

In school, said Jordan, he has "a bunch of kids I always eat with at lunch and all, but nobody I especially hang out with. Some kids were in the same school before, so they kind of stick together more." His mother noted, "Jordan is maybe too serious for most children he runs into, but he gets along well with people in general. I have to say, in high school, in college, I can't picture him ever being the frat boy, rah-rah type, who gets excited about whether the team goes to the basketball playoffs or whatever. But he's OK."

In a survey of his class, Jordan appeared on not a single list—that is, he was not among anyone's top three "I like best" or "I like least" or "I'd like to be friends with" or "I wouldn't like to be friends with" nominees. An apparently happy child who's close to his parents and has pals to talk to, Jordan doesn't seem exceptionally distressed by the fact—which he has indicated he's well aware of—that he's usually not included in the after-school plans of his popular classmates.

Amy's story is somewhat different. She's always been shy, said her mother, and tends to find just one friend at a time. "Amy's a good, generous child, and she knows how to have fun," her mother explained, "but her friend will start to branch out, and then Amy gets sort of dropped. This has happened three times over the past four years."

Amy's mother was an active—or "ferocious," by her own account—playdate arranger when her child was younger: "We had lots of kids over to our house. Now the kids are going on nine, and they're arranging these dates themselves. In our circle, it's no longer really appropriate for me to be setting things up. Amy doesn't want me to be calling someone's mother." But nor has Amy been especially successful at connecting with other children on her own. Recently, a classmate invited her home with her after school; afterward Amy reported to her mother that the get-together had been "OK," and that she planned to ask the girl, Karen, to come over the following week. That invitation didn't go well, as her mother described: "Amy told me she went up to Karen and said, 'You want to get together tomorrow after school?' And Karen looked at her, didn't smile, and replied, 'You got together with me last week,' and turned away to join some other kids."

Her daughter, she said, "is a little trouper, though. I see her trying to jump to this new level of socializing. It's hard to watch her get the brush-off, but I know she has to kind of struggle through it." Approaching Karen, a popular child, was "tough" for Amy to do, said her mother. "She thought out beforehand what she was going to say—she told me she had heard other kids invite each other home in this kind of casual way—and then the rebuff set her back!"

Amy's class also took part in a sociometric survey; she, like Jordan, appeared on no one's "best liked" or "least liked" lists.

Both Jordan and Amy, in their respective classrooms, were categorized as *neglected*.

Researchers have painted a portrait of neglected children: These young-sters have fewer interactions with other kids than do their average peers, and they tend to avoid aggressive encounters. Their classmates, it seems, have no strong feeling about them one way or the other; neither shunned nor embraced, these boys and girls are simply not much noticed. At the same time, they are usually rated by peers as well motivated and self-assured. Neglected boys, concluded one study, "seem to be a peaceable, reserved group and are less likely to give offense to peers than other chil-dren." Other research has found that neglected children are neither espe-cially wary or mistrustful nor particularly lonely or anxious; nor do they actively withdraw from their social worlds. And unlike their unpopular peers, according to some studies, they seem able to make a fresh start once they move into a new group or a new setting where their reputation hasn't preceded them.

From early childhood through adolescence, as we saw in an earlier chap-ter, some children are simply less sociable than others. And some find sup-port, friendship, and validation in connections outside the classroom, as Jordan seems to. Such a youngster might feel perfectly comfortable in the peer milieu; he or she might, in fact, show up as *fifth*-best-liked (or *sixth-*

most-disliked) in peer rankings, but students are not asked for such nominations, and our studies are not designed to assess these vaguer indications of popularity. Consequently, this basically *average* child is labeled
neglected. In the case of Jordan, certainly, the label is a misnomer; the description given above does not, I can only assume, conjure up a typical image of a neglected individual.

Other children—and Amy would seem to be one of their number—*are*
truly neglected, by the real world of peers as well as according to the somewhat arbitrary measurements of social science. In truth, such a child is tac-
itly *rejected*, not in the "official" sense of being disliked by most children,
but in the actual sense of being ignored, despite making efforts to participate in group activities or to engage another child's attention.

These tend to be sensitive boys and girls, though they may not share all
the characteristics, listed earlier, of the temperamentally fearful youngster,
who has great difficulty regulating feelings of anxiety and wariness. They
may have had the benefit of supportive, child-oriented parents who encouraged them to establish connections with their peers, and, like Amy's
mother, remain keenly aware of and responsive to their children's nature.
They may or may not be deficient in social skills, but in any event there is
something about them that makes them fairly invisible to other children—they may be inadequately assertive, for example, or a step or two
behind their agemates in terms of social maturity. Then, too, they may
have some physical anomaly, or even just lack the sort of looks that other
children find attractive (in which case a retiring nature may amount to a
second strike against them).

Certainly, as Amy's mother noted, children who are neglected in these
ways do have to "struggle through it" and over time, ideally, learn the lessons that only peers can teach. The child who, like Amy, is clearly capable
of making friends, is observant of what other kids do that "works," and
keeps trying even after sustaining some emotional bruises, will probably
turn out fine in the long run. The child who doesn't keep struggling
through, in contrast—the one who reacts to small social failures over time
by increasingly withdrawing—is likely to miss out on important learning
experiences, with damaging results.

Jordan's mother was wise to take the full measure of her child and to
recognize that essentially, and so far, he's "OK." Amy's mother did well to

stay tuned in to her daughter's increasingly self-generated social life; this child is fortunate to have, clearly, a parent who she feels is emotionally available to her, a mom she can talk to about her difficulties.

Any parent who has observed that his or her youngster often seems to be invisible or ignored in groups may want to adopt some of the strategies and approaches geared toward helping the "moving-away-from" or withdrawn child. We'll turn to these in the next chapter.

A high profile: the controversial child

Some children get many positive ("I like this person a lot") and many negative ("I can't stand this person") nominations from their peers: Based on sociometric ratings, they are, both paradoxically and simultaneously, popular among some peers and rejected by others.

Controversial kids, it seems, tend to be of two types. The first is the troublemaker who bosses and bullies his way through life; basically, he (and most *are* boys) is an aggressive child. Most classmates know him to be mean and cruel, and most want little to do with him. In a school with a very large population, however, such a child may find himself a niche among a behavioral subgroup of other mean and cruel peers. With his high visibility within his grade or class as a not-nice guy, on the one hand, and his sizable number of equally not-nice friends, on the other, he ends up with many nominations on both ends of the likability spectrum.

The second type of controversial child, the one usually described in the very sparse research data concerning this category, presents a different profile. Socially flawed in some ways, he or she nonetheless has "something" that attracts others—most likely, it seems, a talent for leadership or the ability and willingness to be supportive of classmates when a little support is needed. This child's status, as I've noted, is not particularly stable. But everyone knows who he or she is.

In their study of first and third grade boys, the psychologists John Coie and Ken Dodge relied on three sources of feedback—peer ratings, teacher ratings, and in-class observations—to understand how the controversial child behaves. Children were asked to list their three "like best" and "like least" nominees, and also to write down the names of the classmates who best fitted eight different descriptions: "Starts fights, is disruptive, angers easily, is cooperative, is a leader, is good at sports, is funny, is unhappy." Then the observers noted how each boy acted in class and during lunch and physical education, including how often and in what manner he approached other kids or was approached, and so on.

The controversial boys, like the rejected ones, were greatly more aggressive, disruptive, and prone to breaking rules than their average peers. At the same time, their classmates also rated the controversial kids, like the popular boys, *above* average in terms of cooperation and leadership. Apparently these high-profile youngsters were thoroughly engaged with their peer groups, in ways that other children found variously pleasing, admirable, and disagreeable. And there was another piece in the complex puzzle of the controversial kid: Although these boys were often "off-task"—fooling around, not sticking to the work at hand, dawdling—their teachers reported that they did very well in their schoolwork.

"The overall picture of controversial boys," concluded the researchers, "is one of socially and intellectually or athletically talented boys who also are more active, as well as more prone to anger and violations of rules, than their peers or teachers [might] like. Not surprisingly, they have a high impact on their peers and receive a mixed evaluation from them."

The controversial child, it seems, is one who's veering toward the opposite end of the continuum from the neglected child. Parents of youngsters who fit the controversial profile will find some useful pointers in chapter 10, on how to help a child rein in negative or aggressive behaviors and foster positive ones.

**The one who thinks he's popular but really isn't:
the aggressive-rejected child**

In chapter 3 I told the story of Brett, a lively, battling boy who was mostly unsuccessful in his attempts to fit in with groups of peers during visits to our lab. In "real life," such youngsters frequently receive low popularity ratings; they are *rejected*.

In student evaluations, teacher ratings, and direct observations, aggression—comprising incidents of acting up or being distracting in the classroom and other school settings; getting into physical fights; verbally threatening others; or using commands and bribes to achieve goals—is the reason most commonly cited for peer rejection. Furthermore, there appears to be little doubt that those hostile or unfriendly behaviors are what *cause* other children to keep their distance.

You may recall that by the end of the peer-quartet session including seven-year-old Brett, the other boys were steering clear of him; this kid, they seem to have concluded, was trouble, or didn't know how to play right. Other lab studies, also involving children previously unknown to one another, have shown that after *several days,* some kids gradually became popular while others—aggressive children—became increasingly disliked and avoided. Similarly, when researchers studied the emergence of popularity in a group of young-adolescent boys and girls just entering the same middle school, they found that combative behavior during the early days of school was the single direct link to a child's rejection later in the year.

But while they're still relatively young, kids like Brett, as I've noted, tend to feel good about themselves. For one thing, when this youngster initiates a move toward other children, he's often successful. Instrumental aggression—pushing, grabbing, and threatening to get a desired item— works well for him in the short term, if only because no one wants to get in his way. And he's fairly oblivious to the fact that most others really don't like him; in fact, he thinks he's popular. Although he is ranked at the top of the disliked/rejected list by the majority of his peers, typically he has pals—who are just like him. If his school population is large enough and includes a fair number of similarly aggressive boys of the same age, he may even make it into the controversial classification: Three or more classmates say they like him a lot, while most kids say they don't like him at all. The nature of his friendships, however, may be less than desirable, and over time, the aggressive youngster will likely stop feeling quite so good about himself.

In one long-term study, my colleagues and I tracked a group of about a hundred children from age four to age eleven. Among other things, we wanted to learn how these youngsters, by middle childhood, perceived the emotional support available to them. Aggressive children who had troublesome relationships with their parents—or whom we had earlier identified as being insecurely attached—indicated that they relied heavily on their friends for support. While it certainly sounds preferable for a child to have friends than *not* to have them, in fact these friendships were characterized by the kind of negative, acting-out, and pugnacious interactions that the majority of children don't like.

Aggressive kids stick together—but they don't do one another much good in terms of teaching and learning more appropriate and generally admired ways of acting. That conclusion has been supported by recent findings that a certain kind of peer therapy, a common "intervention" for children with behavioral problems, hasn't worked very well. When highly aggressive kids are brought together as a unit—rather than in a heterogeneous mix of children, some of whom are highly competent and popular, most of whom are average, and a few of whom are aggressive—attempts to get them to understand the consequences of their actions and the feelings of others generally fail. Tough kids in a group feed off one another, model one another's behaviors, act in even more hostile and aggressive ways in efforts to be accepted, and exacerbate each individual's problem.

Over time, aggressive-rejected as well as withdrawn-rejected children tend to develop skewed notions about the intentions of their average classmates. The elbow in the ribs or the jostle that's understood by most to be a friendly greeting or harmless bantering is interpreted by this child as, "Here's another example of someone trying to hurt me." Both sensitive, withdrawn children and aggressive children tend to see what are probably benign, teasing interactions as intentionally malicious.

Studies in recent years, many conducted by the psychologist Ken Dodge, have examined "intention cuing," or how a child perceives what peers mean by a given interaction and how he or she responds. In interviews, children are presented with hypothetical situations—for example:

Imagine that school has just let out, and you're walking home. As you cross the street, a tennis ball smacks you in the back. Looking around, you see, on the corner, someone you know from school, and he's looking over at you.

Another scenario: You're working hard in class on an art project, for which you will receive half your semester grade. Just as the hour is ending and you're putting some finishing touches on your work for the day, a kid at the same table spills some paint on your project.

And say you're at the school water fountain, and as you're leaning over to take a drink, someone pushes you from behind and knocks your face into the spray of water.

For each scenario, the children surveyed are asked: Would you think this event—the ball smacking you in the back, the paint spilled on your project, the shove at the fountain—had happened on purpose, or would you assume it was an accident? How would you feel about it? What might you do?

The majority of kids will give responses like the following:

"I'd probably think it was an accident, unless the person who did it was someone I knew was a mean kid, and then I'd probably think it was done on purpose."

"How would I feel? I'd be really upset. Nobody wants to get hit with a ball, have a project messed up, or get a face full of water."

"What would I do? Well, if it was an accident, I'd give the kid back his tennis ball; I'd tell the teacher paint had gotten spilled on my project, and I'd ask the kid who did it to come with me, too, and explain to the teacher what'd happened; I'd just dry off my face. If it was somebody I thought did it on purpose, I'd probably ignore the whole thing, because that's what I'd expect from somebody like that. And I'd make sure I didn't have anything to do with that kid in the future; I wouldn't want to be around him."

The aggressive-rejected child makes a very different set of inferences about the intentions of the instigator, and commits to a very different response: "Of course he did it on purpose," this youngster will tell us. "That guy has it in for me. I'm really mad, and I'm going to make sure he pays. I'll get even with him." And so the cycle is reinforced: As these children perceive most actions coming their way as hostile and intentionally hurtful, they strike back in genuinely hostile and hurtful ways, further entrenching their unpopularity and their reputation as aggressive individuals.

Boys, it seems, may be able to get away with such behavior with less damage to their social standing than girls. Some researchers have reported that peer nominations for the item "starts fights," for example, are more strongly associated with popularity for boys than for girls. Children in general apparently see aggression as being less appropriate for girls (just as mothers and fathers, we've found, tend to excuse or even admire rough behavior by sons, and react with dismay and disapproval to the same behavior by daughters). Still, the older kids get, the less accepting they seem to be of *any* child who strikes out against another.

The one who suffers most from being unpopular: the withdrawn-rejected child

You'll remember, too, Derek, the fearful, wary, and watchful boy who stayed in the corner or pressed himself against the wall or looked teary while his four-year-old and seven-year-old peers were playing with toy planes and describing their birthday parties. In those sessions, Derek displayed behaviors that we know are likely to make him unpopular as time goes on.

In preschool or kindergarten, the withdrawn child usually isn't actively rejected by other children. Some withdrawn children are truly reticent; they keep their distance from classmates and observe them from afar. Others are what I described earlier as *solitary-constructive* players, who spend at least some of their time drawing pictures or pursuing other independent activities, perhaps because they are not always interested in extensive social interaction and are more comfortable on their own. Other children seem to find nothing peculiar about these forms of solitude; they don't especially notice that one of their peers usually keeps to himself.

A few years later, however, it's another story. Peers begin to realize that their classmate doesn't join in games or is always on the outskirts of activities, and in various ways they let this youngster know that he isn't acting in a normal fashion. The recognition of others' poor opinion in turn brings on *more* displays of social anxiety by the withdrawn child—a twisting or tugging of the hair, nail-biting, finger-sucking, lip-biting, a worried look.

He may have trouble speaking, may seldom initiate a conversation, or may freeze up when addressed by another child. Perhaps he waits to be invited to join a game of tag, or to be asked for input on what a group of kids should do next—but the problem is, more assertive, less fearful average peers aren't inclined to invite or ask. Typically, the withdrawn one now spends his time watching and hovering, remaining inactive and at some physical distance from the group.

Eventually, the child perceived by peers as a loner becomes more actively disliked. From playing alone, he has moved—or *been* moved, by peers— into another state, one of isolation.

Like their aggressive peers, withdrawn-rejected children come to be suspicious about the intentions of others. When presented with the scenarios described above—you're hit in the back with a tennis ball, another child spills paint on your project, someone knocks you into the water fountain—these youngsters, too, believe the unpleasant incidents were no accidents, but rather were meant as personal attacks. When asked how they feel about that, however, they let on that while they may be a little angry, mostly they're scared. Considering what they might do about the matter, they indicate that they would essentially take no action or run away and try to keep a very low profile in the future.

Withdrawn, socially reticent kids like Derek feel poorly about themselves and blame themselves for their troubles. Any small social success they may experience seems to them a fluke, not something they pulled off because of their positive qualities or skills, and surely not something they expect to be able to repeat. They run into spiraling difficulties in their groups, as negative self-regard leads to further withdrawal, which leads to further rejection.

The withdrawn-rejected boy, in particular, is likely to be viewed by bullies as an easy mark, especially if he is less than adept athletically or physically. But even if such a youngster escapes the extreme misery of victimization, his social life very probably will not be a happy one: By the ages of nine and ten, and certainly by early adolescence, these children almost invariably express loneliness and social despair.

At the end of Derek's story, I suggested one potential saving grace for the reticent child: a solid bond with a responsive peer. A trusting friendship that provides a milieu within which a withdrawn kid can talk about his feelings and thoughts, get advice and help on school- and non-school-related matters, and explore new activities and behaviors can take the pressure off and alleviate the loneliness. Withdrawn-rejected children generally don't feel the need to be popular or loved by all. And the quality of their one-on-one relationships, our studies are beginning to show, tends to be normal, especially if their friends are average, nonaggressive children.

I've described two reasons children become rejected—for behaving in aggressive ways and behaving in withdrawn ways. But two further points are in order:

First, there are other pathways to peer rejection. Some children are disliked because they behave or dress in ways that deviate from group norms:

They may be latter-day hippies in a conservative community, for instance, or conservatives in an "alternative" one. They may belong to a racial, religious, or ethnic minority. They may be immature, or they may act too old for their age.

In short, there are a number of factors that might mark a child for being disliked. Sometimes rejection is deserved, but at other times it can be the product of an unsympathetic peer group or climate. In these cases, it is the group itself that requires coaching and education, not the rejected child. Reeducating the group, of course, isn't generally within a parent's power; nor is moving to a more accepting community or school environment always within the realm of possibility. But the child who doesn't fit in, through no shortcoming of his or her own, can survive the unpleasantness of rejection given a secure relationship with understanding parents, a decent friend or two, and some opportunity to form supportive relationships with peers outside of school.

Second, and more significant: Not all aggressive and withdrawn children are rejected. In their interactions with peers, some seem to have enough of the "right stuff" to compensate for their more disagreeable or unadmired qualities. Almost without exception, these are the children of parents who have learned how to offer well-timed, supportive assistance, and who are motivated to help their youngsters onto a better, more adaptive social track—the subject of the following two chapters.

If not every child wants or needs to be ranked among the "most popular" by peers, all children really do want to be liked. Learning how to solve social problems in a better way can help your "moving-away-from" or "moving-against" youngster achieve that goal.

Chapter 9

The Moving-Away-From Child

Helping Your Withdrawn Son or Daughter

When Courtney, who is now in fourth grade, was a seven-year-old second grader, her mother poked her head in her bedroom door one evening and was dismayed to see tears streaming down her daughter's face. "I asked her what was wrong," this parent remembered, "and she said, 'Nobody likes me. I don't have any friends.'"

As it happened, that day's mail had brought the midyear report from Courtney's school—grades accompanied by a written comment. Her mother was encouraged by much of what she read: "Courtney's gentle nature and wry sense of humor make her a pleasure to have in class," her teacher had written. "Her stories are infused with imagination and charm, and her craft projects show her attention to detail and her ability to work well independently." Other remarks, however, seemed cause for concern: "She is timid in class and hesitates to answer questions, though when she does, her answers are correct. She is a bit anxious in her dealings with classmates. She's often distracted by them, and that interferes with her approach to schoolwork."

None of this was news to Courtney's mother, who had been hearing similar observations since Courtney was in preschool. She would have liked for her daughter to be more of an outgoing, ready-to-meet-the-world kind of kid, she said, and had hoped she might start feeling more sure of herself around other children as time went along, but now here she was in fourth grade, still as cautious and reserved as ever. A parents' discussion group arranged by the school plunged this mother into gloom: "All these other mothers were *complaining* about how their daughters were on the phone to one another all evening. 'They should be doing their homework,' was the message, 'but all they're doing is talking with their friends.' And I was thinking, *I* should only have that problem!"

Reviewing her own performance as a parent over the years, she wondered if she'd done too little, or entirely the wrong thing, to help her daughter enjoy greater social success. Meanwhile, she began formulating new plans: "I want to involve her in some outside programs. I'm thinking that a children's theater group might be good, might help her gain some poise or confidence."

Here's what might be said about Courtney:

- This young girl has difficulty regulating her feelings of wariness and fearfulness and acting in a socially skilled manner.

- She is suffering negative consequences among her peers.

- And she is fortunate in having a parent who is concerned and thinking hard and long about what might be done to improve matters.

One significant key to a child's increasing social success lies in his or her ability to regulate emotions. Indeed, learning to control the display of negative emotions, as well as the natural tendency to act on them, is a significant developmental milestone. Courtney, for example, finds it very difficult to overcome her fear of social interactions—a fear that's taking a real toll on her. But she can come to understand that even if she *feels* anxious and fearful, she needn't let that stop her from having relationships with other kids. This is a lesson that parents play a very large role in teaching their children.

As a parent, you can assuredly help your shy and withdrawn child learn to deal more effectively with situations that provoke fearfulness and withdrawal. First, however, you need to appreciate these realities:

- Helping your child regulate his or her emotions, especially when he or she is easily upset, will take caring determination and consistent attention over time. Change *is* possible, but it won't happen overnight.

- The younger your child, the more effective your efforts are likely to be.

• You may find *yourself* experiencing powerful and upsetting emotions.

Parents do have feelings about their children's social lives, and the particular feelings that youngsters such as Courtney are likely to stir up can be hard to manage. It's *painful*—and often embarrassing, disappointing, and guilt-provoking, too—to see a reticent child all alone in a group of kids, or to hear those heartbreaking words "I don't have any friends." A mom or dad can find it understandably difficult to respond in a truly constructive and supportive way.

The point is this: Helping your child change her behaviors may call for you to modify *your own* thoughts, feelings, and behaviors as well. You may have to bite your tongue occasionally, and make a determined effort to remain in the background, so your youngster can have the opportunity to resolve her own social/emotional issues outside of the home. You may also need to engage your child in dialogue about, or even have "rehearsals" for, social interactions—which will take thought and time.

Ideally, such efforts will seem a bit easier once you recognize that your son or daughter may have come by his or her temperament honestly, as I've put it—meaning that the behaviors that often make his or her life among peers so difficult may be prompted, in part, by biological factors. Accepting your child's unique nature will put you in a better position to help him or her shape or channel the social and emotional behaviors that keep other children at a distance.

All children benefit from parental warmth and control, supervision or monitoring, encouragement of exploration, and empathy as they learn to balance their personal wishes and goals with the needs of a friend or the requirements of a peer group. Withdrawn children need especially thoughtful guidance and support in these areas. The sooner you, as a parent, begin to implement some of the following suggestions, the sooner you'll help your youngster begin the process of change for the better.

Believe that your son or daughter requires your help.

Most parents of children like Courtney do very much wish their sons and daughters found it easier to make friends. Especially in the years of middle childhood, a youngster's feelings of loneliness or self-critical thoughts become difficult to ignore. But those same parents may also believe, or at least hope—though not so realistically—that their child's reticence will fade over time, and that he or she is merely "a late bloomer." Some may worry that suggesting there's a problem will itself add to the child's discomfort or embarrassment, and feel it's better to rely on the feedback of peers to teach social lessons.

The truth is, however, that without empathetic parental support, a youngster's experiences among other children are more likely to be discouraging than instructive. Researchers consistently point to an insidious and dynamic pattern of continuous and reciprocal influences, a spiraling cycle in which:

- Social wariness, anxiety, and uncertainty compel the withdrawn child to behave in ways that most other children find unappealing.

- Those peers consequently choose to ignore, avoid, or actively rebuff the child.

- Stung by that peer rejection, he or she backs away from further efforts to connect with others.

- Such withdrawal leads the child to miss out on the very experiences that might succeed in strengthening his or her social skills and making that child feel more confident among agemates.

- And that, in turn, may cause the youngster to feel increasingly worse about himself or herself, and to remain isolated.

For the child who has difficulty breaking this cycle, the costs are high. It's terrible for a youngster to feel like an outcast, and to come to believe over time that it's simply not within his power to improve matters. The internalizing of such difficulties—in the form of loneliness, for example—can have devastating and lasting effects on a child's self-esteem. It can make going to school a painful business and in some cases affect academic performance.

All of this means it's imperative for *you* to know that your son or daughter will benefit from your attention.

Take a look in the mirror.

Think of the following brief checklist as a bit of personal stock-taking, an exploration of some actions or attitudes that aren't always easy to recognize but that may nonetheless be pertinent to what's going on with your child:

- Do I believe that my child is overly shy? Do I expect my child to react with fearfulness in social situations?

- Do I attempt to shield my child from social situations that I sense may prove anxiety-provoking?

- Do I anticipate that when my young child is in new situations, she is bound to feel anxious and that the worst is about to happen? And do I respond to such feelings by keeping her close to my side?

- Do I believe that encouraging my child to stay near me will be reassuring for him? Do I deliberately *not* encourage exploration of unfamiliar places and things for fear that any such encounter will lead to unhappiness and failure for my him?

- Am I in small, almost unconscious ways pressuring my elementary- or middle-school-age child to be popular because I never was myself? Do I frequently and impatiently push my child to join other kids, and feel annoyed and resentful when she hangs back?

- Do I feel tense and stressed when my child is about to enter an unfamiliar situation, even before anything unpleasant has happened? Do I anticipate rejection for him, even if hasn't happened?

- Do I often tell my child what to do, both around the house and when she is with other children? Do I criticize her impatiently when she comes home looking sad after another lonely day at school?

- Does it make me uncomfortable to invite other children to the house?

If *any* of this sounds remotely familiar to you—if you're thinking, Yes, that's me—be aware that such habitual feelings and reactions may need some adjustment. Your wary, tentative child requires your gentle, consistent urging to venture forth, to build gradually the social confidence that will enable her to move toward, not away from, peers. While your daughter is still very young, that encouragement may mean letting her know—perhaps just through a smile and a nod—that nothing dire will happen if she explores the preschool playroom she's just entered. When your son is older, it might include making sure that your home is a welcoming place for him to bring friends.

In other words, you need a new attitude. You must work to overcome your own discomfort about your child's lack of ease in social encounters. Try to look at her anew, not as a child crippled by shyness, but as a young person who's having some difficulties putting socially competent behaviors into practice, and who could use your help.

Encourage your young child in play, taking care not to be overly directive or intrusive.

You'll remember that in our lab observations involving preschoolers and their mothers, each parent-child pair spent part of the time in what we called free play, when they could do whatever they wished. And our research suggests that during this potential free-for-all in an unfamiliar but entirely safe playroom, moms were wise to encourage their children's independent exploration while monitoring from some distance away. The alternative, the behavior of mothers who kept their youngsters close by, constantly hugging them as if to send the message "You'll be OK in this dreadful place," seemed entirely too controlling and restrictive. The results of our studies enable us to offer the following advice:

- *Do* play with your young child. Parents who play with their young children, and who enjoy this playtime, have playful kids whom other children like to be around.

- When, let's say, the two of you are down on the living-room floor with the dollhouse, the building blocks, or the plastic kitchen set, let your child lead the way. In this familiar, safe, unstressful environment, allow him to set the tone and choose the activity. A young child's play is often repetitive, and as such, it may not seem like a whole lot of fun to an adult, but go with it anyway: Try to match your child's rhythm, and refrain from taking control, directing the action, or prescribing the absolutely "right" way to do something. At the same time, encourage him to try new things and explore new objects.

• Do set up playdates or get-togethers with other children; supervise the kids from a distance and offer the sort of warm encouragement that will help them focus on the activity at hand—but beyond that, stay out of things as much as possible.

Play is the activity of childhood; it's how children explore objects and people and begin to learn social lessons. In these earliest peer encounters, and when you and your child are playing together, let her call the shots as much as possible.

Offer reasoned and reasonable support on task assignments.

Task assignments—household chores, schoolwork—are another matter: Here your child may benefit from a bit of parental help and direction.

The mother of six-year-old Brandon described her son as a timid boy who is always "watching and worrying—about everything, including doing homework." She remembered that she herself, as a child, had approached school assignments with a great deal of anxiety, and that her own mother had reacted to her obvious distress in a manner she had found confusing: "I think *my* nervousness made *her* nervous, and also annoyed. Sometimes she just let me stew and struggle away on my own. Sometimes she jumped in. Once, for example, I was supposed to draw a map of my neighborhood, and I was so tense about not doing this right that I was crying. So she did the drawing for me, but she told me that was OK because it was something I *could* do if I had more time."

This parent is determined not to repeat that pattern with her own child: "I have to squelch the temptation to give him too much help. To be honest, the easiest solution is for me just to do the thing for him sometimes. That way, neither of us gets too upset. But I know he really wouldn't learn anything. So I try to just sit with him and give suggestions. This calms him down."

These are decent strategies. The inhibited child needs to practice confronting nervousness and anxiety, in order to learn that he or she can move forward and act appropriately despite those feelings. When faced with a task that must be completed, your child will benefit tremendously from your measured, supportive, and consistently displayed guidance—manifested, for example, by your sitting with your daughter as she does homework, offering a suggestion or two to get things started, and conveying the clear message by your attention that *you* know *she* can handle things. Being left to stew and struggle with a task alone may only make your youngster feel overpowered and choked into inaction by her emotions. And your doing the job *for* her is an even worse choice.

Some of the tasks that children face in the course of daily life, quite frankly, are not all that critical, or at least do not necessarily have to be accomplished right then and there and to a parent's satisfaction. In his peer interactions, your socially uneasy son needs to feel more comfortable about being assertive, speaking up, negotiating, and getting into the action. He may benefit from having a little more say on certain things at home, especially matters of relative unimportance—tidying up his room, for example.

Be appropriately warm and responsive to your child's emotional signals.

In our discussion of attachment theory, I noted that children with *insecure attachments* have often experienced parenting behaviors that are somewhat unpredictable. Such a child's mom may react appropriately in some instances to her son or daughter's signaled need for attention and comfort; at other times, though, believing that such a signal is *about* to be given, she may anticipate the worst and rush in with hugs and kisses where they *aren't* needed.

Our observations have taught us that inhibited toddlers and socially reticent preschoolers very often have mothers who are hovering and overly affectionate, staying right beside their children at all times. Hugs and kisses and closeness (usually coupled with lots of control) are inappropriate, however, if nothing particularly endangering is happening. These parents appear to take over situations in which they expect their children *might* feel anxious, allowing their youngsters scant opportunity to develop their own techniques for coping with fear-related emotions and behaviors. Instead, the children continue to rely on their parents for comforting.

In a nutshell, then, it's critical that you not be excessively protective of your reticent youngster. Of course your child needs a hug and a kiss sometimes! But avoid oversolicitous displays of affection. And resist the urge to solve her problem by speaking out on her behalf—by asking other kids for information she desires, for example, or obtaining a toy she wants, or requesting that other children let her play with them.

Help soothe your child's natural apprehensiveness about unfamiliar places, things, and experiences.

What *will* help a highly inhibited child learn over time to cope more successfully with his or her fears is a parent's sensitive and consistent reassurance that the world is knowable, manageable, and not really so frightening. That kind of reassurance starts very early and might need to be continued, in one manner or another, throughout your child's school years.

As toddlers, children—of any temperament—aren't yet able to regulate their emotions and behaviors very well on their own. They need external assistance—from parents or other adults. A parent can be a wonderful soother when a youngster expresses fear, for example. But soothing is very different from smothering; Mom and Dad can calm a child in all sorts of ways *without* being excessively demonstrative. If her son is frightened by a clanking, noisy robot toy he hasn't seen before, Mom can say, "You know, this toy looks like fun; let's try it out together." Or if her daughter shrinks back shyly from a play encounter at the park, Mom might encourage her to venture forth by engaging all the children in a little conversation about what they're doing, indicating to her child that it looks like everybody's having a good time, and then remaining a visible and comforting but nonintrusive presence as she gets into the swing of things.

If you're consistent in helping your young child learn to regulate his or her emotions and behaviors in these soothing and supportive ways, something rather magical will begin to happen: In time, you might hear your son telling *himself,* "It's all right, that robot won't hurt me," or watch your daughter seem to be silently reassuring *herself,* "Those kids are having fun, I can go over there." He or she is learning to *self-regulate* fearfulness and wariness.

These are examples of a phenomenon that the Russian psychologist Lev Vygotsky referred to as *self-directed private speech,* or the tendency of individuals to settle themselves down through reminders that everything is really OK. The premise is that we learn to control our feelings and behaviors by talking to ourselves. In times of stress, adults do it all the time; so do adolescents. Sit in on a high school classroom in which students are taking a really difficult exam, for instance, and you may hear a background of whispering and murmuring. These young people aren't trying to crib the answers from one another; rather, the murmuring student may be attempting to calm himself down and get back on track to come up with the correct answer ("Well, it can't be item B or C, so it must be A or D . . . let's see, now"). Essentially, the child is telling himself, "Take it easy, focus, you can do this."

Parents of highly fearful younger children can set them on the path toward self-regulation by helping them ease themselves into activities they find uncomfortable. Talking in a reassuring manner about events can be soothing, as can giving a child a "trial run," or letting him or her case out and rehearse being in a new place or situation, because times of transition are often highly anxiety-provoking for inhibited children.

When her son was about to enter middle school, for example, the mother of eleven-year-old Jack could hardly help noticing that her son was "a nervous wreck. He was very quiet, worried-looking, didn't feel like eating. He knew a couple of kids who'd be going to this school, but not very well. He was not happy!" She called the school and found out that it would be open a few days before classes started: "I said to Jack, without making a big deal of it, 'Let's drive over there and have a look around; I'd like to see the school myself.'" So they did, and once there, they ran into a friendly teacher. Jack seemed more relaxed after that. Just knowing where the bathroom is located can reduce the strangeness and lower a child's wariness a notch.

Don't try to embarrass your child into acting the way you wish he or she would act.

Some kinds of *psychological control*—such as criticizing a child's internal characteristics or feelings, or expressing the expectation that he or she should behave differently by referring to those aspects—are truly demeaning. Most parents are sensitive enough to *know* that it's damaging to tell a clingy youngster, "Don't be such a baby! All the other kids are over there playing; you should be out there, too." But impatience with a child's timidity and fearfulness can make it all too easy for a parent to slip across the line from gentle, supportive encouragement into goading. Sometimes the intention may be to jolly a child into more assertive behavior through what feels, to Mom or Dad, like a little good-natured teasing: "What happened, did the cat get your tongue again?" Such psychologically controlling statements or reactions can, however, make an inhibited child feel quite awful—ashamed, guilty, inadequate, and even more anxious than before. ("Even *Mom* thinks I'm acting like a baby; those kids are going to laugh at me," or "Mom says I should be more like those kids, so she must like them better").

If your reticent child is facing a peer situation that's clearly making him or her uncomfortable, you may need to be especially careful not to let slip a comment that will be unsupportive or even hurtful.

Resist the urge to alleviate your child's social disappointment by offering parent-oriented interpretations or reassurances.

Smothering a child with hugs and kisses and doing something difficult *for* her aren't the only ways of providing a quick fix for social anxiety or rejection.

A mother who said she herself had been "a socialphobe all my life," and who described her nine-year-old, Hope, as shy, admitted that a particular challenge for her as a parent "is to sometimes stop myself from getting caught up in my daughter's unhappiness and hating the kids who behave badly to her!" Like Brandon's mom, she had had a maternal role model that she felt it would be best *not* to emulate:

"Here's an example. In elementary school one year, my class was putting on a play version of *Little Women*. All the girls wanted to be Beth, because Beth was fragile and sickly and she got to die! The teacher handed out a list of the parts, and had written down her suggestions of who should play what, but she said it was up to the class to decide. She had me down for Beth, but I was voted out by the other kids. I got home, burst into tears, and told my mother, who said something like, 'I know you'd be the most terrific Beth, and so did the teacher, and that's what counts.' That made me feel better, momentarily. But in the end it didn't help, because the real issue was that I wanted the other kids to accept me, and actually nobody liked me much."

Although no doubt motivated by a loving intention to comfort her daughter, that parent had in fact tried to reinterpret the world for her, by telling her how to feel and effectively suggesting that peer acceptance was of little significance.

When your socially wary child has suffered a rejection or been presented with some other presumed evidence of his unlikability, the best support you can offer is to listen to your child's story with empathy. First, however, you may need to encourage him to tell it. While some sensitive kids are generally eager to let their parents know what's bothering them, others may be less forthcoming and more inclined to keep their woes to themselves. But it's not difficult for you as an observant parent to recognize when something of an upsetting nature has happened in your child's day, and then to let it be known that you are available to listen. Coming at a child with lots of questions is usually a poor idea; taking a drive down to the mall or a walk to get some ice cream is much more likely to produce the kind of relaxed and affectionate atmosphere that will encourage him to open up.

After you have heard your youngster out, gently encourage him to explore aspects or angles of the situation that the child may not have considered. For one thing, self-conscious, withdrawn children, like their aggressive peers, may consistently misread the intentions of others. This is the girl, for example, who will interpret an unpleasant but benign event as an indication that nobody likes her.

Hope's mother told this story: After a school-sponsored evening ice skating party, her daughter came home looking sad. At first, she said, she had skated mostly by herself, while other classmates were in pairs. Then, midway through the event, "Jen, who I thought was my friend," had called out to her to grab on to the end of a line of kids playing "whip." Forced to skate the fastest, Hope had trouble keeping up and was whipped off into the fence surrounding the rink. After that, she sat out the rest of the party. Hope's mother described her own response:

"I think I showed I was sympathetic to the fact that she didn't have a great time at this affair, but I didn't overdo it. Then I asked her if skating into the fence had hurt her physically. She wasn't actually hurt, but she said it was embarrassing. Then we talked a bit about Jen. And it came out that Jen has made some really friendly gestures to Hope during school, and Hope thinks she's a nice kid. I said it sounded to me like Jen was just having fun, and she agreed. We left it at that. I wanted to just help her get her head screwed on straight about what really happened."

That was no doubt a useful lesson in perspective-taking. Helping your child figure out what *she* might do differently next time is promoting social competence. But encouraging her to consider other people's emotions and intentions—and to understand that not all negative occurrences are proof that others don't like her—is the first step.

Build a bridge to other children.

More than most kids, your wary child will feel a small surge of courage and confidence if you sometimes help him or her break the social ice. You could, for example:

- Initiate conversations with other children and their parents. If the two of you are waiting for an elevator in the presence of another youngster and parent, let's say, your son probably won't speak, even to say "Hi." Rather than telling him to do so, you could start a conversation yourself—perhaps by asking the child his name and where he's going—and thereby model friendly behavior without putting your child on the spot.

- Sit in on a first playdate between your daughter and a possible new friend. Be a nonintrusive but visible source of available comfort and security.

- Be the parent who hosts a backyard barbecue for your seventh grader's soccer team, or who volunteers to monitor the field trip and supply refreshments.

Such types of supportive behavior on your part can continue across a child's school years. If they're made not with the aim of boosting your youngster's popularity but rather in an effort to provide a helpful, secure bridge to his peers, these gestures can be an enormous boon to the child who has difficulty initiating his own approaches and contacts.

In peer connections, encourage your child to focus on better, not more.

Most parents wish for their children to have a social life that is both better *and* more—good, fun-filled, lasting friendships, as well as general acceptance and popularity. But not every child is going to be popular. If your child seems to be having problems with "more," go for "better."

"Better" can be promoted in various ways. You can let your school-age child know that making friends isn't always easy, and that some find it harder than others. You can talk, when the opportunity arises, about the real meaning of relationships, explaining that being a friend involves trust, validation, caring, helping, and being able to patch up arguments in a good way—and adding that anyone who has one or two friendships like that is doing pretty well. And then bend your own focus toward helping your child nourish a solid relationship with one or two compatible peers.

Find a gentle environment in which your child can spend gentle time with other kids.

When her son Robbie was four years old, a parent remembered, "the thing to do among the mothers I knew was to enroll our kids in a music program. They went twice a week, an hour each time. The children were given little instruments. There were two lovely ladies who led them in singing, rattling their tambourines, and banging their drums. Cheerful, marching-type music was played on a tape machine." On arriving to collect her child toward the end of the first session, she was upset by what she saw: "All the kids were marching around with their drums. And there's Robbie sitting in the middle of the floor, sobbing his heart out. The two lovely ladies seemed to think they should just let him sit there."

She did reflect later on that scene and other, similar ones, and decided that fewer and quieter activities would be better for Robbie. Fewer and quieter might be better for your child, too.

- Do arrange for your withdrawn child to be in the company of peers by enrolling him or her in out-of-school activities—but realize that a chaotic situation with a lot of noise, a lot of kids, a lot of activity, and perhaps a bunch of people watching and passing judgment will probably not be the happiest environment for her.

  The withdrawn, inhibited child—the youngster who's always look-ing over her shoulder, minding the store, never relaxing—needs less "stuff" to worry about. A younger child of this temperament may flour-ish, for example, at a traditional preschool where children are allowed to explore at their own pace, and where there's a relaxed emphasis on group interaction.

- If your wary child resists going to other kids' homes, invite other kids to *your* house. Over time, those children will come to think it's sort of fun to visit, because your home is a nice place to be. Once your child has be-gun to feel more comforted and comfortable being with peers in his own space, encourage him to venture out. Being more at ease in the company of particular peers may persuade your child that it might not be so bad to accept invitations to *their* homes.

  That kind of sensitivity to the best social environment for your child is something you really should maintain right through his or her school years. For the socially anxious boy or girl who's not terribly happy at school, or hasn't found a comfortable niche there, extracurricular activ-ities can be wonderful—but not all will pay dividends. Urging an in-hibited preadolescent to sign up for ice hockey or another sport that calls for assertiveness and a lot of physical contact, for example, is al-most surely a mistake. Activities involving *small* groups—especially of *mixed ages*—might be a better fit.

Encourage your child to foster a friendship or two
outside of school, perhaps with a slightly younger child.

One thing we know about inhibited children who are not terribly competent in their social skills and who don't feel secure in the world of peers is
this: Although they may *want* to spend time with their agemates, sometimes they're better off playing or being with slightly younger kids.

Our children live in an age-oriented culture. Enrollment in a particular
school grade, for example, is determined largely by the calendar. Consequently, a child born in the last month or two of a school-defined entry
year will be in the same grade as many children who are seven, eight, or
nine months older. And among the less well accepted children in any
classroom or grade are those who are that much younger and less mature
than the oldest kids in the same group. Such children might feel more
competent and comfortable in the company of somewhat younger kids,
even those in a lower grade, but parents are often bothered if their sixth
grader, say, makes friends with fifth graders. The truth is, though, years
and grades are far less important than levels of maturity—and in any case,
the youngest sixth grader is far closer in age to the oldest *fifth* grader than
to his or her own oldest classmate.

It's good to remember that in the broader scheme of things, those whom
children will end up socializing with as adolescents are not simply agemates, but individuals with whom they share attitudes, opinions, and values. When cross-sex friendships begin, dating pairs are not necessarily
exact contemporaries. In college, freshmen spend their time not exclusively with other freshmen, but with students who are taking the same
classes or belong to the same clubs. Younger children should have the
same advantage.

As a parent, you can help your shy, socially wary child by promoting
opportunities, right up through the teen years, in which she can interact
with a companion a year or two younger. It may do your child good to
spend time with a kid who will look up to and respect her as the possessor
of more advanced information and knowledge. Within that slightly different peer setting, your child can gain more confidence in herself and feel
more secure in her standing.

Now, I'm fully aware that some parents will consider such advice intolerable. That being the case, permit me a brief digression concerning three studies, one a little further removed from the issue at hand than the other.

Some years ago, Steve Suomi, a researcher at the National Institutes of Health who investigates the social and emotional behaviors of primates, conducted a study involving a group of monkeys that had been raised in isolation since shortly after their birth. Some of the monkeys were placed in social situations with normally raised agemates, and others with younger (also normally raised) monkeys. The isolated individuals fared far better with younger monkeys than with agemates: They were more sociable and more assertive, and basically appeared to derive greater benefit from being with younger peer "therapists" than with same-age ones.

Clearly, monkeys are monkeys—and a monkey raised in isolation is not the same thing as a child who isolates himself or herself from peers. In the late 1970s, however, the psychologist Wyndol Furman and some of his colleagues at the University of Minnesota decided to borrow Suomi's monkey-therapy model and apply it in the preschool. They paired socially withdrawn preschoolers with classmates who were either the same age or younger, and compared both of these groups with a third group of socially withdrawn youngsters who received no "treatment." Basically, Furman and his colleagues simply allowed the children to play with their partners freely; then, over the course of time, they observed the children in their regular classrooms. They found that the children with the younger peer partners became less withdrawn and more sociable in class. The children paired with same-age partners, meanwhile, did *not* fare as well, though they did look more sociable than those withdrawn preschoolers who had received no "peer therapy" at all.

Later, my colleagues and I repeated the Furman study in an effort to understand *why* those children with younger play partners made the gains they did. We videotaped the play sessions and then coded them to track any signs that the initially withdrawn child was becoming more sociable, more dominant and initiative with his or her play partner, and more affectively positive—in a word, happier. In a nutshell, we found that over time, withdrawn children (both preschoolers and second graders) who were paired with younger playmates became more confident in their social initiations, even as they developed close relationships with those juniors. When we paired them with another playmate, they picked up where they had left off with the first "peer therapist"—that is, they demonstrated social initiations and confidence at the level seen in the *last* play session with the *previous* playmate, not at the level of their first play session with that child. In short, social confidence transferred from one partner to the next. The same was *not* the case for withdrawn children paired with same-age playmates.

The results of this research make sense: When wary children are provided with peer experiences that are *nonstressful*, they begin to develop competence. We may note, too, that play sessions involving only one other child, rather than many others, simplify the social environment for these children. I suggested earlier that the best friend for a withdrawn child is not necessarily another withdrawn child—that while two such friends may enjoy each other's company and explore their universe together, it won't be a terribly wide universe. By contrast, spending time with a socially average child (and particularly, it seems, one who is somewhat younger) can help the wary child gain confidence—a kind of confidence, moreover, that is transferable to a broader milieu.

Practice assertive, expressive behavior.

Withdrawn children like Courtney—the youngster who told her mother, "Nobody likes me"—often display a kind of deference or submissiveness around their peers, acting too eager to please and be accepted. They have trouble putting themselves forward, making themselves heard, and influencing the action. Much of the time, they just hope to be noticed.

In our own Waterloo Longitudinal Project, we observed striking differences between withdrawn and average children in play encounters. When a withdrawn youngster who was paired with an average child made a social overture, for example, her goal usually was merely to gain the other's attention—to get the peer simply to glance her way. The withdrawn child made few attempts to ask for a toy or to suggest a game. These children harbored what we call relatively "safe" or "low-cost" social goals—little was ventured, in other words, and relatively little could be gained. Yet even so, the members of this group were *less* likely to achieve their goals than were other, more sociable children. Furthermore, the average children directed more "high-cost" goals (taking possession of a desired toy, for example) toward their withdrawn partners than toward others—that is, the normally sociable youngsters appeared to regard their withdrawn playmates as pushovers, and were more likely to be assertive and, by that standard, more socially successful with them.

Being noticed, or getting another kid's attention, is obviously a good start to a social interaction. But if a withdrawn child lets it go at that, he or she is not likely to enjoy very rich encounters with peers, and is also apt to be perceived as submissive—someone others can dominate.

Perhaps, then, the following hints may be helpful:

- Suggest to your young child that when you're together in social company, he must ask you clearly if he wants something—no whispering or tugging at your sleeve to make himself understood.

- Ask your youngster for her opinion about various things, and respond to her observations with interest.

- Use "spare" times—such as when you're driving in the car—to engage your child in conversation, about anything at all. The idea is to help him feel more comfortable with the back-and-forth, give-and-take nature of sustained verbal interaction.

- Talk about real-life "what if?" situations, and get your youngster to tell you what her solutions might be. Then ask what she would really, *really* do at such times:

    "If that kid pushes me out of the line tomorrow, I'll say, 'Cut that out. I don't like getting pushed.'"

    "If I want to talk to that new girl, I'll just go over and say, 'Hi, I'm Laura, what's your name?'"

    "If he says he doesn't want to shoot baskets after school, I could say, 'OK, maybe next week.'"

    For an inhibited child, rehearsing—and simply hearing the sound of her own voice—can be a great confidence booster.

Encourage your child to *look* confident.

Shy kids really do know a lot about how they *want* to act. When asked how they would go about solving a social problem—getting a kid to return a ball, joining a group, asking a classmate for help—they're able to come up with all manner of strategies. Unlike aggressive children, they can think about their dilemmas constructively, but their emotions may prohibit them from putting what they know into action. Remembering simple social skills gives them a leg up.

The father of a "bashful" ten-year-old remembered that when *he* was a kid, "grown-ups were always saying to me, 'Smile, it's not that bad!' and comments like that, because I guess I always looked serious and glum. Actually, I was just too shy to act more friendly. Now I tell my own kid that sometimes you have to fake it till you make it!" He has suggested to his son, in a gentle and supportive manner, that it's good to look directly at others, to smile, to stand up straight, and to walk into a room with one's head up.

That isn't bad advice. The typical withdrawn child slouches, displays nervous habits (nail biting, hair twisting), and avoids eye contact in social company. These are all signals to others that "I'm here for the taking." Your child needs to understand that it's in his power to project an image of competence and confidence, even if he doesn't *feel* competent *or* confident. It's another way—and sometimes a useful way—of coping with being socially anxious and wary.

Applaud a small risk taken.

All children need to know that their parents are behind them, serving as their personal cheering section. When your inhibited child takes some small, appropriate action to move herself out of character, as it were, give her a pat on the back, a little encouragement, or maybe just a "Nice job!" Without making a mountain out of a molehill—by saying with a smile, perhaps, "I saw you go up to those kids in the park this afternoon. I know that was hard to do"—make it clear that you recognize her efforts and admire her for making them.

Parental support really can help shy children increase their degree of social comfort and expand their social connections. Our research bears that out again and again, and shows us, too, that a child's small successes—step by step toward greater courage and confidence—can have a wonderfully cumulative positive effect.

Chapter 10

The Moving-Against Child

Helping Your Aggressive Son or Daughter

The parents of Douglas, now in third grade, had received school reports about their child that bothered them. Douglas was especially friendly with two classmates, and collectively the three boys were considered by their teacher to be a rowdy bunch. Earlier in the year, during a school conference, the teacher had told Douglas's parents that she found it necessary to seat the boys far apart from one another. Sometimes their son's two friends came over for a weekend afternoon, and the parents had seen some wild behavior themselves on these occasions, but Douglas's father, in particular, didn't perceive this in a negative light: "They're just exuberant, pumped-up kids with a lot of energy to burn," he said. "When they get together, they jazz one another up, and then they need to let off steam. They're not *bad*."

There had been several incidents over the years in school, however. When Douglas was in prekindergarten, for example, the teacher had called his mother one afternoon to talk about something that had happened that morning: Douglas had been seen "accosting" another child in the class, waving a push-pin type of thumbtack in front of the other boy and pretending he was about to stab the tack in his face. His parents were inclined at the time to dismiss this behavior as not terribly significant. "*Accosting* was a strong word to use, it seemed to me," said his mother. "He just thought this was kind of funny, and of course it wasn't funny, as I told him later, but he wasn't actually going to poke this kid in the face." Often, however, Douglas's sense of fun led to battles at home with his younger brother, and their mom said she often had to reprimand her older son for being bossy and playing rough.

A recent event had brought them up short. Douglas and his two friends had been kicking around a volleyball in the schoolyard during recess, and then had started throwing it at another child. The ball had hit the boy on the side of the head, hard enough to push the wire frame of his eyeglasses into his cheek, where it broke the skin. Other children who had witnessed the incident reported it to the teacher, the injured child's parents called the school, and Douglas's parents were asked to come in and speak to the principal about the matter. Now they *were* concerned. "We didn't pay much attention to those earlier incidents, but this was like a red flag," said his mother. "Maybe he really *was* trying to hurt that other boy." They had some things to think over, she said, including the possibility of sending their son to a private school in order to separate him from his current friends.

Some observations that might be made about Douglas:

- This is a boy who has difficulty controlling his emotions and acting in a socially skilled manner.

- His difficulties are causing him to acquire a reputation with his teacher and among some of his peers as rowdy, maybe even a kid who wants to harm others.

- Douglas is fortunate in that his parents are paying attention to all of this and starting to consider what role they might play in eliciting more acceptable behaviors from their son.

Developing the ability to regulate or control emotions, and consequently the tendency to act on them, is a milestone in a child's progress toward social competence. Emotionally reactive kids like Douglas—children who are quickly aroused to anger or whose instinct is always to barrel ahead impulsively, with little awareness of what others are thinking, feeling, or doing—*can* learn to put a brake on actions that will lead, sooner or later, to peer rejection. That learning process begins with parents, the initial influences on a child's emotional displays and accompanying behaviors.

If your youngster sounds something like Douglas, you can certainly encourage him to act in more acceptable ways. You can, without question, help him understand that even if he's feeling angry, upset, or "pumped up," those feelings don't always have to be accompanied by corresponding behaviors or actions. At the same time, *you* need to understand certain realities:

- Helping your child behave in a more controlled, less aggressive way will take time, patience, and sensitivity. Don't expect a miracle overnight.

- The younger your child, the more effective your efforts are likely to be. Uninhibited, emotionally reactive aggressive children become more difficult to influence once they have experienced peer rejection in the early school years.

- You may need to recognize and attempt to counter your *own* upsetting emotions.

It *is* difficult to remain calm, affectionate, and focused on a child's needs when he or she is bouncing off the walls, often out of control, or maybe even developing a reputation with other children or in school as being too bossy, a bully, or someone who causes trouble.

As I explained in detail in chapter 3, understanding the connection between temperament and behavior can help parents appreciate that much of what their child is like has to do with inborn biological factors. From that perspective, and by putting into effect the strategies described below—ideas that are, in fact, based on much recent research in the area of child development—you can work with your child to make his or her friendships and life among peers a great deal more successful.

Believe that your child should have your help.

When a child is still quite young, aggressive behavior is often excused; it's viewed not as a characteristic or a stable trait but rather as a *state* that's specific to the situation. The child is considered simply "wound up" or "full of energy" at the time of his or her outburst. Parents may interpret a youngster's aggressiveness as the byproduct of a bad day or the fault of other kids. Some may even consider it endearing—a sign that their child is a little leader. Even when they believe it's wise to curb such behavior, they may send the child a mixed message through the words they use or the (lack of) consistency with which they impose punishment for the rough stuff—a message that conveys, "I don't want you acting like that, but I must admit it's kind of cute."

Or perhaps Mom's and Dad's efforts to teach a youngster social skills have been less than successful, and the confrontations are a nightmare, so they back off, opting to wait out what they hope will be a passing phase.

We do know a few things for certain:

- Parental toleration of a young child's impulsive, acting-out, over-the-top behaviors is an excellent predictor of child aggression.

  Left to continue on this course without a parent's wise and sensitive intervention, the aggressive child may run into serious trouble.

- Behaviors that may have seemed appealing from a toddler don't go over well with teachers and peers a few years later.

  The child who is "difficult" temperamentally—meaning inadequately or only intermittently able to regulate emotions and quiet herself down—will exhibit an inclination to anger within the peer group, which will lead to rejection by average kids and possibly to a budding reputation with teachers as a little troublemaker.

- Increasingly, the aggressive youngster will adopt a suspicious, chip-on-the-shoulder perspective on the world, and peers will in turn form a suspicious view of him. Thus, he will be convinced that others harbor hostile intent toward him, even in situations where they don't; and they will assume this child's behaviors are hostile, even when they're not so intended.

- And finally, childhood aggression and peer rejection are very strong predictors of future difficulties, both in adolescence and later in life.

The aggressive child caught in this cycle of suspicion and reciprocal ill feeling is at high risk for developing the kinds of problems that lead to delinquency, academic troubles, and "bad-crowd" associations.

Believe that your child, at any age, will benefit from your help.

Take a look in the mirror.

Think of the following brief checklist as a bit of personal stock-taking, an exploration of some actions or attitudes that aren't always easy to recognize:

- Do I view my child as a problem? Do I have difficulty calming him down once he's upset and furious?

- Do I have a great deal of trouble getting him to cooperate and do things around the house?

- If he fails to comply with my requests or demands, do I become angry? Do I use physical punishment in the hope that it will settle him down and make him think about "the next time"?

- When my child acts in a hostile way toward a playmate, is it just what I expect from her?

- Am I disappointed in my child? Is it because she seems not to measure up in comparison to other children?

- When I watch my child among other kids, do I feel annoyed? Concerned? Embarrassed? Guilty?

- Do I hear and see *myself* in the way she talks to her friends?

- If he's domineering and critical with other children, am I that way with him? If he's bossy with his friends, am I bossy with him? Or do I let him boss *me* around?

- Does my child see eruptions of hostility and lack of respect between my spouse and me? What is the prevailing atmosphere in our home?

If you recognize yourself in the descriptions of these attitudes and reactions, you'll be able to change your child's behaviors only if you start by making adjustments in your *own*. The last item in the list above, concerning the tone of the family environment, is especially important here.

Administrators at institutions that deal with "troubled and troubling" children frequently observe that many parents of such youngsters would rather not recognize that a problem exists. Expressions of anger and hostile accusations between various family members—even, perhaps, cycles of violence—may be common, the stuff of daily life in such households. These parents are likely to maintain the expectation that their child is a troublemaker—so that the boy who inadvertently spills juice on the table, for instance, like toddler Brett, is seen as purposely trying to enrage his mother. And this incorrect inference, of course, is just what a child living within an atmosphere of persistent suspicion carries into his or her peer interactions.

Social intervention programs help parents break these habitual thought patterns, reflect more broadly about what's really going on with their child, and come to understand that not every troublesome act is intentional mischief. In turn, that mother and that father can, with effort and over time, begin to think more abstractly about their parenting strategies, as well as about the consequences of *their* actions—by asking themselves, for example:

- "If I hit my son or shut him in his room, what will the costs be for our relationship?"

- "If I'm harsh with my daughter this morning, what will the rest of the day be like for her? For her peers? For the rest of the family when she gets home from school?"

- "What model am I setting of the proper way to behave?"

If your home is clouded by anger, if you are perpetually caught up in power struggles with your child or with your spouse, it's essential that you yourself begin to demonstrate greater self-control. Physical punishment is abusive, not only to your child but also to *you*. It suggests that you cannot deal with your youngster in a way that will inspire his or her respect and trust; it suggests that *you* are out of control. Verbal abuse is similarly destructive. It demeans you and does long-term damage to your child's sense of self-worth. Resolving to change your own actions will put you in a position to help your child change his or hers. And patience *is* a virtue.

Let your young child know that aggressive behavior is not acceptable, and that it carries a cost.

It's entirely possible that your child simply doesn't realize that name-calling, being rough, or tormenting another is an unacceptable and intolerable behavior. In many situations—such as Douglas's pretend-stabbing of a thumbtack in his schoolmate's face—the protagonist thinks that all he is doing is having some fun. In that case, what's needed is a clear, consistent parental message that such behaviors aren't allowed, and one of the most effective ways of getting that message across to a young child is by talking about the consequences of aggressive actions, both for the child himself and for his peers.

Instrumental aggression—achieving a desired end by threatening, grabbing, or pushing—is a treatable problem. Your child really can be taught that there are other, and better, ways to resolve interpersonal dilemmas, though it's a principle she may not easily grasp at first, because the clear and simple truth is that threatening, grabbing, and pushing work pretty well most of the time! The immediate result of these actions is likely to be the attainment of the primary goal, which may be to possess a toy or gain access to an activity. Ask an aggressive child, "Was that the right thing to do?," and even if she understands that it's in her best interests to satisfy Mom by saying, "No," she may be thinking, Sure, I got what I wanted, didn't I? Similarly, if you tell a young child, "Stop being so bossy," she will wonder why it's necessary, especially if you fail to provide an explanation.

Get across to your child, over time, the point that such behavior just doesn't work very well—because it pushes people away, because it will cause most other children not to like her, and because it's unacceptable to you and all the other members of your family.

"Other kids aren't going to like being around you if you do that" is a powerful message to convey. There's a lot to be said for the idea that no child really wants to be disliked. So impressing upon an aggressive youngster early on that the eventual price of continuing her behavior may be a lack of friends—or rejection by someone she *wants* to befriend—can provide some real motivation for change.

Of course, aggressive behaviors have other consequences as well. The child on the receiving end may get hurt and thereafter will be afraid or angry, and reluctant to forgive. But perspective-taking, or considering one's actions from another's point of view, is something that aggressive children find particularly difficult to do. Discussing *consequences*—for herself and for others—will help your child better appreciate why such behavior is basically good for no one.

Provide structure and support when you need
your child to comply.

You'll remember the behavior of uninhibited Brett in our lab visits. When faced with an assignment—tidying up the playroom, replicating a Lego construction—this young boy never got down to business. He ignored the request, let other kids do all the work, and generally seemed not to hear what was being asked of him. Children like Brett have a great deal of difficulty paying attention and sticking to a task, which of course causes them problems in their classrooms and among their peers.

Compliance—doing the job that has to be done—is an excellent marker of a youngster's developing abilities to regulate emotions and behavior. But it's a frustrating matter for the parent of an extremely uninhibited child who is prone to easy anger or who turns a deaf ear to the parent's requests. The temptation is either to demand compliance—"Just do it!"— or, out of frustration, annoyance, or impatience, to jump in and do it *for* him or her. But what this youngster needs, more than most children, is direction, a helping hand, and warm encouragement.

The mother of one such preschooler recognized her own "Just do it!" tendencies, and also a persistently negative pattern of interactions between herself and her child: "I'll tell him five times to stop flinging his toys around the den and to get into bed. Nothing happens. Then I lose it and give him a swat on the behind, which at least gets his attention." Unhappy about that pattern, she began working to change it: "I tell him once, and if he's not cooperating, I'll go in and I might say, 'Let's get started on this together, suppose you pick up your action figures and I'll put the books back on the shelf.'"

In adopting this approach, this parent was providing well-timed, supportive assistance that facilitated her child's actions and made it easier for him to comply. She is now more able to "get his attention," but through behaviors that show both control and warmth.

Most young children, as I noted earlier, find it difficult voluntarily and easily to stop doing something pleasurable (such as playing or watching TV) in order to go along with a grown-up's command to do something less pleasurable (tidy up, get ready for bed). If you issue a request and follow up with several reminders, and *still* your child refuses to comply, the scene is all too apt to turn angry. But if you can offer your child a helpful boost to get with the program, you may find that things will go better.

Saying something like, "OK, this room needs to be straightened up now. How about if you put the blocks away, and I'll get these clothes off the floor?," conveys a useful message: "This task needs to be accomplished, and you, child, are expected to accomplish it. But if it's too difficult for you to abandon what you'd rather be doing, I'll give you some help to get you started."

And if he or she still doesn't get moving, there's a consequence: "I'm afraid we're not going to have time for reading tonight, because it took too long to get cleaned up. Maybe tomorrow night we'll see if we have more time."

All this is not necessarily going to proceed pleasantly at first, or even smoothly. Your child's initial reaction to this new and different behavior coming from Mom may be loud protests or whining. But start with one issue or sticking point in the day that invariably leads to frustration, and maintain your calm determination to change the old pattern—your nagging and shouting, your child's refusal to comply.

Set limits and clear and consistent expectations for behavior in the home.

Both too little and too much parental control are likely to exacerbate children's problems with self-regulation. The worst-case scenario for the highly uninhibited child is a parent who behaves in anything *other than* an *authoritative* manner—that is, offering the right degree of control in an appropriately warm way.

Permissive ("Do what you want") and *authoritarian* ("Do what I say") parenting, we know from much research, both exacerbate aggressive behavior. "Do what you want" will not provide an uninhibited youngster with the limits and structure he or she so desperately needs, while "Do what I say" imposes so *much* structure that the child has little opportunity to practice self-control and self-regulation.

In some families with easy-to-anger, running-wild children, parents have been observed to act erratically. A child's "bad" behavior may be dealt with in some instances and ignored, or even rewarded, in others—when Mom is attempting, say, to prevent a blow-up between siblings. Or a child may be punished for being pushy or bossy in the home, even though the same behavior is encouraged in the peer group; conversely, a youngster may be allowed to get away with murder around the house but draw a quick and harsh reaction if a parent sees him or her acting in a bullying manner toward peers.

If you're engaging in constant power struggles with your child, if no day goes by without a dozen angry standoffs, most likely too much parental "Do what I say" is going on. Picking your battles more carefully may noticeably reduce the confrontations and aggressiveness and lead to an all-around more pleasant atmosphere. A mother who described her child as "bullheaded," for example, elected to keep a diary, a short list of the fights that occurred between her and her daughter. Reviewing the list at the end of a week, she decided that in the future she would retreat from certain habitual arguments: "I won't allow her to hit her sister or call her nasty names. Other stuff—such as when she takes a bath—I'm letting go of. And on a couple of other things, I'll give her a choice of two or three options."

For another parent, setting clear limits meant not allowing her five-year-old to "rule the roost." Justin, said his mother, "constantly tells everybody what to do, including the grown-ups. We had a large family dinner party recently, and Justin started instructing people on where they had to sit, which in fact was not according to the way I had arranged the table." Having resolved to curb her son's tendencies to take control of any and all situations, without losing her calm, she talked to him: "I said, 'Well, Justin, we're not going to do that at this dinner. Maybe next time we can try it your way.' This didn't go over very well with him, but I stood my ground."

Parental permissiveness and indulgence—or letting a child dictate how the family should be run—almost inevitably increase a child's belief that he or she is in charge and no one else matters much. When Mom and Dad neglect to lay down any rules or express any expectations about the proper way for their youngster to act, they may be legitimizing or encouraging the very behaviors they don't want to see.

In order to set appropriate limits for your child—and strike the tricky balance between too much and too little parental control—you have to be clear in your own mind about what's acceptable behavior and what isn't. Once you've established those limits, you need to enforce them consistently.

Find fault with the behavior, not with the child.

As I suggested in the previous chapter, on inhibited children, it's crucial that parents avoid falling into the trap of exerting *psychological control* by referring to a child's characteristics in a critical (and often public) way. Parents of aggressive kids, we know, are inclined to exert that kind of control through words that devalue or undermine a child's self-esteem and sense of security.

Eliminate from your repertoire any comments that are belittling or sarcastic or draw negative comparisons, all of which are likely to threaten your child's sense of trust and security in the family. Such remarks—from "Why can't you be more like your sister?" to "Daddy doesn't love you when you do that" to "Come on, act your age"—are debilitating and require a child to spend his or her energies coping with hurt or stung pride instead of learning.

Help your child tone down and slow down.

The mother of six-year-old Frank said she thought of her son as being not aggressive, exactly, but rather "a kid who wears everybody out, pushes everybody's buttons, and gets on everybody's nerves. He's too much of everything—too loud, too in-your-face. Even when he was very little, you'd wish you could just switch him off sometimes!" The behaviors of her "too-much" son often caused other children to either stay out of his way or flat out tell him they didn't like playing with him. Watching Frank at birthday parties and other social events, his mother observed a pattern: "He gets to a point of no return. He doesn't realize it. He'll be happy, laughing, having a great time, the other kids are having a great time, and then all of a sudden he goes over the top and he's pushing and shouting."

For children like Frank, approaching a social situation or an unfamiliar setting is no problem. In visits to our lab, these are the toddlers who walk right up to a researcher, someone they've never seen before, in order to get hold of an intriguing toy; they are the seven-year-olds who within moments are in the thick of things in the company of three previously unknown peers. *Inhibiting* the inclination to approach—reining in that in-your-face instinct—and calming down when overly excited, upset, or frustrated are what give this child trouble. Here are few pointers for parents:

- Step into any situation that seems to be on the verge of turning ugly.

     If Frank sounds like *your* child—if you often see appropriately assertive behaviors veer suddenly into unpleasantness—try to be on the spot and ready to intervene with supervision that includes a specific consequence. When he's with a friend and fast approaching the point of no return, let him know what the problem is—for example, "You're being very loud and getting a little rough." This is not a criticism or a judgment call, but a statement of fact—necessary because your child, like Frank, most likely doesn't "hear" himself very well.

- Next, explain to your child what he needs to do and what will happen if he doesn't do it: "You have to stop the pushing and shouting, because Joey may get hurt, and maybe you will, too. If you can't settle down, Joey will have to go home."

- If matters don't improve, enforce the consequence, which may be that your youngster won't get to spend the whole afternoon with his pal, or that for the next couple of days he can't invite a friend over.

- Before the next playdate, you may want to work out a signal with your child—a little reminder you can use as a gentle warning, without your child's playmates even knowing, that things need to settle down.

     Frank and his mother agreed on this one: "When I was in another room and I heard Frank getting too boisterous, I'd go, 'Hellooo.' This was our secret code, and Frank knew it meant he needed to take things down a notch. It worked very well."

     The goal is not to tell your child to stop, but rather to encourage him to take better note of what he's doing and to realize that if he can't manage to change the behavior, it may cost him something pleasant. Over time, such parental reminders will prompt your child, ideally, to self-soothe and start to regulate his own behaviors. Frank's mom, for example, was amused and delighted one afternoon to hear her son give *himself* a quiet little "Hellooo."

In fact, this is a wonderful example of a phenomenon I described in the previous chapter—*self-directed private speech,* or talking to oneself. A valuable tool for controlling emotions and behaviors, it's a skill that children develop over time. In toddlerhood, it's expected that a child's emotions and behaviors will be regulated by external sources—chiefly his or her parents. When her highly uninhibited young son is getting angry because he can't get his hands on a toy he wants, for example, a mother may redirect his attention to another activity. When he's determined to climb onto a glass table, his mom or dad may strongly advise him not to try it ("Because it's dangerous, and you could hurt yourself"). And if he's lobbing spoonfuls of oatmeal onto the kitchen floor, or grabbing his older brother's homework, either parent may issue a verbal prohibition: "No, that's not how we act around here." If he complies, he may earn a pleasant "Good for you, I'm proud of you."

Such consistently demonstrated parental regulation ideally leads, in time, to the next stage, when the child begins to regulate himself or herself externally, through self-verbalization. Thus, the youngster who's about to do something she ought not to do may suddenly issue a verbal prohibition to herself: "No, Amy, it's bad to tear up Mikey's schoolbook." (This was essentially what young Frank did to help himself out, with his quiet "Hellooo" reminder.)

Eventually such expressed speech goes "underground": Self-regulation, the Russian psychologist Lev Vygotsky wrote, has reached maturity when the need to speak out loud to oneself during problem solving or in moments of anxiousness is internalized and transformed into planned thought.

This same regulatory sequence, in fact, is often applied by psychologists working with children who are too quick off the mark, or apt to run through social interactions without giving them enough thought, and thus likely to get into trouble with others.

Allow your child to expend energy in an acceptable way.

The temperamentally exuberant and easily angered youngsters we see in our lab visits tend to be lively children. Even as babies, they resent being constricted or held firmly. They're on the move, and quickly frustrated when they can't be. Often they're kids who "need to let off steam," as Douglas's father said of his son and his friends.

Early theories about children's play had much to say about this "letting off steam" notion: It was thought that everyone needed a time and place to release "surplus energy." And indeed, some researchers have demonstrated that if young children are cooped up in their classrooms because of inclement weather, their behavior when they're finally allowed outside to play is far more rambunctious than on a normal day, when they're free to run around as usual.

All of which is to say that it may actually make implicit sense to buy into the "letting off steam" idea. For the high-energy child, the fast-moving competition of a soccer league, for example, might be an appropriate venue for energy release, whereas piano lessons requiring serious concentration might be anything but! Many kids in our culture are overscheduled and left with little free time, but your child may be one who would benefit from more rather than fewer organized extracurricular activities—provided that they let him or her run around and have some "good," regulated fun.

Help your child read social situations with greater accuracy.

An average elementary-school-age child will take in feedback from a friend or from the peer group and use it to adjust behaviors that he or she perceives to be unappreciated. An aggressive child, however, has trouble making adjustments, probably due to an inability to read the relevant social cues. He may, as I've noted, have one or more friends who are also aggressive, a milieu that leads him to conclude that such behavior is just fine. If this child does become aware that his actions are turning others off, he may simply become even angrier and conceive a good-guy/bad-guy explanation for why things aren't going well for him: He is the good guy, and everyone else is the bad guy. Sensitive, withdrawn children may look inward and ask, "What's the matter with me?"; aggressive children may look outward and find fault with others.

- If your youngster frequently comes home from school with angry or hostile complaints about classmates—"They're dumb; I don't want to play with them anyway," "They're jealous of me," "They made me do it"—start a dialogue that will help him or her get a more accurate reading on what's actually going on. Let's assume your son looks angry, and you're hearing about the "bunch of jerks" in his class. Ask simple, information-gathering questions:

"What went on at school today?"

"And how did that start?"

"Hmm . . . what did he say after that?"

"What did you do then?"

Your goal here is to review the bit of social business that turned nasty or had an unpleasant outcome and break it down into discrete steps, to underscore the point that things don't "just happen" magically or spontaneously, but can in fact be understood as the end result of a series of interactions between two people. This will put your son in a better position to figure out how matters could have taken a different turn, starting with the moment when he might have recognized that the situation was about to go sour—when, for example, the other child complained, began to fret, or became visibly upset. Let your child know that that was the point when the warning light should have come on—when he should have realized, in effect, "This is not the way things should be."

And then *you'll* be in a better position to give him some help working out how he might have solved the problem differently.

Practice "What are all the things you can do . . . ?" problem solving.

Some years ago, my colleague Linda Rose-Krasnor and I outlined the process by which a competent child deals with social situations. First, the child has in mind what he or she hopes to achieve—John would like to play PlayStation with his friend, for example, or Tammy wants to get acquainted with the kid waiting behind her on the cafeteria line. For the average child, the hoped-for goal is often something pleasant and prosocial, such as persuading a pal to have some fun, or establishing a new relationship.

Next, the child accesses from memory those strategies that may help him or her achieve that goal. From these, he or she chooses the one that seems the most appropriate to the specific context, and then implements it: John suggests to his friend that they could have a game; Tammy asks the classmate on the cafeteria line how she did on yesterday's math test. If this strategy doesn't work, the child may either repeat it or else put plan B into action—John, for example, may agree to rent a video now if his pal promises to play PlayStation later. Alternatively, the youngster may abandon the effort entirely if his or her social goal seems unattainable or not so important or desirable anymore—in Tammy's case, if she discovers that the kid she wanted to talk to was unresponsive or not that interesting.

If all of this sounds rather automatic, that's because for most children it *is*. Once learned well, the problem-solving process does not necessarily involve a great deal of thinking or conscious deliberation. There are times, however, when *social information processing* is not automatic at all. If a child expects a friend to do one thing, for instance, and the friend does something entirely different, the automatic response may be inappropriate. For example, if Millie asks a friend to join her later to go shopping, and the friend says, "I can't, I'm going to Vanessa's house after school," Millie's expectations may be violated. But after stopping to think of an appropriate response and pausing to get over her disappointment, Millie—a self-regulated and socially competent child—may offer a counterproposal: "Well, maybe we can get together tomorrow."

For the easily angered, aggressive child, in contrast, the only conceivable response may be the first one that comes to mind: "Well, that's it for you, then. I don't need you anymore." In short, the aggressive child is likely to have many deficits in social information processing. For one thing, aggressive youngsters' goals or motives are more likely to be negative in nature—they very often want to "get even with" another child, or one-up him or her. And once they're frustrated by not getting what they want, their scripted or automatic reaction is to respond immediately and negatively; they don't pause to think about alternatives or other ways of solving a problem.

In our own studies, we've noted that when aggressive children are presented with an imaginary social dilemma or hypothetical goal and asked how they would go about solving or achieving it, they generate few ideas. Moreover, the plans they *do* come up with tend to be unkind ("I'd just grab the toy," "I'd shove him back") or to involve bargaining, bribes, or commands ("You better help"). When asked to explain how they would go about initiating a friendship with someone, they often outline strategies that are somewhat bizarre, and certainly not what we hear from average kids ("I'd buy her a belt," "I'd sneak into his room at night").

In other words, these children fail both to *act* and to *think* in ways that are likely to be acceptable to other kids. They also fail to pause, take a breath and calm down, and consider alternatives when another child responds to a social overture in an unexpected way. The basic problem, then, is that aggressive children seem unable to take themselves off "automatic pilot." And when their attempts to resolve an interpersonal dilemma fail, their emotions overwhelm them, and they respond either by using the same strategy that didn't work the first time around or by striking out.

Thinking in the right way about the whole matter of friendship and peer acceptance is at the core of prosocial behavior. You may recall the statement, in an earlier chapter, by Jonathan, a twelve-year-old participant in our studies who described what he'd do when faced with a choice between shooting the possible winning basket for his team and coming to the aid of his friend. What was most important, he indicated, was repaying his friend's trust, honoring their friendship, and being supportive and helpful. Put to the actual test, Jonathan might, it's true, make a different choice, but the very fact that this young person could reason that way means he's more likely to *act* that way.

- Help your child learn to think better, and to increase his or her repertoire of good, adaptive strategies, by engaging her in "What are all the things you could do . . . ?" conversations.

   This need not be a heavy-handed, "Now we're going to practice" kind of talk. Say you've obtained a reasonably clear picture of an incident that left your youngster feeling angry or got her into some other kind of difficulty earlier in the day. You might begin by stating your position regarding her behavior and promoting a little perspective-taking: "Knocking someone down isn't the right thing to do. How do you think Janie felt about that? How do you think she's going to feel about seeing you tomorrow?"

   If the actions that led up to the problem involved, for example, your child's taking back something that another youngster absconded with, you might say, "OK, she took the Harry Potter book you were reading, and you wanted it back. What else do you think you could have done at that point? What do you think you might do if the same thing happened again?"

Your child may come up with some less-than-wonderfully-prosocial strategies at first—"I could tell her I won't be her friend anymore"; "I could tell the teacher what she did"—but if you encourage her to keep thinking things through, maybe she will get to something like "I could ask her if she wanted to read the other Harry Potter book," or "I could say we could read together," or "I could say, 'I'll be happy to give you the book tomorrow.'" If so, be pleased with that; it's real progress.

Getting your child into the habit of thinking about other possibilities for action is building a social strength that will be needed right up through adolescence and beyond. In addition, when a youngster generates her own problem-solving ideas, she will tend to follow them more readily and feel better about them—and about herself. And all the while, your child will be regulating her own emotions and behaviors.

Applaud prosocial actions.

Notice when your child starts getting better at self-calming and inhibiting the instinct to confront and move against, and let your child know you noticed and think he or she is doing great. This is no small feat, I know, for the parent of an emotionally reactive boy or girl! First, changes are small and come slowly. And then, focused as you have been for so long on what's going wrong, it's easy to overlook what's going *right*. But do remember to offer a little applause (though without suggesting that the accomplishment is the most remarkable thing in the world):

"I saw you help Diana pick up all those crayons she spilled. That was a nice thing for you to do."

"You know, Jim, it's good that you didn't blow your top when that kid knocked into you. You're handling things really well."

Encourage your child to apologize.

Aggressive children very quickly develop unpleasant reputations among their peers, though they themselves often remain oblivious to the fact that they've been pegged as mean, or kids to stay away from. Apologies don't come easily for these children, and having to offer one may *not* be an ego-boosting action.

But children have long memories. If your eleven-year-old son punched a classmate out of frustration and anger, that one-time event will be remembered and will cause others to react to him in negative ways. Physical aggression—as distinct from the bantering, rough-and-tumble pushing and jostling that normal children engage in and recognize as benign—is conspicuous and truly out of character for the vast majority of human beings. Children may see violent behavior on TV, but they really don't expect any of their peers to strike out physically. The child who does so, even once, will have to prove he or she isn't really "that kind of kid."

When a child starts a fight or acts physically aggressive in school, and the incident is witnessed by or otherwise comes to the attention of a teacher or coach, the youngsters involved may be brought together, and the perpetrator advised to apologize. But much more often, only the kids themselves will be aware of what's taken place.

- If you've learned—after noting his or her angry or bad mood, or after your information-gathering talk—that your child was the perpetrator in an unpleasant incident, suggest that apologizing might be a good way to begin to reverse other children's perceptions: "Do you think you can repair the situation? Do you think you should tell your classmate you're sorry? I know that's something you probably don't want to do, but if you think about it, you may see that it's really a good idea."

Help your child learn to be in the group without taking it over.

The report from Meredith's kindergarten teacher was for the most part one that any parent would be thrilled to receive. This child was bright, verbal, and friendly, said the teacher—but then she added that she needed to learn some social skills. "When Meredith approaches several children," the report read, "the group tends to disperse." As it happened, parents' visiting day was coming up, and Meredith's mom decided to take the opportunity to observe her child's behavior toward her classmates. During recess, she saw that her daughter was often both domineering and physical, telling other kids what to do and once actually moving another child, clearly against his wishes, into the space she wanted him to occupy. And indeed, this parent did see a group "disperse"—three girls who were having a lively conversation drifted away as soon as Meredith joined them.

Children like Meredith usually have few qualms about entering a group of peers. They enjoy being around others; they're ready for fun. The trouble starts when they attempt to integrate themselves into an activity that's already under way. Our own lab studies have shown that such youngsters are frequently intrusive—that is, they set out to interrupt or change what other kids are doing, and because they're determined and forceful, they're often quite successful at it. But being socially intrusive typically does not make one well liked.

Meredith's mother decided to draw her daughter's attention to her behavior in order to help her recognize that there was a better way of approaching others: "I just talked a bit about what I had seen in school that day. I said that when she was with a bunch of kids, it was good to be helpful and kind, to suggest and not just tell someone what to do or where to stand. And when some of her classmates are already busy playing a game or talking, she has to keep herself on the edges for a little while, watch what they're doing, and see how she can fit in." Being bright, verbal, and friendly, Meredith was able to accept this sound advice.

Encourage friendship with a socially competent child.

In writing about Derek and Brett, the reticent and uninhibited boys we observed over a period of some years in our lab studies, I noted that each child might benefit tremendously from finding a close friend who was not just like him. When two aggressive kids pair up, the combination may promote—or "jazz up," as Douglas's father said—the negative behaviors that throw them off track with most of their peers. Furthermore, while they may *seem* to be friends, our work in the Friendship Study suggests that such relationships may not be truly supportive.

Bonds between aggressive children may in fact be fragile, because in terms of day-to-day communication, these youngsters tend to be much less predictable than more competent kids. For example, they may be unable to get past the conflicts, accidents, and misunderstandings that happen all the time within any friendship pair or small group. The aggressive child's inclination to blame others and to react with anger may make it difficult for him or her to resolve such dilemmas—especially with *another* aggressive child—in a way that would sustain and perhaps even strengthen a friendship.

• If your uninhibited youngster is often in the company of friends who are equally impulsive, acting-out, and oppositional, see if there's a child of another stripe in his or her peer world with whom your child might be able to get together.

  You can't *force* two kids to become friends, of course, and attempts to push such a connection will often backfire. But there's everything to be said for observing the social landscape keenly, becoming friendly yourself with the parent or parents of a more mature or controlled child, and inviting that family over for a potluck dinner or the like. (This strategy may not work with older elementary and middle school children, since by this age, other kids and their parents are apt to want to avoid the child who has a reputation for being aggressive.)

  Even if the two children don't become fast friends, it's a good idea for your youngster to expand his or her horizons. He or she is much more likely to learn about socially competent behaviors by engaging in interactions with a normal child than by spending all of his or her free time with a similarly uninhibited and undercontrolled friend.

Spend good, friendly time with your child.

Many of your interactions with your child probably consist of, on the one hand, preventing him from doing something he shouldn't do, or, on the other hand, getting him to do something he *has* to do. A fair proportion of them may involve your intervening in fights or talking to him about what he didn't get right. Much of what your child perceives as coming from Mom or Dad, in other words, is a corrective, perhaps expressed with anger or impatience.

If that sounds like the prevailing tone of your parent-child relationship, consider whether and how you might increase the number of pleasant times you have together. Take the time to go places with your child, just the two of you. Enjoy a special meal at his or her favorite restaurant. Tell jokes and talk about neutral things that happened in the course of the day. Explore how the two of you might be together in a notably more relaxed, quiet way.

Stay in touch with the other adults in your child's life.

Like the parents of Douglas, the mom and dad who found themselves sitting in the principal's office after the volleyball incident, you may discover that your sole contact with your child's teacher or sports coach, or any other individual who observes him in action each day, comes about when something unpleasant happens—or when you meet for the annual parent-teacher conference and hear general comments about your youngster's "being noncompliant" or "clowning around too much."

Teachers, overburdened though they are, really may be on your side, and can be encouraged to be part of the process of improving your child's behavior. At the beginning of sixth grade, one set of parents who had been hearing such complaints about their daughter on a regular basis determined to "stay on top of things this year," in their words, "and put us and our child and the school all on the same page." They asked their child's teacher to meet with them for a few minutes early one morning in the first week, told her a bit about some changes they were working on with their daughter, and said they'd appreciate it if they could e-mail her every couple of weeks just to get her feedback on how things were going in the classroom. She was amenable to the idea. The parents and teacher thus established a flow of information between school and home, and as a result, the child had her most successful school year yet.

Talk to a professional.

Self-help is often not enough effectively to alter an aggressive child's behaviors, especially if the child is in the preteen years. Although I know from over twenty-five years of observing parents and children that the measures described here can have powerful positive results, it is also the case that reading *any* book can take a parent only so far. Some aggressive children and their parents *do* need to talk to a professional, be it a psychologist or some other type of counselor who can discuss specific issues and explore solutions.

Fathers especially, we've learned, are resistant to the notion of seeking help. But if matters in your household aren't improving, if your child is actively getting into trouble, it really is in his or her best interests for you to find someone who can help you on an ongoing basis.

Uninhibited children have a great deal going for them. Their typically sociable, outgoing personalities can be a big plus *if,* with parental support, they can learn some critical social skills.

Chapter 11

Bad Influences

When a Child Falls In with the "Wrong Crowd"

Upsetting though a child's lack of popularity or difficulty making friends can be to parents, what really makes them frantic is the suspicion that their son or daughter is caught up in—or drifting toward—a bad crowd. Your normally sweet, reliable, self-confident child is hanging around on weekends with kids you don't like the looks of; he is acquiring habits or adopting an attitude or mannerisms that you think are foreign to his nature and to everything he has learned at home. You may be concerned that your son is being unduly influenced by peer relationships that aren't good for him or that he's emotionally not ready for, or maybe you're becoming deeply worried that your daughter is headed for real trouble.

But how can parents know with certainty that the kids *their* child is spending time with are either "troublesome" or "in trouble"? The truth is, it's often difficult to make clearheaded, objective assessments of a child's peer group and of those seemingly bad influences within it. Some issues, such as substance use, need to be taken seriously of course, but others, including a child's preferred style of dress, should probably be viewed with relative detachment, hard though such a stance may be to take. However, here's something to keep in mind:

- When your child begins to act in ways that you consider too independent-minded, even risky, it can actually be a sign that development is proceeding as it should!

In large part, after all, your youngster's behaviors are a product of your encouragement, throughout his or her young life, to revel in creative exploration, to call up friends, to become involved with peers—to develop social competence, in other words.

In this chapter we will consider the parenting skills that come into play during the years when a child is typically associating with wider peer groups, when pressures to conform to "what everybody's doing" may be intense, and when talking things through is the main avenue of parental influence.

Pushing the envelope: a good kid's brush with a wrong crowd

Often, the company a teenager keeps can affect his or her whole family. That was the case, for example, when fifteen-year-old Erica became involved in a scene that deeply disturbed her parents.

Since their kindergarten days, Erica and a child named Carrie had been close friends. Although Carrie and her family had moved to another community about an hour's drive away after the girls finished fourth grade, the two children had kept in touch over the years. The families were friendly; Carrie often spent weekends at Erica's house, and vice versa, and they had attended the same sleepaway camp for several consecutive summers.

Recently, however, the friends had been growing in different ways or at different speeds, said Erica's mother: "Carrie was always smart as a whip, a terrific student. She also had a wild side, even as a youngster. In high school, she went a little crazy, it seemed to us. It was almost as if she were living a double life, going to school and pretty much keeping up her grades, then hanging around the rest of the time with a very different crowd—mostly older, mostly boys, all with cars. A couple of these kids were school dropouts."

Erica's parents were aware of all this because, for one thing, Erica's mother made a point of staying in touch with Carrie's mother, who was frank in expressing her concerns about her daughter. In addition, after spending a weekend visiting Carrie, or sometimes after chatting with her on the phone, Erica would talk to her mom about what was going on with her friend. According to Erica's mother, "It was obvious that Carrie was sexually active, maybe even promiscuous. Erica would say she was worried about her, but at the same time, I could tell she was tremendously intrigued by that whole scene.

"You know that song lyric from *Oliver,* 'I'm reassessing the situation'? That's what her dad and I were doing during those months—keeping our ears open, listening and talking to her, and talking to each other about whether or when this situation might need some reassessing! Our daughter always had other friends, though—good kids, most of whom we knew—so we didn't worry that she felt isolated or desperately in need of hooking up with this other crowd."

They believed that forbidding their daughter to associate with Carrie would be the worst possible move they could make. "First, she wouldn't agree to do that and also would probably clam up as far as we went," said this parent. "And there was a history here that I thought had to be respected. Those two girls had shared a lot of talk and a lot of experiences." The fact that Carrie lived in another community was both a boon and a disappointment: "During that year, when Carrie seemed to be veering out of control, she and Erica really couldn't get together much, and their contact was mainly over the phone, which I was glad about. But if Carrie had still lived nearby, I would have wanted to have her come over to the house more, maybe spend some family time with us."

One Saturday morning, Erica told her parents that she was going downtown to spend the day studying with her classmate Susan, and would probably sleep over at her house. Instead, she took the train to Carrie's city and appeared on her doorstep. Erica's parents found out about it when Carrie's mom called that evening to say, "You do know that Erica's up here, don't you?" The two friends were out and didn't get back to Carrie's until late. "We were having phone calls and tears at two in the morning, apologies and shouting," said Erica's mother. "Her father and I had calmed down somewhat by the next day when she got home, and the three of us talked. What was apparent was that Erica was deeply upset about having lied to us. And of course, *we* were unhappy about that, too. There was really nothing we needed to say on that score. She knew how we felt, she knew she had let us down, she recognized the breach of trust she had committed—she saw it in our faces. She told us, in tears, that it made her feel terrible. She said it would never happen again. And it didn't."

The following day, Erica told her mother that she thought there was something wrong with her eyes. "It came out that a boy in Carrie's crowd had had some substance—she wasn't sure what it was," said Erica's mother. "They had all taken this stuff. Apparently Erica was experiencing visual distortions—the peripheral images were sort of flattened out. I could tell she was embarrassed, and very scared. I took her that afternoon to the eye doctor, and I told her she must explain to him exactly what she thought had caused this. The doctor spoke to her and then to me separately, and I gather he attempted to put the fear of God in her. There was no lasting harm done, but he talked to her about the damage drugs can do to the body's organs."

Erica's mother was far from unhappy about the doctor's lecture: "As a parent, the temptation is to say to your child, 'You idiot! Don't you have any sense?' And of course, that would just get everybody angry and stirred up. Going to that doctor was a perfect opportunity to say to my daughter, in effect, 'OK, you did something very foolish, we are going to take this very seriously, and we will first and immediately find out if there have been physical consequences related to your actions.'" Later in the week, she said, "We went out to dinner as a family, and we talked about a lot of things, including what she was thinking now about her friend. We told her that if she wanted to spend time again with Carrie, first she must discuss that with us, and we'd see what we thought about it. And we told her we loved her—which of course she knows—and that we're responsible for her, and it's our job to keep her safe, as much as we can." There were no further visits with Carrie for some time.

That was several years ago. Said Erica's mother about her daughter, now a twenty-year-old college junior, "You really couldn't have a more delightful daughter. It's a joy to be her mother. She's funny, smart, hardworking, great company, very loyal. Her friends are terrific young people. I gather the partying at college, especially the first two years, was all about drinking, and she and her friends just haven't gotten into that. She's a fine young person. Carrie got herself straightened out eventually, and the two girls are still friendly, but they live very different lives now."

Some points of relevance to *all* parents might be drawn from this family's story:

- "Good kids," with good parents and good friends, aren't immune to the temptation to associate with peers who are doing unacceptable things, or to the appeal of a crowd that seems to be exciting or even somewhat dangerous.

  One thing we know from our own work: Children from middle school on often tell us that they like hanging out with certain peers who may not necessarily be the finest of friends for them. They may enjoy being with individuals who are popular or highly visible in the social milieu, who are risk takers and experimenters, or who have something else to offer that the "regular" kids think they lack. Thus the studious boy and good student may begin to spend time with kids who cut class or are careless about their homework. The clean-cut girl begins dressing like the "partiers" in her school who frequent the downtown club scene. The attraction may be real enough when a child needs to push the envelope of acceptable behavior and try on another persona for size—but often the influence is fleeting. Although to a parent, "fleeting" may seem like a millennium, we're talking here about a relatively short developmental period, perhaps a year or two.

- Parents who stay in touch with their kids have a much better chance of influencing their choices.

  Erica's mom and dad kept their ears open, gathered information and were interested in what their daughter had to say, and weighed what they knew about her over her whole life against what was going on in the moment. They were at once, it seems, realistic, tuned in, and flexible.

- Children who have a sense of *felt security* with their parents, and who perceive them as being available, are less likely to get too far off-track.

  That Erica could talk to her mother and father about her friendship with Carrie, that she was unhappy and remorseful about lying to them, and that she turned to them for help when she was worried about her physical well-being—all of these things point to a solid relationship nurtured over the years. That bond served *everyone* well.

- In some cases, young people can come away from a brush with a wrong crowd relatively unscathed, and perhaps even strengthened in their feelings of both *individuality,* or autonomy, and *connectedness* with their parents.

That's not to suggest, of course, that Erica's mom and dad didn't experience trying, uncertain, and even scary moments. But in the long term, *this* story ended happily.

The roots of parental influence

During the years when your child is testing the limits, however confident you may be in the strength of your relationship with him and in your own repertoire of skills, there may come a time—or more than one—when you worry about his susceptibility to bad peer influences.

What needs to be said at the outset is that even through a child's teen years, parents can continue to encourage her friendships with peers who are basically well adjusted and competent, and express their support for those connections. And they can also discourage allegiances to less well adjusted, less competent kids, *provided* they do so in a manner that is not intrusive and judgmental but rather reasoned and reasonable—by pointing out in a calm, concerned fashion, for example, why it might be best for their son or daughter not to pursue certain involvements or engage in certain behaviors. Such influence doesn't come out of the blue. The sensitive and responsive parent of an adolescent was almost surely sensitive and responsive to that child when she was a toddler, a preschooler, and a fourth grader. A history of trust, respect, and, really, mutual admiration will almost always allow for good communication.

But communication isn't only or simply a matter of "sitting down to have a talk." In fact, having a talk—if it's suffused with a parent's disapproval, or if it comes across as a scare tactic—can backfire and actually push a child *further* in the very direction Mom and Dad don't like. And lecturing a child about the dangers of hanging around with kids who drink or smoke, for example, is likely to have little effect if a parent isn't modeling sober or cigarette-free behavior himself or herself. More than what parents say, it's what a child *believes* his or her parents believe, and how the child observes them conducting their own lives, that *most strongly influence* what he or she chooses to do. This internalization of clear adult expectations and conventions, psychologists think, serves as powerful protection when a young adolescent faces peer pressures to participate in risky or dangerous activities.

What you as a parent believe is right for your child comes through in all the countless small ways you demonstrate love, warmth, caring, and sensible living on a daily basis—the means by which, that is, you foster your child's connectedness with you and the family to which he belongs. When the connection is strong, you're in a good position to engage your youngster in conversation about aspects of his life that concern you, and to let him or her know what you think. How such communication takes place is a matter partly of style and partly of history.

Hard-and-fast rules about how to "talk teen," or how to have productive conversations on difficult topics with adolescents, often fail to take into account the fact that there really are no hard-and-fast family profiles. Some parents and children exchange important information in an offhand, joking manner. Some adolescents may have become accustomed to parents who are strikingly forthright about and forthcoming with their opinions. How parents choose to address an immediate worry may have much to do with how they have handled issues of concern in the past, and how their child responded on those occasions.

Whatever the style and the context, what matters most is that parents convey consistent warmth, support, and caring, even as they offer nonintrusive guidance and monitoring.

Displays of bravado: a risky age

The mother of a high school freshman happened to be driving by her daughter's school shortly after classes had ended for the day, a time when many youngsters "apparently like to loiter and watch the passing parade," as she put it. "And there was Jamie in a group of about six or seven kids, all hanging off a stone wall across from the school, all smoking cigarettes. I just stared. She didn't look like my own kid anymore." Her daughter has always been "a social animal," this mother said, "and she's been loving high school, joining lots of clubs." Jamie left the house before eight each morning and usually didn't return until early evening, but now her mother was wondering "if there's less constructive activity and more loitering going on than I thought. And it seems she's gone from being a little health nut—a kid who wouldn't let a fried anything pass her lips—to being a smoker."

Whether Jamie is at risk of becoming a dyed-in-the-wool cigarette addict remains to be seen. What is certain is that she's toying with behaviors that she believes proclaim her burgeoning independence. And "social animals," or the most socially competent and popular children, are sometimes the most eager to make that proclamation. Many youngsters who explore and *experiment*—with cigarettes, with beer, even with marijuana—are confident individuals who enjoy engaging in risk-taking. In particular, smoking frequently seems to a public display of bravado, an action that indicates, "I'm an adult now, and I can make up my own mind about this kind of thing—just watch me."

For many young people, the beginning of high school may be the most active period in this regard, and the peak of conformity to peer pressure as well—the time when they're feeling, or wishing to feel, less dependent on their parents, but not yet sufficiently self-assured to react relatively independently within the group. Many youngsters' displays of bravado are motivated by a strong desire to seem in sync with school norms, or conversant with the practices that appear to be accepted by and acceptable to older students. Research also tells us that a young teen may not yet be able to process information in a mature manner. According to recent studies by the National Institute of Mental Health and other research laboratories, the parts of the brain that influence emotional control—including the ability to inhibit behaviors—continue to develop through midadolescence.

Jamie's mother remembered an incident from her own days as a high school student: "Smoking was definitely the thing to do for a while, though of course never at home, and I'd keep my pack at the bottom of my book bag. One morning in school I was getting something out of my bag, and I found a note from my mother, taped to my pack. The note said, 'Since when did you start smoking?' And that evening and forever thereafter, nothing was ever spoken about this between us." She was embarrassed by the note and infuriated by the fact that her mother had gone through her bag, she said, "and also both relieved and somewhat disgusted that she never had the nerve or whatever to talk to me."

Teenagers as a rule react badly to parental sneak attacks or invasions of their property. Taking a different approach with her daughter, this mother decided to speak to her directly that same evening. She told Jamie she hoped she would lose her interest in smoking, because unquestionably it was a bad habit to start; then she asked her about the classmates she'd been with that afternoon. Jamie briefly described them to her mom, who was happy to hear that "actually they sounded like all-right kids." She felt she had made her thoughts known to her child, and also opened up a dialogue about her new friendships. Besides, she said, her own "cigarette phase ended during my first week in college, when someone casually remarked that my clothes smelled like smoke all the time, and so I stopped, just like that. Forget about the state of my lungs—the idea of having bad-smelling clothes was horrible." If peer pressure can make a kid start smoking, sometimes it can encourage him or her to quit, too!

Another child thought smoking wasn't a bright thing to do, but he liked being with a crowd of classmates who puffed away at every opportunity. There were two guys in particular, he told his mother, whom he really admired and would like to have as friends. His parent asked her son if socializing with these boys would put pressure on him to smoke as well. She recalled, "He said, well, he wasn't sure—probably not. So I asked him if he could talk to these boys about why they were smoking, what they were trying to prove, and he looked at me with an expression that clearly indicated, 'You have *got* to be kidding!'"

She opted to let the matter drop at that point, explaining, "My son is a sensible kid who's always had decent friends. And he and I have a good relationship. I felt it was wise for me to back off and let him make his own decisions right now about this new group." Trusting in her child's good judgment—and, by extension, in the way she'd raised him—was the best course for this mother. The associations that her son hoped to forge, too, might prove to be genuinely pleasurable and supportive.

Parents do well to remember that there's more to friendship than whether a child's friends smoke, wear black nail polish, or listen to what sounds to their elders like bizarre music. Some individual predilections, in other words, do not necessarily define the quality of a relationship, nor should they be automatic grounds for ruling out a potential friend for your child.

Partying, drugs, and alcohol . . . and how to say "don't"

Drinking is another concern that raises the hair on the back of many parents' necks. And obviously, that worry is well founded. Since alcohol alters both clarity of thought and emotional control, drinking can affect on-the-spot judgments in dangerous ways. And teens become intoxicated more quickly than adults.

Your teenager may suddenly have a social life that encourages him or her to be more independent than ever before, even as it brings him or her into contact with kids who drink. But declaring, "You can't go to that party if there's going to be alcohol" or "You can't associate with that crowd," or "If I find out you've had a beer, you're grounded for a month," amounts to delivering a lecture, and it probably won't get you the result you want. At the very least, most such ultimatums are difficult, if not outright impossible, to enforce. You'd be wiser to accept that your teen may very well be around peers who drink, and to give some thought to what you want to say about that and how you want to say it.

In an informal interview, several adolescents were asked how they would respond if their parents offered them a great deal of money not to drink until they were twenty-one. One boy said he'd agree to the deal, drink anyway if he felt like it, but do it on the sly, and then collect the money. Another believed that parents had the right and the duty to insist that their child not drink, and that if he or she disobeyed, the parents should do anything to stop him or her, including revocation of all privileges or humiliation in the presence of friends. A third teen thought it was a shabby tactic for a parent to try—essentially translating to blackmail—and said *he* would expect his mother and father just to tell him, "Don't drink."

The first two of these reactions are clearly suggestive of badly flawed parent-child relationships, connections characterized in the first instance by the child's lack of honesty and in the second by the parents' lack of respect. The teen who was scornful of the whole premise seemed to be on more solid ground. Implicit in his response was the insightful notion that any parents who would offer such a bribe in the first place must have scant confidence in their ability to influence their child's behavior by better means.

"Don't drink" *is* an appropriate message to impart to your adolescent, but it's one that needs to be conveyed in a reasonable manner.

⑥ PARENT SKILL: Engage in "what if?" talk with your teen.

Anticipate with your child, some of the pressures he or she might run into, and encourage him or her to consider how best to deal with them. The *distancing strategies* I outlined earlier—"What will happen if . . . ?" and "What are all the things you might do . . . ?"—can be just as useful with a partygoing adolescent as with a playdate-going second grader. Rather than letting your child find himself or herself clueless and unprepared in a tempting situation, help him or her to think things through a bit beforehand—guidance that might include providing important information.

One father, for example, recalled his own earliest experiences with alcohol: "Three guys and I had jobs cleaning trash off the beach in this town we lived in over the summers. One afternoon after work we all went back to one fellow's house; his parents were away for the weekend driving his sister around to visit colleges, and he decided we should all have gin and tonics. A couple of hours later, there were four kids with their heads hanging into the bathtub. I was sicker than I had ever been in my life, or in fact have ever been since. It occurred to me later that nobody had ever told me drinking could make you feel like that."

When his son began coming home with party invitations, this parent decided to bring up the subject of partying and drinking: "The gist of our talk was, 'You're going to be in social situations where somebody may say, "Come on, have a beer." And it may be very tough to say "No thanks" or "See you later." It's right for you not to go along, that's the wise course. And it's a measure of your strength as an individual that you can do that. However, if you feel under a great deal of pressure to do what other kids are doing, have just a sip, and don't drink anything else.' I explained to him that having a lot of beer or combining drinks can have disastrous consequences—you feel dizzy, nauseated, really quite sick. And getting to that state is a big mistake, because you're not in control of your actions at that point."

He had thought about whether he might be sending a mixed message with this advice, but in the end he decided that it was in fact "a *realistic* message that was also saying to my kid, 'I trust you to be smart,' which I do."

Significantly, there is some evidence that fathers are especially good at helping adolescents develop the strong sense of self that encourages independent thought and behavior, or the ability to hold on to their own ideas when pressured in another direction. There's an interesting history to this: In Western cultures, we know, fathers and mothers tend to interact with their children in different ways. When they spend relaxed time with their young children, for example, mothers are likely to get them to play with toys, read to them, or help them with art or crafts activities. Fathers, in contrast, are more likely to engage youngsters in physically challenging games or outdoor activities, and to be more boisterous and more freely joking and teasing. Furthermore, when they're with their children, they spend a greater *percentage* of that time in play than mothers do—in short, they're more "peerlike."

According to some researchers, the kinds of involvement that mothers and fathers have with their children continue to differ, in complementary ways, into adolescence. During this period, teenagers are working at becoming separate from their mom and dad, while at the same time staying connected to them—the developmental "tasks" of these years. It may be that fathers promote "separateness" by expressing trust through peerlike talk and exchange; they're more likely than mothers to convey the feeling that they can rely on their child—to say, in effect, "I trust you to be smart."

ⓖ **PARENT SKILL: If you disapprove of the kind of parenting that's going on in a friend's home, let your child know how you feel.**

Regrettably, peer pressure to go along with the crowd is sometimes compounded by an atmosphere of parental permissiveness in other children's homes. This is a fine line to walk, pointing out to your child what you consider to be inappropriate behavior on the part of other adults, while at the same time allowing her the freedom to make her own friendship choices. But in this situation, you're right to make your views known.

That's just what the mother of one sixteen-year-old did. Her son was involved with a group that threw weekend parties, she said, and he "thinks these kids are cool. He's thrilled to be one of them, because he's never been one of the cool crowd before! I've met some of them, and they certainly don't seem like bad kids at all, but the parties are something else." Picking up her son after one such event, she saw that a large van, with an adult driver, was on the premises, waiting to return the teens to their respective homes. "I talked to the father of the boy who was hosting the party, and his attitude was, 'It's good for the kids to be in a private home. They're going to have beer wherever they are, and we don't want them driving, so we've arranged for this transportation for them.'" She was appalled: "Of course, safety is paramount, but you should not convey the impression to kids that it's OK to drink as long as you don't drive."

She spoke to her son later and explained why that action on the part of his friend's parents was misguided: For starters, she said, it's illegal for underage children to drink, and any adult who condones the underage use of alcohol and has it available for teens to drink in his home is, in fact, subject to arrest. "And just as important," she added, "I wanted him to understand that those grown-ups were being really dumb, they were not cool at all. They were irresponsible—perhaps nice, but definitely stupid." She insisted that she or his dad would continue to drive him to and from these affairs, but she made it clear that they expected he would not drink while he was there.

Taking a realistic approach, acknowledging that your teen may encounter pressures to experiment—with alcohol or with "street" or "recreational" drugs—and supporting your objections to those behaviors with relevant information all make a great deal of sense. In the talk they had with their daughter after her experience with her friend Carrie's crowd, Erica's parents discussed the possible effects of drugs. "After the meeting with the eye doctor," said her mother, "I did some research of my own. And her dad and I brought up these issues in a factual, concrete, and vivid way—explaining that some drugs can affect your heart rate, for example, and some can cause convulsions. And that when drugs take effect, you may do things you would otherwise not choose to do under any circumstances in which you *were* in control. We wanted to let her know that since she is the one making many decisions about the people she's going to be with, she needs to have a clear picture of some very real fallout from those decisions."

Parent-initiated conversations like these really amount to a parent's being an authority figure in an appropriate, teen-oriented, and supportive manner—which is what every child has a right to expect from a parent. The message is, in so many words, "I cannot be, and don't want to be, your policeman or your conscience. Many of the choices you make about the individuals you spend time with are yours alone. But here is the kind of behavior I encourage you to display. Here's what I know about the consequences of other kinds of behavior. I realize that you may face difficult situations, and that it's not easy always to resist those pressures. And I want you to be safe, and I love you."

Moving at quick speed: the fast crowd

From middle school through the middle of high school, studies show, girls feel that their female friends, and boys feel that their male friends, are their strongest sources of peer support, as we have noted. With the development of opposite-sex friendships, however, the emphasis shifts; often a teen will indicate that his girlfriend or her boyfriend is just as important as, or more important than, close same-sex friends when it comes to his or her personal sense of well-being and happiness.

Some of these boy/girl pairings offer teens their first sexual experiences as well. In late adolescence, sexual activity may occur within a relatively secure relationship—a friendship based on emotional intimacy and trust—or it may not, depending on the maturity of the individuals involved. At younger ages, or within less strongly friendship-based and emotionally trusting relationships, sexual experiences are inevitably more troublesome. Such young people rarely possess the self-confidence or self-knowledge to cope with the complex feelings that often go along with sexual activity. Some children say "it just happened"; others feel pressured to *have* it happen, by the peer groups of which they are a part.

While reports indicate that sexual activity among high school students is generally on the decline, many children are evidently engaging in sexual encounters at even earlier ages. According to data from the Division of General Pediatrics and Adolescent Health at the University of Minnesota, 17 percent of respondents in a national survey of thousands of seventh and eighth graders said they had had intercourse. In a study conducted by the Centers for Disease Control, a greater percentage of ninth-grade than twelfth-grade boys and girls reported that they had had sex *before* the age of thirteen—suggesting that within that brief span of three years, there had developed a cultural climate that either permitted or encouraged a rise in sexual activity at younger ages.

This is a climate that many children may find confusing and upsetting during their school years. The mother of one sixth grader, for example, said that a number of her daughter's classmates "were already pairing off at the beginning of the year. After school, it was impossible to avoid seeing these boy-and-girl couples, in little groups, draped all over each other. The atmosphere created tension and unhappiness for the children, like Lexie, who weren't in a couple." But other parents weren't all of the same mind concerning the appropriateness of such displays, this mother discovered: "Some parents I've talked to are alarmed at the thought of eleven-year-olds' being involved in romantic relationships. And some others seem to think, Well, if this is what it takes for my kid to be in and doing what the crowd is doing, I'm not going to interfere."

Midway through that year, her daughter acquired a boyfriend and was drawn into the "in"-crowd, a small group of classmates who often spent a couple of hours together at one child's apartment after school. Lexie, said her mother, "was excited about this development, and also, I think, uncomfortable about it. I knew where she *was* in the afternoons, because she always called me at my office to tell me she was at this girl's apartment, and she was always home on time. But when I asked her what they did, she would seem tense. She said they just hung out and played music; sometimes they danced. I figured there was more to it."

She initiated another kind of conversation one evening by talking to her daughter about the boyfriend: "I said that Gil, whom we had met, seemed like a really nice boy; I liked his sense of humor, it seemed as if she really enjoyed being with him, and so on. And she started talking. Apparently several of the kids in this crowd are extremely precocious, there's some mutual masturbation going on, and Lexie doesn't know what to think about all that. Nor, I gather, does Gil." They went on, she said, "to have a pretty amazing mother-and-daughter conversation, about love, sex, friendships, relationships." Although she was spending time with a fast crowd, Lexie was not comfortable with the behaviors of some of its members, and her mother felt their talk strengthened her resolve to act in a way that felt right to *her.* In the weeks that followed, Lexie and her boyfriend drifted away from that group.

This mother's daughter, like the majority of children in our culture, had come by a good deal of knowledge about sex and reproduction in school. But parents need to understand what their children are and aren't learning in school, where instruction is guided mainly by state and local school board policies:

- Some schools, by law, must provide sex education, or information about anatomy and conception.

- Some schools, even in the absence of mandated sex-education courses, must provide information to students concerning sexually transmitted diseases and HIV and/or AIDS.

- Some schools must teach students about contraception; others must teach them that abstinence is the only sure way of preventing unplanned pregnancies and sexually transmitted diseases.

Most important, *all* such instruction, worthwhile though it may be, must be considered only the most elementary introduction to the complex issues that go along with sexual intimacy.

Ⓖ PARENT SKILL: Broach the subject of sex with your child, even if both of you find it uncomfortable.

Engaging an eleven- or twelve-year-old in conversations about friendships, romantic crushes, and peer pressure to become sexually active is a good idea. It's a good idea with teens, too. You may discover, to your surprise, that your seemingly confident, know-it-all adolescent is actually eager for some guidance—or wants to know what *you* really think.

Lexie's mother had a relatively easy time opening up a conversation with her teenager about "love, sex, friendships, relationships." Some children will bring up the topic themselves, but most won't—and many will find even the *notion* of talking about such matters with Mom or Dad acutely embarrassing. Parents may be equally uncomfortable; many of us, understandably, have our own inhibitions about discussing sexual activity with our children. Speaking frankly to a teenager is a far cry, after all, from sitting down with a five-year-old to page through a children's book about how babies are born.

But if your child has not come to you to air his or her own worries, pressures, or questions regarding sex, and especially if you sense that such issues are on your child's mind or in his or her life, *do* initiate a conversation. You may even want to start it off by acknowledging that it's difficult to talk about all this and that you feel somewhat awkward (if you do) about raising the subject. After that, you should probably cover at least the following basic points:

- Sexual needs and urges are normal and to be expected.

- Having sex with someone is an intimate act that involves emotions and feelings.

- It's imperative to be responsible for one's own body and safety, and also for one's partner's.

Your teen or preteen may also need your guidance in finding the right way to say no or otherwise resist a partner's pressure to have sex. Here you might tell your child, "You could say, 'I really like you, and I want to keep seeing you, but I'm not really comfortable with the idea of having sex, and I hope you'll understand.' If your relationship is a strong one, your friend should be able to accept your decision and not feel rejected."

Finally, your conversation might include an expression of your own thoughts and values. If, for example, you believe strongly that people should not have sexual relations before marriage, let your child know where you stand.

But remember, in all of this, that you can't force your adolescent or preadolescent to do what *you* think he or she should do, and that it's critical—to your relationship as well as to your child's growth and development—that you respect your child's judgment and ability to make good decisions for himself or herself.

ⓖ **PARENT SKILL:** As you encourage talk, convey information, and express opinions, always make it clear that you are there for your child.

Whether you're concerned about your child's smoking cigarettes or trying marijuana, having a few beers or becoming sexually active, or all of the above, keep in mind these general thoughts:

The kinds of conversations described above really amount to educating a child about risky or dangerous behaviors, in order to supply some of the wherewithal he or she needs in order to make intelligent choices with peers.

If you're aware that your adolescent has already experimented with risky behaviors, see it as an opportunity to have an open discussion with him or her. Saying nothing is not very competent parenting. At the other extreme, your reacting in an outraged or hand-wringing manner, as if a disaster had occurred, is most likely only to convince your child that in the future he or she should keep you in the dark about his or her activities, and that it isn't safe to approach you with difficult questions or real problems—a conviction that really *could* lead to disaster.

Your children need to believe that first and foremost, you will be there to help them if they do find themselves in trouble. You want your son or daughter to trust you and your relationship enough that he or she can call you from a party and say, "Please come and pick me up, I can't get home on my own," or confide in you about a possible pregnancy. Any young person will feel more secure if the parent finds a way to say, "You know you can always come to me if there's a problem. I'll help you. We'll work it out together." No adolescent should ever have to feel compelled to turn elsewhere for help or advice—or worse, feel there is *nowhere* to turn—because "my parents will kill me if they find out."

Collective rudeness

Teenagers, as any parent knows, often like to present a general appearance that's difficult for adults to accept. The mother mentioned in an earlier chapter who talked about her daughter and her friends—the kids in head-to-toe black, with the preference for lurid makeup, body piercings, and leather neck bands with metal spikes—knew what these young people were really like, because she was often around to hear what they had to say and observe how they spent their time together. "But I could without a lot of difficulty imagine them walking down the street in a little pack," she conceded, "and old ladies crossing to the other side!"

During some years, when the pack mentality is strong and their son or daughter, perhaps, thinks looking "bad" is the height of cool, parents must tread this territory with care and work very diligently at viewing those aspects of their child's life from the child's own perspective. It takes *very little* to shake a young person's sense of felt security: Make a disparaging comment to your sixteen-year-old son in front of his friends, for example—"That tattoo on your shoulder makes you look like a thug; five years from now you'll regret getting it"—and he'll feel angry and embarrassed. Exert psychological control over your thirteen-year-old daughter—"Why are you hanging around with those losers? You can do better than those kids"—and *she'll* feel angry and unsupported.

Parents really do need to be cognizant of the fact that their child will interpret their behavior or remarks in a way that will be *either* comforting *or* distancing. And distance, once created, takes a great deal of time and effort to repair. Nevertheless, there are certain lines that must be drawn in the sand, and expectations that need to be made clear. These might involve bad language, "back talk," or bad manners.

When her son entered junior high, said one mother, he fell in with a crowd that seemed to her to embrace below-par standards in terms of civilized behavior—"and Craig sank right down to their level." She felt that her child's friends were not properly respectful of boundaries, for one thing: "One boy would come in, give me kind of a slap on the back, and say, 'Hey, what's up?'—which is not the way to act with an adult. Also, they always looked disheveled, and proud of it, and Craig picked up that look right away. They just came across as kind of crude kids who were trying to get a rise out of the grown-ups." One Saturday afternoon, some neighbors were visiting when Craig and his friends walked in after attending a sports event. Craig's mother recalled, "They came into the living room, grunted in acknowledgement of these people, grabbed up handfuls of nuts I had put out for my company, and disappeared into Craig's room."

After everyone had gone home, she spoke to her son about his friends and their actions. "He accused me of being overly concerned with appearances and with what other people think. And he said he really liked these boys—they were friends," she said, "and they were 'good guys.' And maybe they were, for all I know. It's hard to tell."

This last was an accurate perception on her part: It *is* difficult for a parent to take the true measure of a child's friends, or to know—in the absence of clear-cut evidence of real mischief—whether they are genuinely nasty or not. Generally speaking, however, adolescents who fail to display decent social skills in the company of adults are more likely to get into trouble, and less likely to be merely "going through a phase," than teens who act appropriately.

Ⓖ **PARENT SKILL: If your child has taken up with friends whom you find rude, crude, or obnoxious, let your child know what you expect.**

That might mean making it clear that your child's manners also leave something to be desired. Craig's mother, for example, might have told her son, "Yes, I do have some concerns about how our neighbors and friends perceive our family. I believe it's right and courteous to act in a way that makes other people comfortable. That means being polite, looking at people, saying hello, and recognizing what others may find annoying or offensive. I'd like you to think about that.

"About your friends—it's true, I don't know them the way you do. And I have to say, I don't think they'll ever be favorites of mine. But I trust your judgment about them and your good instincts about people, and I respect your feelings about wanting to be their friend."

Letting your child know where you stand might also involve saying something like, "I really don't like the kind of language I hear you and your friends using with one another. And I think people who don't know you are going to think less of you if you talk that way."

Not liking a child's friends is one thing; believing that a child is being used or taken advantage of, or coming to understand that the crowd she has cast in her lot with is doing unacceptable things, is something else entirely. Again, taking the hard line—"Stay away from those kids, you're ruining your life"—will almost guarantee that you'll lose the battle, along with any possibility of holding your child's attention. What's critical here is that you engage in the *kind* of conversation your youngster will understand. A sympathetic approach might be to say, "This is what I've observed. I'm not very comfortable about these friendships; I understand that you feel differently, but I want you to know my feelings, and please be careful." Or, "This is why I'm concerned; this is what I've heard," and then maybe, "You can alleviate a lot of difficulties for yourself if you change the way you behave, and that probably means spending less time with those people. I can't tell you whom you can or can't spend time with, but I want you to think about what you're doing, think about the possible consequences, and think about alternatives for yourself."

That kind of discussion can have a particularly powerful effect on a child up through the years of middle school (fifth and sixth grades, when kids are between the ages of ten and twelve). Beyond that—in the junior and senior high school years—the dialogue becomes more difficult.

Crossing the line: when a child is slipping away

Her usually chatty son, said Thomas's mother, "turned overnight into what I thought was a typical teen who didn't want to talk to us." He returned home later and later after school each day; in response to her questions about where he went and what he did during those long afternoons, he replied, "I just hang around after school." When she asked him anything at all, in fact, he usually said "I dunno" or, "Nothin'."

His mother and father no longer heard about or saw the two children who had been Thomas's closest friends the previous year. In addition, they became aware that their son, who had always been a good student, wasn't spending much time doing schoolwork; his midyear grades were surprisingly mediocre. "But even with all that," said his mother, "I thought he was just going through a rebellious, growing-up phase." One evening, a neighbor called with disturbing news: That afternoon, she had seen Thomas with a group of about a dozen boys in a public park miles away from either his home or his school, drinking beer, being noisy, and tossing pebbles at passing cars. Two of the boys had jumped onto the rear bumper of a bus as it pulled away from a stop.

Thomas maintained his customary stony silence when his parents questioned him about all of this. Two days later came an even more alarming phone call. Returning home in the early afternoon, his mother found a message on the answering machine: "This is Sergeant Rollins at the Tenth Precinct. Please call regarding your son." She made the call, rushed to the station, and found Thomas sitting there with three boys—"all looking blasé," she said, "eating chips and drinking soda, as if nothing out of the ordinary were going on." She learned that the four had been spotted by a patrol car in a city park, apparently selling marijuana to two other children, who had run off.

Said Thomas's mother, "The officer was nice. I think the idea was to give these kids a shaking up. By the time we left, none of the parents of the other boys had shown up. And I had no idea who those kids were." Over the next couple of days, Thomas's parents took some steps to mop up after the incident. His father called the school, which wanted an explanation for his disappearance that afternoon, and then he checked with the police department to ascertain whether his son would have "a record." Thomas himself, meanwhile, appeared unconcerned and continued roaming about with his friends.

As time went on, the boy's parents began to argue over the best approach to take regarding their child's behavior. Thomas's father increasingly adopted what his wife called a "head-in-the-sand, this-too-shall-pass" attitude, while she herself became both more genuinely frightened for her son and more tentative about her own actions. Insisting on a curfew simply didn't work, she said, and so she bent her efforts instead to "just making sure he was home at night. I told him he could have his friends stay over if he wanted. There are bunk beds in his room, and the problem was that I never knew who was in there. I met one of these boys one night and asked him if he'd called home to let his parents know where he was, and he said he didn't have to."

This mother felt as if she were holding on to her son by a very slender thread: "I was just keeping things together at that point, so he wouldn't slip away entirely—or run away, or do something crazy. We had to hang on until we could figure out what to do, or understand why this was going on."

We know a great deal about kids like Thomas, who are on troubled paths. In many respects, there isn't much mystery about them: Researchers consistently point to the parenting patterns and styles I described earlier as *neglectful, permissive,* and *authoritarian:*

- Disengaged parents who are focused primarily on their own needs; permissive ("Do what you want") parents who maintain an anything-goes attitude about a child's behavior; hard-line ("Do what I say") parents who react angrily to a child's perceived transgressions and who inappropriately demand compliance with adult-centered goals—all are inadequately, insensitively, or inconsistently responsive to the needs and the nature of their child. And that is the child who is most likely to be vulnerable to "bad influences," or to become a bad influence himself or herself.

- Adolescents with harsh, uninvolved, or neglectful parents are far likelier than average teens to drink to excess, to hang out in public places with a "wrong crowd," to cut school, and to be arrested.

- Teens and preteens whose parents do not monitor their whereabouts during the evening hours and do not know their children's friends are far likelier than others to have unstable, problematic peer relationships.

- *But importantly:* Not every child who suddenly takes up with a wild crowd can be understood from this perspective.

Thomas would seem to fall into this last category, as the son of caring, involved parents who by and large, did right by him.

This mother and father believed in the importance of education, attended school conferences and teacher meetings, and offered their son support as needed. Equally certain that their child's friends were a significant part of his life and development, they throughout the years welcomed other children into their home and were happy to witness those connections. Describing the child who seemed to have changed so dramatically, Thomas's mother spoke sadly: "He always loved math. Once, when he was in, I think, fourth grade, his teacher gave him an A-plus-plus for the year, and he said to me, 'I'm a kid with perfect math in his head!' He was actually tutoring two of his classmates, and was very proud of himself."

At the same time, Thomas was always a child "with a defiant streak, a willful kid," she said. "He didn't like going along with the rules in school, for example, as teachers were always telling me—just simple things like lining up, raising your hand. He got annoyed easily. Also, I think other people found him annoying sometimes, or at least hard to take. Once the father of one of his friends remarked that I had a little Roman candle of a son, always shooting off sparks."

When he was younger, Thomas had needed a lot of structure to his days, in order to help regulate his behavior. He had required "containment," his mother said. But containment no longer worked.

Thomas might be a temperamentally uninhibited and easily upset child, a boy who had difficulty controlling his emotions during early childhood and refused to conform to rules and regulations. Despite being intelligent, considered a leader, and willing to help others, he may gradually have fallen out with most of his peers because of his more unruly behaviors. Perhaps he suffered from a mild learning disability, or displayed the impulsivity that sometimes accompanies an attention-deficit disorder. There may be any number of reasons for peer rejection, with a simultaneous need to find solace and comfort with agemates.

By the time he reached early high school, when he could come and go relatively independently and range farther afield, Thomas had aligned himself with a group of boys who had never had much in the way of parental rules, expectations, and structure in their lives. He found in the company of that uncontained crowd a degree of freedom that enthralled him: These kids could do what they wanted, which he saw as the measure of success.

Pulling back a child who is "slipping away" is no easy task. Certainly, it was greatly in this family's favor that Thomas had had the benefit of reasonably responsive parenting all along, and that his defiant streak crossed the line into genuinely unacceptable activities only in early adolescence. Indeed, his father may not have been entirely off the mark in thinking that his son's behaviors marked a passing phase. We know from self-reports that the *majority* of teenage boys, and many girls, have engaged in some kind of criminal behavior—which, of course, includes underage drinking, but which may also involve setting fires, theft, vandalism, and other more serious activities. In that sense, being "a little delinquent," say some professionals, is almost par for the course for a teen.

This is not to suggest that a head-in-the-sand approach is the correct reaction—or, in fact, anything but misguided. Feeling ineffectual or even powerless to influence an almost-young-adult who's associating with a bad crowd, parents may be tempted to throw up their hands or throw in the towel, become detached or laissez-faire—just when their teen most needs their support and guidance. Giving up, or saying "There's nothing more I can do," is far different from making a conscious decision to stand back, watch and wait, and keep open the lines of communication—often the wisest and most sensitive line for a parent to take when he is concerned about some aspect of his child's behavior.

Thomas's parents did eventually "figure out what to do," after consulting with their son's guidance counselor in school and with a psychologist who suggested some workable ways for them to establish clearer limits and closer monitoring. Thomas drifted back to his former friends, and the family was able to resume the happier relationship they had once enjoyed.

⑥ PARENT SKILL: Make it clear that you expect a change in behavior.

Any parent whose child seems to be headed for trouble should first and above all reinforce a relationship of trust and caring. That means saying, in so many words, "I'm here for you; I will help you; I will not give up on you, no matter what happens."

Beyond that, psychologists who counsel young teens and their families often prescribe a number of potentially useful steps for parents to take, beginning with reasoned and reasonable parent-child discussions and progressing to specific parent-imposed consequences. They also describe some actions that parents should *avoid* taking. For example:

- Choose a time to engage your child in talk about his friends and their activities. Do *not* do it at a moment when everyone's emotions are running high and the air is filled with accusations and hostility.

- Do *not* confront your youngster in the midst of a social situation or when she is with friends—public confrontation will do far more harm than good.

- Discuss very specifically the behaviors that must be changed, and provide reasonable and logical explanations of why it makes sense for your child to change them.

- Do *not* get drawn into an argument about any of this.

- Explain what will happen if your child continues with the activities that got him into trouble, or that are causing you and your spouse warranted concern. The consequences may include loss of privileges; restricted access to the car, the phone, and/or the TV; or grounding.

The specifics of these steps—*what* is said, *how* it's said, how it's received, and what should happen next—will have much to do with the interpersonal histories and relationships of the particular parents and child. If a child clearly *knows* right from wrong; if her inappropriate, unacceptable, or even illegal behaviors are happening only in the company of certain friends outside of school; and if she has enjoyed good friendships in the past, then almost surely there will be a reservoir of parent-child trust and respect that can be drawn on now. For example, parents who typically have not imposed a great many rules, such as hard-and-fast curfews, because they've never been necessary, may need only to invest in such rules, and perhaps only temporarily. In other words, let your child understand: "If you're doing well, we'll relax; that'll mean to us that you don't need a lot of structure from us. But if you're not doing well, or if you're behaving in a way that we think is dangerous, we'll tighten up. Then you *will* need rules and structure from us, and we'll provide them." In a way, this goes back to the issue of *self-regulation:* If a child can't adequately self-regulate, then she needs some help from an external source.

⑥ PARENT SKILL: Consider seeking professional help.

Some children need more than parental guidance and advice. When a child is highly oppositional, sees nothing wrong with the kids he is hanging out with, or is uninterested in or apparently bored by reasonable and logical input from his parents, there's everything to be said for those parents' seeking the help of a trained professional. Fairly quickly, this individual should be able to take the pulse of the family, "read" the way the parents and child communicate, and suggest workable strategies tailored to the particulars of the situation.

Many if not most preteens, teens, and even younger children will be highly resistant to the idea of seeing a therapist. If matters have reached the point where you feel that your efforts to influence your child's behaviors are having little effect, and you believe he or she (and you) might benefit from outside help, by all means set something up—just don't expect your child to respond with enthusiasm, or even willingness. Psychologists and others who work with troubled children have some useful tips and encouraging observations to offer on this score:

- First, tell your child in no uncertain terms that a visit to a counselor is going to take place.

  This might mean saying, "I think we need to talk to somebody about what's been happening lately, so I've made an appointment for us with a counselor tomorrow at four-thirty. I'll meet you after school so we can go see this person together." Such an action has an important subtext, which your child cannot fail to appreciate. It states, in effect: "I am your parent, I'm responsible for you, and sometimes I must decide what's best for you. We've talked about the behaviors that are unacceptable; they must change, but so far I haven't seen any improvement. Now we're going to figure out what to do next." You're saying, really, that the dialogue (or the battle) is moving to a new plane, because things have gotten *that* serious. *In itself,* according to psychologists who work with oppositional children, that message—a wake-up call—can begin to move a child onto a better track.

- Simply getting your child to a therapist is a big step. If she can't stand the idea of therapy, it may be necessary to continue the "I'll meet you after school and take you there" arrangement for a while. If your child still persists in digging in her heels about going, you may need to take your insistence to a higher level: Explain—again, in a reasonable way—why such a step is necessary and in everyone's best interests; then make it understood that if your teen refuses to comply, you will need to restrict her access to certain privileges and perks, such as having the freedom to see friends on weekends, the use of the car, or watching TV.

  Typically, after an initial session involving both parent(s) and child, the therapist and the child will work alone together. And the therapist may at first hear from your youngster more of the "I dunno" and "Nothin'" responses to which you yourself have become so accustomed. But trained therapists and child psychologists (your child's school counselor or pediatrician will probably be able to refer you to a good one) are skilled at developing over time the kind of relationship that leads to truly productive therapy, and to changes for the better.

- If your child absolutely refuses to see a therapist, no matter what carrot or what stick you brandish, make an appointment for yourself and talk over with this professional the circumstances that have brought the family to this impasse. You will, at the very least, learn more about how you or your spouse may be contributing to the problem. And you may also pick up some pointers on how to help your child become more comfortable about the possibility of therapy.

The outcasts

Is my child keeping company with a group of kids who are deeply alienated from the general peer culture? Are they united in a distorted friendship by perceptions of ostracism and rejection? And could they be propelled by feelings of anger, hatred, or a wish for revenge to strike out against their more popular peers?

Such questions strike fear into the hearts of parents who know that their children feel like outsiders at school, either because they're the constant target of jokes, rumors, and teasing or because they're associated with a fringe group that's not in sync with the norms of the school (the geeks, the freaks, the nonconformists). Rejected-victimized children do sometimes end up in small groups with other victims. For the child who is persistently teased by others, who is excluded in a public way, life both in and out of school can become truly hateful. He or she may indeed harbor deep anger toward those who have acted as bullies, or, for that matter, toward those who seem to be "better off" for whatever reason. Given that it is human nature to seek support from others, the rejected-victimized child may find peers who share his or her alienation, disaffection, and often legitimate feelings of hostility.

This youngster may believe that everything that is visited upon her—particularly the dismissal or ridicule of most peers—is intentional, mean-spirited, and deserving of retaliation. In the company of other outcasts, she may begin thinking of ways to strike back at those who have either directly or indirectly made her life so unhappy. Alternatively, she may hope that through a demonstration of perverse power, she will gain the attention or respect of those who have previously rejected her.

What parent could fail to be horrified by the terrible media images of distraught teenagers reeling in the wake of murderous acts committed by their schoolmates? And then there are the headlines: Suddenly we're reading about the "secret lives" of our children; the cover of a national magazine announces, "At schools, in clubs, and on the Internet, a new world is being born. And it's scariest for those who don't yet understand: parents." The message conveyed is that something quite unfathomable is going on in that "new world" that all of our children live in. We're learning about newly instituted zero-tolerance policies in schools, as a news program reports that a group of five- and six-year-old boys who were running around the schoolyard playing cops and robbers, pointing their gun-fingers at each other while making "Ka-POW" sounds, has been suspended for several days. (At the same time, interestingly, many teachers tell us that sociodramatic fun or cooperative pretense is, in fact, just the kind of play they would most like to expect among youngsters of that age. So even though cooperative dramatic play is viewed as cognitively the most mature form of play behavior for young children, some kids are being harshly disciplined for behaving in precisely that manner!)

Pretend violence aside, the singular, appalling type of act directed against peers by one child or a small group of children can be motivated by a number of factors, none terribly well understood. The provocateurs in these instances may themselves have been provoked and victimized—or at least have *felt* provoked and victimized—by those they then actively targeted. The pictures the experts paint of the "causes" of such uncontrolled acts of violence are numerous and varied, ranging from a child's inability to regulate or control emotions, to problems related to neglectful parenting; from behavioral responses to being victimized and rejected by peers, to overly nurturing and forgiving parenting; from the child's thinking that *others* are responsible for all things unpleasant that befall him, to abusive, authoritarian parenting; and from assumptions that such behaviors are the product of inappropriate socialization experiences in the home, peer group, or school, to notions that they are biologically determined and emanate from the family gene pool (the "bad seed" thesis).

In many respects, "all of the above" may ring true to a greater or lesser degree—and not only for teens who plan the abuse or even the murder of their schoolmates, but also for children who go to great lengths to cope with life in the fast lane of peer networks, cliques, and gangs. Life in that fast lane, it should be noted, does not always result in violence directed against others; the result may just as likely be self-degradation and -abuse.

In the widespread search for an explanation for those violent outbursts and killings in schools, the one thing that has become clearest is that such events share no single common cause. Nor is there any one personal characteristic or trait or aspect of personal history that can be identified as a central factor in such behavior. We cannot point to peer rejection, a lack of friends, a certain home environment, or a love of Doom and Quake video games as "the reason" for such actions.

We do know that scattershot violence *almost* always ties in to a history of parental abuse. Harsh, demeaning, critical, or violent behavior toward a child may launch him or her on a developmental trajectory of hatred, distrust, insecurity, inability to develop and maintain relationships, and both felt and actual rejection. But parental neglect and its accompanying lack of appropriate attention—a condition marked by psychological absence and abandonment of parenting responsibilities—may also set a youngster off on such a path.

Case histories of children who have taken part in violent activities yield developmental tales that are long and complicated. If there is one conclusion that can be drawn from the intensive, after-the-fact examination of kids who go off the rails, it is this: Intense feelings of angst and anger do not develop overnight. The notion of the child who is acutely sensitive to peer rejection, who one day—out of the blue—reaches a breaking point and "snaps," may be something of a myth. Breaking points, which have to do with emotional reactions and regulation, may be identifiable phenomena, but invariably, long before a child acts in either outwardly or inwardly destructive or distressed ways, he or she will have displayed serious disaffection, alienation, or anger. And no child should have to reach that point of no return.

Unfortunately, in what some observers regard as an overreaction to the behaviors of the minuscule percentage of children who have committed violent acts, large numbers of fairly normal kids who nevertheless act differently than the larger group have been and continue to be singled out by

school personnel, and peers, as suspicious characters. Adolescents themselves are often keenly, ruefully aware that they're under this microscope:
In one interview, a high school student said that he was sitting off by himself one day, minding his own business and pondering nothing in particular,
when a friend walked over and joked, "Uh-oh, you're showing warning
signs."

In truth, there *are* warning signs. But they have little to do with
whether a teen sits by himself once in a while, or shows a preference for
dark clothes, sullen looks, gothic muses, or cliques that share his inclinations. There may be real cause for concern if your adolescent:

- Says he or she doesn't like, or in fact hates, himself or herself.

- Appears generally dissatisfied with life, or depressed.

- Says all the kids at school hate him or her, and in turn indicates that he
  or she hates them.

- Doesn't want to go to school; fails to complete homework assignments;
  dislikes the teachers and school staff.

- Isn't eating or sleeping properly.

- Shows sudden and puzzling changes in behavior, becoming more hostile, irritable, or disrespectful and distrusting.

- Makes or receives furtive phone calls.

- Is more than typically secretive about his or her room.

These are signs that parents—the people who see a child most over
time and across situations, the people who know what's normal and what's
odd behavior for him or her—can recognize, and heed as a signal that they
need to become involved in appropriate ways. That might mean arranging
for their son or daughter to get professional counseling or to pay a visit to
a favorite aunt or uncle, clearing the schedule for more parent-child time
together, or signing their teen up for new or added out-of-school, structured activities. It might also mean talking over with a child the possibility of his or her transferring to another school.

The basic point here is this: Any sensitive parent who is truly tuned in to his or her child, who is aware of the routines and rhythms of the child's day, familiar with the child's likes and dislikes, acquainted with possessions and friends—in short, any parent who knows what his or her youngster is all about—will not find it at all difficult to detect when that child needs help, or when his or her life is not what it should be.

⑥ PARENT SKILL: If your parent-child relationship has been less than ideal, begin now to establish a connection of greater trust, respect, and communication.

Especially during the preteen and teen years, when children develop strong allegiances to their peer group, the parent who has *not* consistently, over time, interacted with his or her child in an authoritative manner—being sensitive to his or her needs and feelings, being appropriately in control, in an appropriately warm way—may feel ineffectual. Children are often suspicious of parents who suddenly show a heightened interest in what they're up to and whom they're friends with, particularly if those same parents have previously been somewhat emotionally absent, or have tended to operate in a more *authoritarian,* or "Do what I say," fashion. If you're concerned about bad influences and wrong crowds or worried that your child may be slowly drifting away, or if you simply want to convey your thoughts about some of the issues discussed in this chapter, but you suspect you're the *last* person your child wants to hear from, you can build your way gradually toward better communication.

• Talk more with your child.
    But make it casual talk. Avoid asking out-of-the-blue questions about "big" issues of direct relevance to his life, such as "So, who are you hanging around with these days?" Talking can be relatively stress-free if you bring up a movie your child has just seen, or ask for help figuring out how to program the VCR, or describe something amusing or annoying that happened to you that day.

• Demonstrate interest in what she is doing.
    To demonstrate interest, you must genuinely *be* interested, because preadolescents and teens can spot pretense in an instant. Ask questions; make few judgments.

- Take an interest in his friends.

  Try to meet as many of them as you can; ask your child what they like to do and where they live. Encourage your son or daughter to invite friends over. If they're old enough to drive, ask if everyone could stop in briefly to say hello the next time they're all going somewhere together.

- If possible, get to know—or at least meet—the parents of her friends.

- Avoid making harsh or judgmental observations about your child's friends.

  If your youngster is telling you a long-winded, affectionate story about a friend (a child you know to be a decent kid who's not in trouble), and you make a mildly negative comment about that person's behavior—something along the lines of "Well, it sounds to me like she was just trying to act cool"—it will be a long time before you hear another long-winded story about a friend. And you *should* hear those stories.

- If your son or daughter asks you a question that makes your ears twitch in curiosity, just answer the question.

  Your instinct, of course, will be to jump in with your own question in an effort to find out what's going on. If your daughter asks, for example, "Did you ever have a really bad crush on someone?," don't reply, "Uh, sure . . . why? Do *you* have a really bad crush on someone?" Just tell her a story about the classmate you were crazy about in high school, and let it go at that. You'll have a better chance of getting the information you want to know—and it may be something you *should* know—an hour later, or the next day, if you don't pounce.

  Once you've put these principles into practice and established a stronger foundation of trust, respect, and communication, once you've demonstrated that you can and truly will hear what your child has to say, then you can be honest with him. *Then* you can say, "I'm concerned about something that's going on with you and your friends. I want to hear your thoughts about this, and I want to tell you what's worrying me."

Figuring out whether your child is in safe company calls for common sense, perhaps a measure of humor, and, especially, the ability to gather information and pay attention. You will want to view the "bad influences" and worrisome behaviors both with adult wisdom and from a child's perspective, and to make good judgment calls on the extent to which you should become involved. It may help, as well, to keep in mind that you, too, were once an adolescent, and maybe even caused your *own* parents their fair share of worry about sex, drugs, and rock 'n' roll. And you (and they) actually survived to see a better day, didn't you?

Chapter 12

Real-Life Parenting

When Family Problems Enter a Child's Social World

Here's a "Fantasyland" scenario of parenthood: A well-adjusted, optimistic adult sees the world as a most pleasant and knowable place. This individual loves being a parent. His or her child enjoys good health, is of "easy" temperament and reasonably bright, and gets along well with others. The parent, too, experiences limited stress—with no big money problems, a solid marriage or partner relationship, and good friends.

Real life, of course, often falls some distance short of that ideal.

When stressful life forces enter the picture (through the loss of a job, tension in the marriage, illness), a parent's psychological well-being—which, of course, promotes the "tuned-in-ness" that makes him sensitive to his child's nature and needs—can be strained to the breaking point. Adult concerns take over; a mother's or father's feelings of anxiety, anger, or depression can become pervasive. One or both parents may be very much exhausted, preoccupied, or distracted by their problems.

A monkey wrench thus gets tossed into what may have been, if not a perfectly smooth family life, then at least a reasonably predictable one. The grown-ups may behave in alarming ways as their emotions run higher, and the child may not be attended to very well amid all the turbulence. At such times, *even a previously well-adjusted child* of any age can get off track and begin to run into difficulties in her peer relationships. Such changes may not be pervasive or all-encompassing, but they do happen, and they do make life difficult for children.

In this chapter, we will consider what happens to children in terms of their social behaviors when their parents are under pressure—and what sorts of parental behaviors, in turn, can help a child weather a family storm with greater ease.

Experiencing the tough times

Twenty-year-old Amanda, a college junior, said life was pretty serene in her family at the moment, though that had not always been the case: "A couple of years were difficult, when my younger brother got sick with acute nephritis, and another time when my dad lost his job. My brother had a lot of complications, and he had to be home a lot. Then, when my dad was out of work for months, we had to cut back on a lot of things. Then it looked like we might have to move to another state at one point, because he had an offer there." Her parents, she said, "talked to us about what was happening. My other brother and I were expected to help Kenny, my kid brother, so he could study at home and keep up with his class. I'm embarrassed to admit this, but the possibility of moving away seemed worse to me than my brother's being sick. That was my first year of high school, and I had my friends. My parents, my brothers, and I had some discussions about all this. My father said we had to circle the wagons so we could figure out what we needed to do, how to cut back on expenses and all. I ended up feeling all right about the move, which turned out not to be necessary because my father found another job."

Looking back from the perspective of a young adult, Amanda felt that her parents had been "pretty cool. They were stressed out, that was obvious, but we weren't really worried. And they were sympathetic to me, but not *too* sympathetic. Basically, they sort of let me know I was going to survive, whatever happened, and it would be better if I didn't moan and groan so much. It actually was a good learning experience."

Many families confront such upheavals. Occupational stress, in particular, has the potential to permeate the household atmosphere; much research, in fact, has focused on the associations between "parents as workers" and "parents as parents."

In the broadest sense, parents who are happily and well employed experience happier interactions with their children and enjoy the kind of parent-child relationship that promotes a youngster's social competence. Mothers who like their jobs and who want to be working, for example, tend to be more *authoritative* in their parenting styles; mothers who dislike their jobs or would rather not be working at all are likely to exhibit a more *authoritarian* style. Fathers who sense that they're valued for their autonomy at work often value and encourage exploration and independence in their children, and are able to respond to a youngster's unacceptable behaviors with reasoning and appropriate consequences. When men lose their jobs, however, they're apt to become irritable and prone to angry explosions at home. Unemployed fathers may spend more time with their children, but research shows that they're less warm and nurturing than before. Women who experience job loss are more likely to become tense and depressed, or psychologically unavailable to their children.

All of those qualities that lie at the heart of effective parenting, in other words, can be diminished or skewed by completely separate developments in adult lives.

During periods of stress, parents really can ease a child's anxiety—and help him or her understand why Mom and Dad may be acting in certain out-of-the-ordinary ways—simply by being honest and making it clear, at the same time, that they're capable of dealing with the adversities that are upsetting the family.

⑥ PARENT SKILL: **Acknowledge that the family is going through a difficult time.**

Children are almost always keenly aware of underlying tensions. Pretending that nothing is amiss, or not telling a child anything in the belief that it's better to shield him or her from adult worries, generally isn't a wise course; in fact, in the absence of evidence to the contrary, young children are apt to blame *themselves* for the air of gloom that has settled over the household. At the other extreme, burdening a child with an excess of detail and information is no less unlikely to promote a sense of felt security.

Amanda's mother and father, it would seem, made it through their tough times in ways that enabled their children to feel both clued in and protected. When parents are sensitive enough to understand that kids *know* something's wrong and probably have fears and worries about it, they can acknowledge that they're going through a difficult time and still convey a sense of confidence and being in charge—which is exactly the feeling children want to get from the adults who are responsible for them.

The state of the marriage, the quality of the parenting

One of the most powerful positive influences on any family is a united parental front, a bond of mutual trust, respect, and affection between two adults. When parents *can't* pull together, when they're actively in opposition or at each other's throat, everyone suffers.

Many researchers believe that in the middle-class, two-parent family, the state of the marriage is *the* most critical influence on the quality of parenting. Marital conflict—when it's persistent and ongoing, and *especially* when it's characterized by a great deal of hostility and/or outbursts of violent behavior—may indeed affect a child's adjustment to and behavior in his or her peer world.

According to much research, a turbulent and unhappy husband-wife relationship can have a spillover effect, both because it colors the general atmosphere of the home in unpleasant ways and because it may severely impair parenting. Here's what we've learned:

- Negative, hostile feelings between parents are felt by everyone in the family. Even when fighting or arguing is not actually occurring, the air remains heavy with tension.

- Angry partners, distracted by their own animosities and preoccupations, are simply not as emotionally open and sensitive to a child's needs.

- Even if parents consciously attempt to shield a child from their marital discord—by not arguing in front of her, for example—parent-child interactions are likely to be strained and less than competent.

- A mother who in less stressful times might be a reasonably sensitive parent may turn snappish and demanding; she may feel desperate to get the kids to bed, for example, just so the day will finally be over. In such times of partner stress, the child of "difficult" temperament—the boy or girl who has always needed an extra measure of understanding, support, and soothing—may be treated with less patience than before.

- Discipline becomes both harsher and more inconsistent.

  Parents may have trouble marshaling the energy or the determination to influence their child through distancing strategies; they're less likely to have discussions with him about the possible consequences of undesirable behaviors, for example, or to encourage perspective-taking. Instead, they're more apt to resort to high-power and directive strategies, or to punishment, to "get the job done."

- Men in particular seem to be more effective parents when they're happier spouses.

  Studies show that when their marriage is strong and mutually supportive, fathers are more fully and more positively involved with their children than when they feel estranged from, angry at, or rejected by their spouse. If their relationship begins to crumble, or if both parents are engaging in a great deal of hostility, fathers—more so than mothers—have angrier and more intrusive interactions with their children. They're less playful, less involved in caregiving, and less satisfied with their role as parents.

- When they're under stress, parents tend to monitor less diligently, paying less attention to where their children are going and what they're doing.

- One or both parents—but most likely Mom—may become depressed.

  Depressed mothers, in turn, are apt to be unresponsive and distant; they're simply unable to be very emotionally involved with their children. Then, too, a depressed parent, perhaps in an effort to gain some say over what she perceives to be a life spinning out of control, may become intrusively controlling in her child-rearing practices. And that combination—too little sensitivity and too much interference—is one that, as we've seen, bodes ill for a youngster's social and emotional well-being.

- When a parent is depressed, he may find it difficult to "read" his child accurately.

Our own studies have consistently demonstrated that the parent who's looking at life through dark-colored glasses—the father or mother who feels hopeless or helpless—may have a distorted impression of his or her child's behavior. When we ask mothers to complete rating scales for their children—indicating how well they get along with other kids, for example, or whether they tend to be more aggressive, oppositional, and defiant or more tentative and fearful—some reveal by their answers that they believe their children are not doing well at all. And yet the child's world of peers and teachers, as well as objective observers, may rate these same children as perfectly *normal*—kids who by all appearances and most measures are fitting into their social and school milieus in an expected and acceptable manner. Still other moms indicate that their children are fine, with no problems—again contradicting peer and teacher ratings and reports by objective observers, which suggest that *these* youngsters are having all sorts of difficulties in their social interactions and relationships.

Parental perceptions matter enormously, in that they directly influence how a father or mother reacts to a child's behavior. Whether it's skewed toward the negative or toward the positive, an *inaccurate* picture is never a good thing. In the former scenario, a parent's too-bleak assessment may become a self-fulfilling prophecy, encouraging a child to behave more poorly than he or she normally would. And in the latter, a too-rosy view can blind a parent to a youngster's real needs: The mother of a temperamentally "difficult" child, for example—a boy whom peers and teachers know as a little monster—may exacerbate his monsterhood if she remains oblivious to his behavior and fails to provide him with greater structure and support.

The point of all of this is, parents who are unhappy with each other frequently have a hard time providing the very responses and maintaining the very attitudes that we know are most likely to keep a child on track socially. We know, too, that marital *conflict*—that is, the obvious expression of anger and hostility between Mom and Dad—has a direct bearing on a child's feelings, functioning, and adjustment.

How children react to parental conflict

Couples *do* argue—that should go without saying.

Disagreements, even occasionally heated ones, are part of the tapestry of any close, caring, ongoing relationship—between husband and wife, siblings, or friends. Upsetting though it may be for a child to hear parents arguing, it's not always damaging; in fact, in some cases, it may even be instructive. After all, children have conflicts and ill-feelings, too; if two kids are to enjoy a strong friendship, they must be able to manage their differences in reasonable and reasoned ways. And a child can pick up clues about how to do that at home. But parents must understand that marital conflicts, especially those that are hostile and out of control, can be very difficult for a child to witness.

Much research on child maltreatment has focused on the effects of chronically, excessively dismal or abusive homes—families that live in poverty, families in which one or both parents suffer from mental illness, in which parents are socially isolated, in which parents routinely hit and physically punish their children, in which pervasive and multiple stresses lead to minimal functioning on all fronts. But there have also been a significant number of studies done on relatively stable, generally well functioning marriages and families. One of the things that such work has told us is that children *are* resilient. They don't appear to suffer unduly, for example, if the household is only moderately stressful or if family interactions are less than sunny. When parents fight, however, children manage significantly *less* well—and not least in their peer worlds.

More specifically, poor social and emotional adjustment is most likely to be seen when parental conflicts are frequent; when they are intense; when they are over child-related issues; and when they either go unresolved or are resolved in unconstructive or essentially hostile ways. *Observed violence* between a mother and father is especially harmful emotionally to a child.

Almost all kids say they hate to hear grown-ups fighting; they tell us it makes them feel frightened, sad, angry, worried, guilty, and/or ashamed. Controlled lab studies have consistently demonstrated that this is true for children—from very young ages through adolescence—even when the adults who are arguing are not their parents. In such studies of "background anger," some children have been observed to freeze, becoming immobile and seemingly afraid almost to breathe. Others cried, covered their ears, fidgeted, or asked to leave the room. And still others told their mothers that they wished could do something to help or to stop the problem; sometimes they even tried to intervene, taking on the role of comforter.

For some children, however—those of "difficult" temperament, or boys and girls who have a great deal of trouble regulating their emotions—background anger is not only distressing; their responses can lead them to act up *and* to act out against others. Uninhibited/emotionally reactive children, after witnessing a "staged" hostile exchange between adults, have been observed to career about the room, to be destructive with playthings, to behave more angrily toward peers—shoving and pinching—and even to try to hit the researchers. It may be that a child's biological characteristics serve as either a buffer against or a risk factor regarding adult conflict. Temperamentally "easy" children may be concerned and upset about what they're hearing, but they do not behave inappropriately because of their distress. For temperamentally difficult (or what I have called emotionally dysregulated) children, the same scene may provoke aggressive outbursts.

Such observations in lab settings suggest how children may react closer to home, or wherever they witness frequent, intense, and unresolved conflict between parents:

- Children who hear a great deal of parental arguing become keenly sensitive to background anger *outside* the home and have difficulty coping with it.

  Such youngsters may interpret even benign peer interactions negatively; they may feel unable to influence their social situations in the directions they wish. In addition, they may pick up from their parents an antisocial behavioral model: Mom and Dad deal with their differences by fighting, they reason, so that must be an acceptable way to act.

- While many youngsters who live in constantly anger-infused homes become more aggressive, others become quieter and more withdrawn, more anxious, or depressed.

  And boys and girls, it seems, present different profiles in these regards, and at different ages. Young boys, for example, are often thought to experience more negative outcomes than young girls as a result of their parents' marital unhappiness. Sons in general are more likely than daughters to witness adults' arguments and fights, simply because mothers and fathers both tend to be more reserved in the presence of the latter. Furthermore, according to some research, the less satisfied a mother is with her marriage, the more apt she is to be harsh with her son. And yet the reality may be that young boys merely *appear* to be the more troubled because they usually express negative feelings through more visible, *externalizing* behaviors such as starting fights, teasing, posing distractions in class, and generally acting in a manner that attracts the attention of teachers and other adults. (These behaviors may in turn result in their being referred for counseling, which in the long run, of course, can prove most helpful.) Young girls more typically exhibit *internalizing* problems—sadness, for example, or depression, loneliness, or withdrawal. They suffer silently.

Adding another dimension to this picture are recent studies by the psychologist E. Mark Cummings and his colleagues, whose results indicate that from early adolescence on, girls report feeling mainly *angry* about parental conflict, while boys admit to feeling *sad*—an apparent reversal of the pattern during younger years. Possibly, the researchers concluded, "adolescent girls' anger reflects a greater sense of responsibility for others whereas adolescent boys' sadness reflects a more detached or withdrawn, albeit sympathetic, reaction."

Externalizing and internalizing difficulties are both forms of maladjustment, and both, as we have seen, make life difficult for children within their peer groups.

- Over the long term, kids can acquire distorted notions about intimacy and closeness.

Seeing parents battle may evoke questions in a child's mind about whether his own relationships—with parents *and* peers—are truly comfortable, secure, and reliable. He may come to think, If this is what relationships are all about, I don't want any part of them. We know that some children who grow up in angry homes are slow to establish friendships, and that the friendships they *do* make are not of a very high quality. Such children may have a best friend, but the connection may not be deeply satisfying.

In short, witnessing adult anger and conflict can carve a pathway to poor social outcomes for children. But here's the most important point: When occasional parental conflict takes place within a broader context of warmth, affection, and communication, or when two adults have the insight and motivation to resolve their arguments in constructive, appropriate ways, children are likely to suffer no lasting ill effects. In addition, *how* parents resolve their arguments may have a significant bearing on a child's development of the conflict-resolution skills that are so critical to social competence.

The "good" fight: lessons in conflict resolution

Not all parental fights sound the same, as the following examples demonstrate:

Fourteen-year-old Jeffrey said his parents often argue: "It's mostly about my dad was supposed to do something and he didn't do it. But then they make up and they act sort of silly, like they'll start snapping dish towels at each other in the kitchen." He described his family as "a bunch of hotheads, actually. My parents can get into a major battle about when it was we went to Disney World—she says it was five years ago, he says it was six years ago. And they're hollering at each other about this. When everybody gets together on the holidays, my uncles and aunts and the cousins, everybody's shouting at everybody else."

He remembered when he first became aware that his family wasn't like every other child's in this regard: "When I was about eight or nine, my friend Keith came with us for a week when we went camping. By the end of the first day, he was sort of staring at my parents, like he'd never heard anything like this before. That was the first I saw from the outside what we sounded like. It was pretty embarrassing at the time." Now Jeffrey thinks, "This is just the way we talk. It's like we're not very polite or watching our manners with one another; we just let it all hang out and say what we think. Then a little later, everybody could be telling jokes and laughing."

Families do have their own ways of sharing ideas and feelings, and Jeffrey was probably accurate in his perception that what might sound like hostility to an outsider was simply his parents' and relatives' understood and accepted mode of communication. Among his "bunch of hotheads," he knew that arguments didn't signify bad feelings.

Two other children—also fourteen-year-olds—talked about very different experiences of parental conflict in their respective families.

Stuart's mother and father, their son said, "will go into a deep freeze. We don't have any idea what's going on, but they don't talk to each other. It's worst at dinnertime. We have this very small table off the kitchen, and there're my parents and my two sisters and me. When my parents are having a fight, my sisters and I bring our books to dinner and read. It's pretty uncomfortable, because there isn't really room for books on this little table and it's hard to concentrate anyway. But nobody wants to look at my parents. It's not much fun eating, actually. We just want to get it over with and get out of there."

For Julie, her father's angry outbursts were deeply frightening: "My father comes home from work in a good mood or a bad mood. You can tell as soon as he walks in. He goes in the kitchen and fixes himself a drink. And then you can tell if he has any more drinks, because the cabinet where the bottles are makes this little *ting* sound when it's opened. My sister and I listen for the *ting*, because if he's in a bad mood and he has a couple of drinks, he can get very angry."

One recent evening, her parents seemed to be about to hit each other, Julie said: "There's a piano in the living room, and they were kind of circling around it, my father moving toward my mother, and she moving in the other direction, like she was keeping the piano in between them. They were shouting. My father's face was bright red." Their daughter found her younger sister hunched up in the space under her desk in their bedroom—"She thought they were mad at her and they were going to get divorced," Julie said. After a blow-up, "things just kind of gradually improve over the next few days, or maybe it'll take a week."

These accounts illustrate some damaging ways parents can argue—and the powerful effects such conflicts can have on children. They underscore, as well, some points that parents need to be aware of.

ⓖ **PARENT SKILL:** Assume that your child knows that you and
  your spouse are angry with each other.

Many parents believe that their children are better off not hearing them
fight. But the "deep freeze" really doesn't work, because children are keenly
aware of unspoken hostility. Studies have shown that nonverbal expressions of anger are just as upsetting to them as verbal arguments; in fact,
some psychologists have concluded that youngsters may find withdrawal—or a persistent "silent treatment" between parents—even *more*
stressful and anxiety-provoking than an open contentiousness.

   Besides, an emotionally expressive atmosphere, as I have noted, is good
for kids. Parents who suppress any expression of their conflicts provide
their child with a poor model of how to regulate or control his or her own.
And being able to resolve conflict is a key skill for children to bring to
their friendships. Bottling up emotions usually isn't healthy for anybody.

ⓖ **PARENT SKILL:** Control your rage.

Heated fights—the red-faced, shouting, name-calling ones—look and
sound terrifying to children, especially if such scenes seem liable to veer
into hitting or physical abuse. Seeing parents act so out of control is almost always deeply disturbing to a child, who's likely to fear that they'll
hurt or even kill each other. The youngster may feel it's up to her to "protect" a parent, either by distracting the adults in one way or another or by
physically separating the combatants by getting between them. If you're
engaging in this sort of antagonism with your spouse, you can help your
child by taking a few simple (which is not to say necessarily easy) measures:

- Recognize your point of no return.
     Family therapists often advise couples that a key to getting outbursts
  under control is for one or both individuals to learn to spot trigger
  points, or the minutes or moments just *before* things are about to ex-
  plode into real rage. Physical signs are one common clue—for example,
  heart racing, fists clenched, jaw tightening.

- Call a break in the action at that point.

Tell your partner you're going into another room or out for a walk for a few minutes. If your child is privy to the scene, let him know that you're very angry at the moment and you're going out for a few minutes in order to calm down, but you'll be back very shortly.

⑥ PARENT SKILL: Let your child see that you and your partner can come out the other side of an argument in a positive fashion.

When parents successfully put a disagreement to rest, a child's feelings of anger and upset decrease. And children *know* when a conflict has been resolved, whether or not they actually witness their parents "make up."

The researcher E. Mark Cummings and his colleagues conducted a series of studies to determine what kinds of conflict resolution between adults were most reassuring to children: Did children need to hear the adults apologize to each other? Did they want an explanation of what was going on, or was a change in mood from tense to friendly enough to satisfy them that the battle was over?

Assuming that in the wake of an argument, many parents tended to work things out between themselves in private, the researchers examined how children reacted to a "behind closed doors" solution. In lab visits, children between the ages of five and ten were shown several videotapes in which a man and woman (actors) had an angry exchange of words. After the blow-up, one of several things occurred: In one scene, the pair said nothing to settle their disagreement and continued looking angry. In another, the man and woman were seen talking over their differences and behaving pleasantly. And in two other tapes, the couple left the room for a little while and returned acting friendly toward each other. In one of those last scenarios, mention was made of something that had happened "offstage"; in the other, nothing was said about the argument or how it had been resolved.

The children's responses were revealing. All felt angry, sad, or fearful when the two adults made no effort to end their dispute, and all were pleased and relieved when the adults settled their differences; interestingly, it didn't seem to matter whether they witnessed that happening or not. In addition, when questioned, the children said they thought the adults who had left the room were trying to patch things up between themselves—

perhaps because they'd seen their own parents do much the same thing. In a related study, the same researchers found that when the previously quarreling adults appeared on screen together and explained that they had apologized and reached a compromise, the children were satisfied that the problem had been solved.

The lessons we can extrapolate from such studies are clear: Kids feel best when they know that a fight between adults has been resolved—through apology or compromise, onstage or offstage, as evidenced by friendly exchanges between the participants or made explicit in a brief, after-the-fact explanation that everything is OK. Children feel *less* reassured and comforted when an argument does not seem to be truly settled—when, for example, the adults involved simply switch topics. And they remain distressed when a fight continues, even if it does so quietly, through the deep freeze. Resolution, these researchers surmised, "appears to act as a 'wonder drug' on the children's perceptions of adults' fights, putting the conflict in a relatively positive rather than highly negative light in their eyes."

There's one more point to make here about the *way* an argument is resolved: Some couples settle things through discussion and *conciliation*—meaning that the partners reach an agreement that is reasonably satisfying to both. Others' conflicts end, however, only when one partner *appeases* or gives in to the other, and this model is one that will do a child no good. When one parent is always the appeaser, it sends a clear message that mutual satisfaction is difficult to obtain.

As it happens, we do know something about the costs of being a persistent appeaser. In our own research, we've discovered that children who consistently resolve conflicts by giving in to another may develop low self-esteem and negative perceptions of their own social skills and relationships. Conciliators as a rule have a stronger sense of self-regard; they're more popular among their peers, as well.

Whether it's actually *good* for kids to hear their parents argue is open to question, and it certainly has a great deal to do with the particulars of a given family or situation—how heated the exchanges are, for example, and how often they occur. It seems absolutely safe to conclude, though, that knowing that parents have *resolved* a disagreement is beneficial for any child. What's more, the *manner* in which that resolution is accomplished may be more or less satisfying, or even instructive, for all concerned: It seems that older children and adolescents, in particular, may learn much about conflict resolution from observing their parents, and may derive from such experiences a behavioral model they will employ when faced with their own social dilemmas.

Occasional conflicts in the course of an otherwise sound marriage won't harm a child if parents handle them well. When a marriage is ending, however, it may take extra measures of parental strength and resolve to ensure that a child remains on an even keel.

When parents divorce

One mother's memory of the dissolution of her marriage, seven years earlier, showed just how bad things can get. Her marriage had been, she said, "around a six on a scale of one to ten—not the greatest, but sustained largely by love of our kids and what I guess I'd call intellectual compatibility." She and her spouse were also, she said, both "basically pacific types. There wasn't a lot of arguing—just distance, pulling apart." One day she received a phone call from her husband, who was away on a business trip: He would not be returning directly home, he announced, and he felt they should separate. They were officially divorced a year later.

This mother's behavior during the first few months of that year, in her own words, was "insane, bizarre. I was aware that my husband was involved with someone, who in fact is now his wife, and I made numerous phone calls to this person at her office, hanging up when she answered, to see if she was there when I knew my husband was traveling, or whether she was with him. I drove by her house many nights to see if his car was there. I lurked around corners."

One evening her estranged husband came over to their home to discuss matters pertaining to arrangements for the children. She recalled, "We were standing in the kitchen, and the idea came to me that I could pick up the chef's knife that was sitting there on the counter and stab him. I actually put my hand over the handle of the knife and kept it there while we were talking." Meetings between the two often ended in shouting matches, with their children, Mary and Warren—age eight and twelve at the time—looking on.

Eventually they reached a comfortable accommodation regarding the separation, she said, "but it took many months, and I did not behave well during that time. I made sarcastic comments to the kids about their father. The house pretty much went to pieces. Sometimes I yelled at the kids to clean up, and sometimes I ignored everything." Her soon-to-be ex-husband, she suggested, behaved badly in his own way: "Spending the weekend at his new apartment was like being on vacation for the kids, with lots of indulgences. He bought an eight-hundred-dollar leather jacket for our son, over my objections."

During this whole period, she said, both children "were abnormally quiet, like they were walking on eggs all the time."

If each unhappy, dissolving marriage is unhappy in its own fashion, to paraphrase Tolstoy, the experiences of Mary and Warren's mother are not uncommon. Very troublesome dynamics can develop within a family during a time when one or both parents are feeling hurt, angry, and not entirely in control of their "bizarre" actions. Here are some things we know about such situations:

- The months right before a separation and the first year after a divorce are often the most tumultuous times.

- Established household routines are disrupted; parents have difficulty maintaining the structure or expectations their child is accustomed to.

- Separating or divorcing parents often argue *about* their child, as issues of custody, visitation, and financial support come to the fore—and parental arguments having to do with themselves, as I've noted, are the ones children find most disturbing.

- At least initially, parents may alter their parenting practices, with—typically, according to research—fathers becoming more permissive and mothers both more authoritarian and more inconsistent.

- More than the fact that their home as they have known it is breaking up, or that from now on they will be spending time in two separate places, it is the animosity and especially the overt hostility between their parents that children find most upsetting, and that in turn most directly predict behavioral problems for them. Many children react to separation and divorce by "walking on eggs"; a high level of conflict between parents has been related to a child's feelings of tension, anxiety, loneliness, and even physical discomfort. Other children become noticeably more aggressive, particularly during the year or two before things settle down between their parents.

These and other findings derived from research on families and divorce suggest that the best outcomes for children occur when parents can find it in themselves to behave in specific ways.

⑥ PARENT SKILL: Make a concerted effort to work together to understand what's going on with your child.

Convincing research results tell us that men and women typically react differently to high levels of marital hostility: Women confront, while men withdraw. Meanwhile, of course, there's a trickle-down effect on both the parent-child relationship and the three-way relationship of mother, father, and child. Apparently, when Dad disengages or withdraws into angry silence, Mom, perhaps venting her frustration, often acts more critically and/or intrusively toward her child. The child's reaction may be to become or remain impassive, distant, and unresponsive—in other words, to tune out; teacher reports may indicate that this youngster is shy and withdrawn among peers. Dad is likely also to pull back from attempts to cooperate with Mom in helping their child adjust, and both parents are apt to be less effective in supporting their son's or daughter's problem-solving efforts. It is at this point, too, that teachers may begin to observe additional behavioral problems when the child is among peers.

If you're going through a divorce, you and your partner may well be having trouble maintaining a united front. The emotional distractions you're preoccupied with may lead you to assume (or hope) that your child's low profile around the house means that nothing too wrong is going on with her. At such times, though, it's *especially* critical that you do everything in your power to gather some objective information concerning your youngster. In particular, you need to know how other adults in her life perceive her in this difficult period.

A joint visit by you and your spouse to your child's day-care supervisor, teacher, coach, or other such individual is the best way to find out whether your child is experiencing difficulties in school or social situations. Talking to a third party also can put the focus back where it should be—on your child's needs.

⑥ PARENT SKILL: Spend warm, affectionate time with your child.

Among the protective factors that buffer a child from the negative effects and unpleasantness of divorce is the consistent demonstration of warmth and nurturance—*by at least one parent*. Certainly, the child who perceives Mom and/or Dad as affectionate, comforting, and reassuring is likely to feel a lot better about things than the one whose parent or parents act angry with the whole world, including him. We know that even children who live in extremely high-risk environments, amid a great deal of marital discord and stress, are less apt to demonstrate behavioral problems—aggressiveness, disruptiveness, or withdrawal—if they enjoy a qualitatively nurturant relationship with a parent.

⑥ PARENT SKILL: Rely on sources of social support.

Parents, in turn, can be buffered from their own feelings of uncertainty, anxiety, and unhappiness by the active presence in their lives of good friends, helpful relatives, empathetic coworkers, neighborhood or religious-based organizations and groups, or other informal sources of emotional or practical comfort. It may seem obvious that having others to talk to or call on will ease the stresses and strains of a dissolving marriage and a disrupted home. But there's even more to it than that: A number of studies have confirmed that when parents have such support available to them, their *children* also experience direct and positive payoffs.

For example, mothers who have supportive friends or peer networks are more likely to praise their children and less likely to behave in an intrusive and controlling manner with them. Then, too, the more reliable and nurturing adult friends there are in a parent's life, the more contact the child will have with other adults who can help shore him or her up when the going gets rough.

ⓖ **PARENT SKILL: Nourish your child's friendships.**

Especially from the years of middle school on, children turn to friends as a source of support, comradeship, and fun. When a child is trying to weather a divorce, good friendships and peer involvements can provide something even more important: a lifeline. One of the best things you can do for your child at such a time is to welcome her friends into your home and value their presence in her life.

Parents, peers, friends, and family

At the beginning of this chapter, I suggested that the interplay among several factors—parents' personality and well-being, a child's temperamental characteristics, and life forces that are either stressful or supportive—must be considered in any discussion of parenting and, in turn, of why children turn out the way they do. But explaining normal development, and just how those factors work upon one another, is an awfully complex business, as the story of one young man demonstrates.

Several years ago, a *New York Times* piece profiled a teenager named Brian, who was just finishing his senior year in high school and weighing his immediate options: Should he attend a state university near his hometown or enroll in an engineering program in a college farther away? That he was in a position to consider such alternatives at all was in itself no mean accomplishment.

Brian had put a turbulent family life behind him. His father was manic-depressive, a man who, when Brian was younger, would sometimes squander the family rent money and at other times sit in a chair all day long. After Brian's father attempted suicide, his parents divorced, and his mother spent some time in a hospital for the mentally ill. Upon her release, she began living with a boyfriend, leaving Brian and his younger sister alone at home, though she checked in with them by phone once in a while. The two siblings often went without food. Brian's sister got into serious trouble and entered foster care.

By his sophomore year of high school, Brian was one of the estimated eighty thousand children in the United States between the ages of fifteen and nineteen who live on their own. For many years, his salvation had been his love of computers, and he now began supporting himself—living in rented rooms—by running a computer repair service. Few people were aware of the hardships he'd endured; Brian didn't talk much about his life. His high school guidance counselor indicated that he always presented himself appropriately: "He keeps himself clean, dresses well, knows how to get along with people and what he needs." One of the few signs of strain was that the boy, a gifted student, received an uncharacteristic C in math that sophomore year.

Brian's best friend since third grade had been a boy named Zach. An athlete and a highly popular child, Zach had stuck by his friend through the years, even though he'd been teased on occasion for having such a close friendship with someone like Brian. As young children, the two boys, said Zach's mother, had shared a love of books. On summer weekend mornings, Brian would always come calling for Zach, often before anyone in the household was awake. Zach's mom told him not to come by before ten; from that day on, he never appeared a minute too early.

In their junior year of high school, Zach made an unusual request of his parents: He asked if his friend could move in with them. Knowing what Brian's circumstances were and how the two boys felt about each other, Zach's parents agreed, and Brian found himself in a regular, normal home for the first time in his life. He also acquired a girlfriend that year, a classmate he'd known and been friendly with since middle school. The girl's family had now and then provided Brian with a meal, and they bought him gifts on his birthday. "People respond" to Brian, said his school counselor, adding that he "doesn't push himself on somebody." As soon as he could, Brian found a legal-aid lawyer and had himself officially emancipated from his family. Thinking about college, he was tempted by the idea of taking an airplane to visit a campus or two. He had never been on a plane before.

What might be said about Brian? Certainly, this young man's story speaks to issues of inner strength and human resilience. Perhaps he was blessed with all the right dispositional characteristics—a temperament comprising tendencies to react to unpleasant situations in a seemingly controlled fashion, a predilection to move *toward* rather than *away from* or *against* others, and an ability to keep on task and not focus his attention in scattershot ways. He may have been "programmed," in other words, to regulate his emotions and adapt to a chaotic environment in a self-protective manner.

Perhaps, too, teachers responded to Brian's intelligence, discipline and industry, and optimistic personality with sensitivity and affection. Perhaps the praise of adults in the school milieu gave him a foot up the ladder and won him the positive recognition of a few peers. Brian was appealing enough to be offered comfort and solace by the families of friends who lived in, as he put it, "a normal situation." We may also surmise that the presence in his life of one or two close friendships may have enabled him to move forward on a constructive developmental path.

Indeed, psychologists believe that strong friendships may eventually, in late childhood and early adolescence, help children overcome negative features in their home environments. And researchers who study the lives of maltreated children and teens suggest that such high-quality friendships not only are emotionally supportive but also serve a remedial function, helping youngsters compensate for deficiencies in social skills and the understanding of relationships.

Of course, the best of all possible scenarios for a child is this one: During times of family stress and difficulty, he or she has parents, peers, and friends who can be counted on to provide support and security.

A Final Word

At the start of our journey together through these pages, I suggested that in childhood, friendship is where the action is. From the time your child first starts getting together with peers in child-care and preschool settings, on playdates and at the playground, through the busy years of elementary school, middle school, junior high, and high school, he or she continues to learn skills that lie at the core of all of our social and emotional lives. We've seen what those skills comprise: the ability to talk to people, to be assertive without being offensive, to resolve disagreements in a satisfactory manner, to ask for comfort and understanding from a friend and to offer the same in exchange, and to pursue independence while maintaining connectedness.

The more competent a child is in these skills, the more likely he or she is to thrive and be happy. Such social competence, moreover, will serve him or her well not only through those first seventeen or eighteen years, but for a lifetime. We are all products, for better or worse, of a complicated conspiracy among our biologically based individual characteristics, our interactions with others, and the relationships we form because of those interactions. It's a conspiracy that lasts from infancy, through childhood and adolescence, and into adulthood; from parenthood to the evolving connection with our own elderly parents.

There are limits to what you can do with and for your child; a great deal of what he or she will end up doing and being in life will be up to him or her. But whatever shape that life takes, it will surely be more pleasant if your son or daughter can learn to be emotionally regulated and socially competent, and if he or she can rely on friends and family for security, support and love. Helping to ensure that is really, I believe, the best aspiration any parent can have. And in this book, I've attempted to provide some hints that may aid and abet you in achieving that wonderful goal.

References

Chapter 2. The Power of Peers

41   *friends and peer relationships are essential:* Harry Stack Sullivan, *The Interpersonal Theory of Psychiatry* (New York: Norton, 1953).

Chapter 4. The Heart of Parenting

81   *"Secure attachment to the mother":* A. Skolnick, "Early attachment and personal relationships across the life course," in P. B. Baltes, D. L. Featherman, and R. M. Lerner, eds., *Life-Span Development and Behavior,* vol. 7 (Hillsdale, N.J.: Erlbaum, 1986).

Chapter 5. Making First Friends

118   *In a study of the association:* Victoria Finnie and Alan Russell, "Preschool children's social status and their mothers' behavior and knowledge in the supervisory role," *Developmental Psychology* 24, no. 6 (1988): 789–801.

Chapter 6. The New Look of Friendship

125   *Preadolescence . . . is "spectacularly marked . . .":* Sullivan, *The Interpersonal Theory of Psychiatry,* 245–46.

128   *The findings of one study were particularly telling:* Lynne Zarbatany, Donald P. Hartmann, and D. Bruce Rankin, "The psychological functions of preadolescent peer activities," *Child Development* 61 (1990): 1067–80.

Chapter 7. The Sea-Change Years

155   *In a widely read study of American adolescents:* Mihaly Csikszentmihalyi and Reed Larson, *Being Adolescent* (New York: Basic Books, 1984), 157–75.

157   *more than 50 percent of the respondents:* From a poll conducted by *The New York Times* and CBS News. Laurie Goodstein with Marjorie Connally, "Teenage Poll Finds a Turn to the Traditional," *New York Times,* April 30, 1998, A20.

162   *psychologists discovered clear-cut connections:* Catherine R. Cooper and Robert G. Cooper Jr., "Links between adolescents' relationships with their parents and peers: Models, evidence and mechanisms," in Ross D. Parke and Gary M. Ladd, eds., *Family-Peer Relationships* (Hillsdale, N.J.: Erlbaum, 1992), 135–58.

168   *nine different commonly used teen labels:* B. B. Brown, "Peer groups and peer cultures," in S. S. Feldman and G. R. Elliott, eds., *At the Threshold* (Cambridge, Mass.: Harvard University Press, 1990), 171–96.

168   *"Abercrombies, alties, chicas . . .":* Liza N. Burby, "Clique Power," *Newsday,* August 28, 1999.

169   *research . . . on the subject of who should have the final say-so:* Judith G. Smetana, "Adolescents' and parents' conceptions of parental authority," *Child Development* 59 (1988): 321–35.

Chapter 8. Popularity

185   *In her acclaimed book for preadolescents and teens:* Ellen Rosenberg, *Growing Up Feeling Good,* rev. ed. (New York: Penguin Books, 1995), 153–56.

185   *several factors that marked a child for popularity:* Patricia A. Adler and Peter Adler, *Peer Power: Preadolescent Culture and Identity* (New Brunswick, N.J.: Rutgers University Press, 1998), 38–55.

188   *In their study of age differences in peer groups:* Leslie A. Gavin and Wyndol Furman, "Age differences in adolescents' perceptions of their peer groups," *Developmental Psychology* 25, no. 5 (1989): 827–34.

199   *In their study of first and third grade boys:* John D. Coie and Kenneth A. Dodge, "Multiple sources of data on social behavior and social states in the school: A cross-age comparison," *Child Development* 59 (1988): 815–29.

Chapter 9. The Moving-Away-From Child

223   *a study involving a group of monkeys:* S. J. Suomi and H. F. Harlow, "Social rehabilitation of isolate reared monkeys," *Developmental Psychology* 6 (1972): 487–96.

223   *They paired socially withdrawn preschoolers:* W. Furman, D. Rahe, and W. W. Hartup, "Rehabilitation of socially withdrawn preschool children through mixed-age and same-age socialization," *Child Development* 50 (1979): 915–22.

Chapter 12. Real-Life Parenting

293   *girls reported feeling mainly angry:* E. Mark Cummings and Patrick Davies, *Children and Marital Conflict* (New York: Guilford Press, 1995), 37–86.

298   *Resolution . . . "appears to act as a 'wonder drug'. . .":* Ibid., 146–47.

303   *a teenager named Brian:* Michael Winerip, "He's Getting By with a Little Help from His Friends," *New York Times,* April 29, 1998.

Index